# Water Industry Act 1991

## CHAPTER 56

**[A table showing the derivation of the provisions of this Consolidation Act will be found at the end of the Act. The table has no official status.]**

## ARRANGEMENT OF SECTIONS

A

*Pipe-laying*

*Other works powers*

*Powers to discharge water*

*Compulsory works orders*

*Entry to land etc. by water undertakers*

## CHAPTER II

### PROTECTION OF UNDERTAKERS' WORKS, APPARATUS ETC.

#### Protection of apparatus in general

*Protection of meters*

*Obstruction of sewerage works etc.*

## CHAPTER III

### SUPPLEMENTAL PROVISIONS WITH RESPECT TO UNDERTAKERS' POWERS

#### Vesting of works in undertaker

*Damage etc. caused by works*

## PART VII

### INFORMATION PROVISIONS

*Reports*

# Water Industry Act 1991

## 1991 CHAPTER 56

An Act to consolidate enactments relating to the supply of water and the provision of sewerage services, with amendments to give effect to recommendations of the Law Commission.

[25th July 1991]

**B**E IT ENACTED by the Queen's most Excellent Majesty, by and with the advice and consent of the Lords Spiritual and Temporal, and Commons, in this present Parliament assembled, and by the authority of the same, as follows:—

## PART I

### PRELIMINARY

*The Director General of Water Services*

1.—(1) There shall continue to be an officer known as the Director General of Water Services (in this Act referred to as "the Director") for the purpose of carrying out the functions of that Director under this Act.

The Director General of Water Services.

(2) Appointment of any person to hold office as the Director shall be made by the Secretary of State.

(3) An appointment of a person to hold office as the Director shall be for a term not exceeding five years; but previous appointment to that office shall not affect eligibility for re-appointment.

(4) The Director may at any time resign his office as the Director by notice addressed to the Secretary of State; and the Secretary of State may remove any person from that office on the ground of incapacity or misbehaviour.

(5) Subject to the preceding provisions of this section, the Director shall hold and vacate office as such in accordance with the terms of his appointment.

(6) The provisions of Schedule 1 to this Act shall have effect with respect to the Director.

*General duties*

**2.**—(1) This section shall have effect for imposing duties on the Secretary of State and on the Director as to when and how they should exercise and perform the following powers and duties, that is to say—

(a) in the case of the Secretary of State, the powers and duties conferred or imposed on him by virtue of the provisions of this Act relating to the regulation of relevant undertakers; and

(b) in the case of the Director, the powers and duties conferred or imposed on him by virtue of any of those provisions, by the provisions relating to the financial conditions of requisitions or by the provisions relating to the movement of certain pipes.

(2) The Secretary of State or, as the case may be, the Director shall exercise and perform the powers and duties mentioned in subsection (1) above in the manner that he considers is best calculated—

(a) to secure that the functions of a water undertaker and of a sewerage undertaker are properly carried out as respects every area of England and Wales; and

(b) without prejudice to the generality of paragraph (a) above, to secure that companies holding appointments under Chapter I of Part II of this Act as relevant undertakers are able (in particular, by securing reasonable returns on their capital) to finance the proper carrying out of the functions of such undertakers.

(3) Subject to subsection (2) above, the Secretary of State or, as the case may be, the Director shall exercise and perform the powers and duties mentioned in subsection (1) above in the manner that he considers is best calculated—

(a) to ensure that the interests of every person who is a customer or potential customer of a company which has been or may be appointed under Chapter I of Part II of this Act to be a relevant undertaker are protected as respects the fixing and recovery by that company of water and drainage charges and, in particular—

(i) that the interests of customers and potential customers in rural areas are so protected; and

(ii) that no undue preference is shown, and that there is no undue discrimination, in the fixing of those charges;

(b) to ensure that the interests of every such person are also protected as respects the other terms on which any services are provided by that company in the course of the carrying out of the functions of a relevant undertaker and as respects the quality of those services;

(c) to ensure that the interests of every such person are further protected as respects benefits that could be secured for them by the application in a particular manner of any of the proceeds of any disposal (including a disposal before the Secretary of State and the Director became subject to the duties imposed by virtue of this paragraph) of any of that company's protected land or of any interest or right in or over any of that land;

(d) to promote economy and efficiency on the part of any such company in the carrying out of the functions of a relevant undertaker; and

(e) to facilitate effective competition, with respect to such matters as he considers appropriate, between persons holding or seeking appointments under that Chapter.

(4) In performing his duty under subsection (3) above, so far as it requires him to do anything in the manner which he considers is best calculated to ensure that the interests of the customers and potential customers of any company are protected as respects the quality of any services provided by that company in the course of the carrying out of the functions of a relevant undertaker, the Secretary of State or, as the case may be, the Director shall take into account, in particular, the interests of those who are disabled or of pensionable age.

(5) In this section the references to water and drainage charges are references to—

(a) any charges in respect of any services provided in the course of the carrying out of the functions of a relevant undertaker; and

(b) amounts of any other description which such an undertaker is authorised by or under any enactment to require any of its customers or potential customers to pay.

(6) For the purposes of this section—

(a) the reference in subsection (1) above to the provisions of this Act relating to the regulation of relevant undertakers is a reference to the provisions contained in Part II of this Act (except section 28 and Schedule 4), or in any of sections 38, 39, 95, 96, 153, 181, 182, 193 to 195 and 201 to 203 below;

(b) the reference in that subsection to the provisions relating to the financial conditions of requisitions is a reference to the provisions contained in sections 42, 43, 48, 99 and 100 below; and

(c) the reference in that subsection to the provisions relating to the movement of certain pipes is a reference to the provisions of section 185 below.

**3.**—(1) It shall be the duty of each of the following, that is to say—

(a) the Secretary of State;

(b) the Minister of Agriculture, Fisheries and Food;

(c) the Director; and

(d) every company holding an appointment as a relevant undertaker,

General environmental and recreational duties.

in formulating or considering any proposals relating to any functions of a relevant undertaker (including, in the case of such a company, any functions which, by virtue of that appointment, are functions of the company itself) to comply with the requirements imposed in relation to the proposals by subsections (2) and (3) below.

(2) The requirements imposed by this subsection in relation to any such proposals as are mentioned in subsection (1) above are—

(a) a requirement, so far as may be consistent—

(i) with the purposes of any enactment relating to the functions of the undertaker; and

> (ii) in the case of the Secretary of State and the Director, with their duties under section 2 above,

so to exercise any power conferred with respect to the proposals on the person subject to the requirement as to further the conservation and enhancement of natural beauty and the conservation of flora, fauna and geological or physiographical features of special interest;

(b) a requirement to have regard to the desirability of protecting and conserving buildings, sites and objects of archaeological, architectural or historic interest; and

(c) a requirement to take into account any effect which the proposals would have on the beauty or amenity of any rural or urban area or on any such flora, fauna, features, buildings, sites or objects.

(3) The requirements imposed by this subsection in relation to any such proposals as are mentioned in subsection (1) above are, subject to the requirements imposed by subsection (2) above—

(a) a requirement to have regard to the desirability of preserving for the public any freedom of access to areas of woodland, mountains, moor, heath, down, cliff or foreshore and other places of natural beauty;

(b) a requirement to have regard to the desirability of maintaining the availability to the public of any facility for visiting or inspecting any building, site or object of archaeological, architectural or historic interest; and

(c) a requirement to take into account any effect which the proposals would have on any such freedom of access or on the availability of any such facility.

(4) Subsections (1) to (3) above shall apply so as to impose duties on the Director and any company holding an appointment as a relevant undertaker in relation to any proposal relating to—

(a) the functions of the NRA; or

(b) the functions of an internal drainage board,

as they apply in relation to any proposals relating to the functions of such an undertaker; and for the purposes of this subsection the reference in subsection (2)(a) above to the functions of the undertaker shall have effect as a reference to the functions of the NRA or, as the case may be, of the internal drainage board in question.

(5) Subject to obtaining the consent of any navigation authority, harbour authority or conservancy authority before doing anything which causes navigation which is subject to the control of that authority to be obstructed or otherwise interfered with, it shall be the duty of every company holding an appointment as a relevant undertaker to take such steps as are—

(a) reasonably practicable; and

(b) consistent with the purposes of the enactments relating to the functions of the undertaker in question,

for securing, so long as that company has rights to the use of water or land associated with water, that those rights are exercised so as to ensure that the water or land is made available for recreational purposes and is so made available in the best manner.

(6) It shall be the duty of a company holding an appointment as a relevant undertaker, in determining what steps to take in performance of any duty imposed by virtue of subsection (5) above, to take into account the needs of persons who are chronically sick or disabled.

(7) The obligations under this section of a company holding an appointment as a relevant undertaker shall be enforceable under section 18 below by the Secretary of State.

(8) Nothing in this section or the following provisions of this Act shall require recreational facilities made available by a relevant undertaker to be made available free of charge.

(9) References in this section to the functions of a relevant undertaker shall be construed, without prejudice to section 156(7) below, as if those functions included the management, by a company holding an appointment as such an undertaker, of any land for the time being held by that company for any purpose whatever (whether or not connected with the carrying out of the functions of a relevant undertaker).

(10) In this section "building" includes structure.

**4.**—(1) Where the Nature Conservancy Council for England or the Countryside Council for Wales are of the opinion that any area of land in England or, as the case may be, in Wales—

Environmental duties with respect to sites of special interest.

    (a) is of special interest by reason of its flora, fauna or geological or physiographical features; and

    (b) may at any time be affected by schemes, works, operations or activities of a relevant undertaker,

that Council shall notify the fact that the land is of special interest for that reason to every relevant undertaker whose works, operations or activities may affect the land.

(2) Where a National Park authority or the Broads Authority is of the opinion that any area of land in a National Park or in the Broads—

    (a) is land in relation to which the matters for the purposes of which section 3 above has effect are of particular importance; and

    (b) may at any time be affected by schemes, works, operations or activities of a relevant undertaker,

the National Park authority or Broads Authority shall notify the fact that the land is such land, and the reasons why those matters are of particular importance in relation to the land, to every relevant undertaker whose works, operations or activities may affect the land.

(3) Where a relevant undertaker has received a notification under subsection (1) or (2) above with respect to any land, that undertaker shall consult the notifying body before carrying out any works, operations or activities which appear to that undertaker to be likely—

    (a) to destroy or damage any of the flora, fauna, or geological or physiographical features by reason of which the land is of special interest; or

    (b) significantly to prejudice anything the importance of which is one of the reasons why the matters mentioned in subsection (2) above are of particular importance in relation to that land.

(4) Subsection (3) above shall not apply in relation to anything done in an emergency where particulars of what is done and of the emergency are notified to the Nature Conservancy Council for England, the Countryside Council for Wales, the National Park authority in question or, as the case may be, the Broads Authority as soon as practicable after that thing is done.

(5) The obligations under this section of a relevant undertaker shall be enforceable under section 18 below by the Secretary of State.

(6) In this section—

1988 c. 4.

"the Broads" has the same meaning as in the Norfolk and Suffolk Broads Act 1988; and

"National Park authority" means a National Park Committee or a joint or special planning board for a National Park;

and section 3(9) above shall apply, as it applies in relation to that section, for construing (in accordance with section 6 below) any references in this section to a relevant undertaker.

Codes of practice with respect to environmental and recreational duties.

**5.**—(1) The Secretary of State may by order approve any code of practice issued (whether by him or by another person) for the purpose of—

(a) giving practical guidance to relevant undertakers with respect to any of the matters for the purposes of which sections 3 and 4 above have effect; and

(b) promoting what appear to him to be desirable practices by such undertakers with respect to those matters,

and may at any time by such an order approve a modification of such a code or withdraw his approval of such a code or modification.

(2) A contravention of a code of practice as for the time being approved under this section shall not of itself constitute a contravention of any requirement imposed by section 3 or 4 above or give rise to any criminal or civil liability; but the Secretary of State and the Minister of Agriculture, Fisheries and Food shall each be under a duty to take into account whether there has been or is likely to be any such contravention in determining when and how he should exercise his powers in relation to any relevant undertaker by virtue of this Act, any of the other 1989 c. 15. consolidation Acts or the Water Act 1989.

(3) The power of the Secretary of State to make an order under this section shall be exercisable by statutory instrument subject to annulment in pursuance of a resolution of either House of Parliament.

(4) The Secretary of State shall not make an order under this section unless he has first consulted—

(a) the NRA;

(b) the Countryside Commission, the Nature Conservancy Council for England and the Countryside Council for Wales;

(c) the Historic Buildings and Monuments Commission for England;

(d) the Sports Council and the Sports Council for Wales; and

(e) such relevant undertakers and other persons as he considers it appropriate to consult.

(5) In this section "the other consolidation Acts" means the Water Resources Act 1991, the Statutory Water Companies Act 1991, the Land Drainage Act 1991 and the Water Consolidation (Consequential Provisions) Act 1991.

## PART II

### APPOINTMENT AND REGULATION OF UNDERTAKERS

### CHAPTER I

### APPOINTMENTS

*Making of appointments*

6.—(1) Subject to the following provisions of this Chapter, a company may be appointed—

Appointment of relevant undertakers.

(a) by the Secretary of State; or

(b) with the consent of or in accordance with a general authorisation given by the Secretary of State, by the Director,

to be the water undertaker or sewerage undertaker for any area of England and Wales.

(2) Without prejudice to the obligation of a company holding an appointment under this Chapter to comply with the conditions of its appointment, the appointment of a company to be the water undertaker or sewerage undertaker for any area shall have the effect, while the appointment remains in force—

(a) of requiring the company to perform any duty imposed by or under any enactment on an undertaker of the relevant description (that is to say, a water undertaker or, as the case may be, sewerage undertaker);

(b) of authorising the company, for the purposes of, or in connection with, the carrying out of any of the functions of an undertaker of the relevant description, to exercise any power conferred by or under any enactment on an undertaker of that description;

(c) of requiring enactments and subordinate legislation authorising or requiring anything to be done in relation to an undertaker of the relevant description to be construed as authorising or requiring that thing to be done in relation to that company; and

(d) of requiring other references in any enactment or subordinate legislation to an undertaker of the relevant description, or to the area of that undertaker, to be construed, so far as necessary for the purposes of, or in connection with, the carrying out by that company of the functions of an undertaker of that description, as references to that company or, as the case may be, to that area.

(3) The appointment of a company to be a relevant undertaker shall be by service on the company of an instrument in writing containing the appointment and describing the area for which it is made.

(4) A single instrument may contain the appointment of a company to be the sewerage undertaker for an area and the appointment of the same company to be the water undertaker for the whole or any part of that area or for an area which includes the whole or any part of that area.

(5) A company shall not be appointed to be a water undertaker unless it is a limited company or a statutory water company and shall not be appointed to be a sewerage undertaker unless it is a limited company.

(6) As soon as practicable after making an appointment under this Chapter, the Secretary of State shall send a copy of the appointment to the Director.

Continuity of appointments, replacement appointments etc.

**7.**—(1) It shall be the duty of the Secretary of State to secure that such appointments are made under this Chapter as will ensure that for every area of England and Wales there is at all times both—

    (a) a company holding an appointment under this Chapter as water undertaker; and

    (b) whether or not the same company in relation to the whole or any part of that area, a company holding an appointment as sewerage undertaker.

(2) Subject to the following provisions of this section—

    (a) the Secretary of State; and

    (b) with the consent of or in accordance with a general authorisation given by the Secretary of State, the Director,

shall have power, by notice to a company holding an appointment under this Chapter, to terminate the appointment or to vary the area to which it relates.

(3) The appointment of a company to be a water undertaker or sewerage undertaker shall not be terminated or otherwise cease to relate to or to any part of any area except with effect from the coming into force of such appointments and variations replacing that company as a relevant undertaker as secure either-

    (a) that another company becomes the water undertaker or, as the case may be, sewerage undertaker for that area or part or for an area that includes that area or part; or

    (b) that two or more companies each become the water undertaker or, as the case may be, sewerage undertaker for one of a number of different areas that together constitute or include that area or part.

(4) An appointment or variation replacing a company as a relevant undertaker shall not be made in relation to the whole or any part of the area to which that company's appointment as water undertaker or, as the case may be, sewerage undertaker relates except where—

    (a) that company consents to the appointment or variation;

    (b) the appointment or variation relates only to parts of that area none of the premises in which is served by that company; or

    (c) the appointment or variation is made in such circumstances as may be set out for the purposes of this paragraph in the conditions of that company's appointment.

Procedure with respect to appointments and variations.

**8.**—(1) An application for an appointment or variation replacing a company as a relevant undertaker shall be made in such manner as may be prescribed.

(2) Within fourteen days after making an application under this section, the applicant shall—

(a) serve notice of the application on the existing appointee and on every local authority whose area includes the whole or any part of the area to which the application relates; and

(b) publish a copy of the notice in such manner as may be prescribed.

(3) Before making an appointment or variation replacing a company as a relevant undertaker, the Secretary of State or the Director shall give notice—

(a) stating that he proposes to make the appointment or variation;

(b) stating the reasons why he proposes to make the appointment or variation; and

(c) specifying the period (not being less than twenty-eight days from the date of publication of the notice) within which representations or objections with respect to the proposed appointment or variation may be made.

(4) A notice under subsection (3) above shall be given—

(a) by publishing the notice in such manner as the Secretary of State or, as the case may be, the Director considers appropriate for bringing it to the attention of persons likely to be affected by the making of the proposed appointment or variation; and

(b) by serving a copy of the notice on the existing appointee and on every local authority whose area includes the whole or any part of the area to which the proposed appointment or variation relates.

(5) As soon as practicable after making an appointment or variation replacing a company as a relevant undertaker, the Secretary of State or the Director shall—

(a) serve a copy of the appointment or variation on the existing appointee; and

(b) serve notice of the making of the appointment or variation on every local authority whose area includes the whole or any part of the area to which the appointment or variation relates,

and as soon as practicable after exercising any power to vary the area to which an appointment under this Chapter relates, the Secretary of State shall send a copy of the variation to the Director.

(6) In this section "the existing appointee", in relation to an appointment or variation replacing a company as a relevant undertaker, means the company which is replaced in relation to the whole or any part of the area to which the appointment or variation relates or, where there is more than one such company, each of them.

**9.**—(1) Before making an appointment or variation replacing a company as a relevant undertaker, the Secretary of State or the Director shall consider any representations or objections which have been duly made in pursuance of the notice under section 8(3) above and have not been withdrawn.

*Duties affecting making of appointments and variations.*

(2) Before making an appointment or variation replacing a company as a relevant undertaker, the Secretary of State shall consult the Director.

(3) In determining whether to make an appointment or variation by virtue of section 7(4)(b) above in relation to any part of an area, the Secretary of State or, as the case may be, the Director shall have regard, in particular, to any arrangements made or expenditure incurred by the existing appointee for the purpose of enabling premises in that part of that area to be served by that appointee.

(4) It shall be the duty of the Secretary of State or, as the case may be, of the Director—

(a) in making an appointment or variation replacing a company as a relevant undertaker; and

(b) where he makes such an appointment or variation, in determining what provision is to be made with respect to the fixing by the new appointee of any water or drainage charges,

to ensure, so far as may be consistent with his duties under Part I of this Act, that the interests of the members and creditors of the existing appointee are not unfairly prejudiced as respects the terms on which the new appointee could accept transfers of property, rights and liabilities from the existing appointee.

(5) In this section—

"existing appointee", in relation to an appointment or variation replacing a company as a relevant undertaker in relation to any area or part of an area, means the company which is replaced by that appointment or variation;

"new appointee", in relation to such an appointment or variation, means the company which by virtue of the appointment or variation becomes a relevant undertaker for the area or part of an area in question;

"water or drainage charges" means

(a) charges in respect of any services provided in the course of the carrying out of the functions of a water undertaker or sewerage undertaker; or

(b) amounts of any other description which such an undertaker is authorised by or under any enactment to require any person to pay.

Transitional provision with respect to replacement appointments.

**10.** Schedule 2 to this Act shall have effect for enabling provision to be made with respect to cases in which a company is replaced by another as a relevant undertaker by an appointment or variation under this Chapter.

*Conditions of appointments*

Power to impose conditions.

**11.**—(1) An appointment under this Chapter may include—

(a) such conditions as appear to the Secretary of State or, as the case may be, the Director to be requisite or expedient having regard to the duties imposed on him by Part I of this Act;

(b) conditions for the purposes of section 7(4)(c) above; and

(c) conditions requiring the rendering to the Secretary of State of a payment on the making of an appointment, or payments while such an appointment is in force, or both, of such amount or amounts as may be determined by or under the conditions.

(2) Conditions may be included by virtue of subsection (1)(a) above in an appointment under this Chapter whether or not they are connected with the supply of water, the provision of sewerage services or the exercise or performance of any power or duty conferred or imposed by or under any enactment on water undertakers or sewerage undertakers.

(3) Conditions included in an appointment under this Chapter may contain provision for the conditions to cease to have effect or be modified at such times, in such manner and in such circumstances as may be specified in or determined by or under the conditions.

(4) Any provision included by virtue of subsection (3) above in an appointment under this Chapter shall have effect in addition to the provision made by this Chapter with respect to the modification of the conditions of an appointment.

(5) For the purposes of this Act where the same instrument contains an appointment of the same company to be both a water undertaker and a sewerage undertaker (whether or not for the same area), all the conditions included in that instrument by virtue of this section shall have effect, irrespective of their subject-matter, as conditions of both appointments.

(6) Where an instrument of appointment has been served under subsection (3) of section 6 above on any company, the coming into force of the appointment for the purposes specified in subsection (2) of that section shall not be affected by any contravention of the requirements of this Act with respect to the provision contained by way of conditions of appointment in that instrument.

(7) If the Secretary of State considers it appropriate to do so in consequence of any legal proceedings with respect to any such provision as is mentioned in subsection (6) above, he may by order made by statutory instrument direct that such conditions as may be specified in the order are to be treated as included in the appointment in question until there is an opportunity for the provision to which the proceedings relate to be replaced by virtue of any of the other provisions of this Chapter.

(8) Any sums received by the Secretary of State in consequence of the provisions of any condition of an appointment under this Chapter shall be paid into the Consolidated Fund.

**12.**—(1) Without prejudice to the generality of paragraph (a) of section 11(1) above, conditions included in an appointment by virtue of that paragraph may—

Determinations under conditions of appointment.

    (a) require the appointed company to comply with any direction given by the Director as to such matters as are specified in the appointment or are of a description so specified; and

    (b) require the appointed company, except in so far as the Director consents to the company's doing or not doing them, not to do or to do such things as are specified in the appointment or are of a description so specified.

(2) Without prejudice as aforesaid, such conditions may provide for the reference to and determination by—

    (a) the Secretary of State or the Director; or

　　　　(b) on a reference by the Director, the Monopolies and Mergers Commission (in this Act referred to as "the Monopolies Commission"),

of such questions arising under the appointment and of such other matters, including (in the case of references to the Commission) disputes as to determinations by the Director, as are specified in the appointment or are of a description so specified.

(3) Where any question or other matter falls to be determined by the Monopolies Commission in pursuance of a provision contained in an appointment under this Chapter—

　　　　(a) it shall be the duty of the Director, on being required to do so by the company holding that appointment, to refer that question or matter to that Commission; and

　　　　(b) it shall be the duty of that Commission to determine any question or other matter referred by virtue of paragraph (a) above in accordance with—

　　　　　　(i) any regulations under subsection (4) below; and

　　　　　　(ii) the principles which apply, by virtue of Part I of this Act, in relation to determinations under this Chapter by the Director.

(4) The Secretary of State may by regulations make such provision as he considers appropriate for regulating the procedure to be followed with respect to the reference of any question or other matter to the Monopolies Commission in pursuance of provision contained in an appointment under this Chapter.

(5) Without prejudice to the generality of the power conferred by subsection (4) above, regulations under that subsection may, in relation to any such reference as is mentioned in that subsection, apply (with or without modifications) the provisions of any enactment relating to references to the Monopolies Commission under the following provisions of this Act, the 1973 Act or the 1980 Act.

*Modification of appointment conditions*

Modification by agreement.

13.—(1) Subject to the following provisions of this section, the Director may modify the conditions of a company's appointment under this Chapter if the company consents to the modifications.

(2) Before making modifications under this section, the Director shall give notice—

　　　　(a) stating that he proposes to make the modifications and setting out their effect;

　　　　(b) stating the reasons why he proposes to make the modifications; and

　　　　(c) specifying the period (not being less than twenty-eight days from the date of publication of the notice) within which representations or objections with respect to the proposed modifications may be made,

and shall consider any representations or objections which are duly made and not withdrawn.

(3) A notice under subsection (2) above shall be given—

    (a) by publishing the notice in such manner as the Director considers appropriate for the purpose of bringing the notice to the attention of persons likely to be affected by the making of the modifications; and

    (b) by serving a copy of the notice on the company and on the Secretary of State.

(4) The Director shall not under this section make any modifications which the Secretary of State has, within the time specified in the notice under subsection (2) above, directed the Director not to make.

(5) The Secretary of State shall not give a direction under subsection (4) above in relation to any modification unless—

    (a) the modification is a modification of provision contained in the appointment for the purposes of section 7(4)(c) above;

    (b) the modification is a modification of a provision of the appointment which relates to the disposal of, or of interests or rights in or over, a company's protected land and is stated in the appointment to be a provision which cannot be modified; or

    (c) it appears to the Secretary of State that the modification should be made, if at all, under section 16 below.

**14.**—(1) The Director may make to the Monopolies Commission a reference which is so framed as to require the Commission to investigate and report on the questions— Modification references to Monopolies Commission.

    (a) whether any matters which—

        (i) relate to the carrying out of any function which is a function of any company by virtue of an appointment of that company under this Chapter; and

        (ii) are specified in the reference,

    operate, or may be expected to operate, against the public interest; and

    (b) if so, whether the effects adverse to the public interest which those matters have or may be expected to have could be remedied or prevented by modifications of the conditions of the company's appointment.

(2) The Director may, at any time, by notice given to the Monopolies Commission vary a reference under this section by—

    (a) adding to the matters specified in the reference; or

    (b) excluding from the reference some or all of the matters so specified;

and on receipt of any such notice the Commission shall give effect to the variation.

(3) The Director may specify in a reference under this section, or a variation of such a reference, for the purpose of assisting the Monopolies Commission in carrying out the investigation on the reference—

    (a) any effects adverse to the public interest which, in his opinion, the matters specified in the reference or variation have or may be expected to have; and

(b) any modifications of the conditions of any appointment mentioned in the reference or variation by which, in his opinion, those effects could be remedied or prevented.

(4) As soon as practicable after making a reference under this section or a variation of such a reference, the Director shall—

(a) serve a copy of the reference or variation on the company whose appointment is mentioned in the reference or variation; and

(b) publish particulars of the reference or variation in such manner as he considers appropriate for the purpose of bringing the reference or variation to the attention of persons likely to be affected by it.

(5) It shall be the duty of the Director, for the purpose of assisting the Monopolies Commission in carrying out an investigation on a reference under this section, to give to the Commission—

(a) any information in his possession which relates to matters falling within the scope of the investigation, and which is either—

(i) requested by the Commission for that purpose; or

(ii) information which, in his opinion, it would be appropriate for that purpose to give to the Commission without any such request;

and

(b) any other assistance which the Commission may require, and which it is within his power to give, in relation to any such matters;

and the Commission, for the purpose of carrying out any such investigation, shall take account of any information given to them for that purpose under this subsection.

(6) In determining for the purposes of this section whether any particular matter operates, or may be expected to operate, against the public interest, the Monopolies Commission shall have regard to the matters as respects which duties are imposed on the Secretary of State and the Director by Part I of this Act.

(7) Sections 70 (time limit for report on merger reference), 81 (procedure in carrying out investigations) and 85 (attendance of witnesses and production of documents) of the 1973 Act, Part II of Schedule 3 to that Act (performance of functions of the Monopolies Commission) and section 24 of the 1980 Act (modifications of provisions about performance of such functions) shall apply in relation to references under this section as if—

(a) the functions of the Commission in relation to those references were functions under the 1973 Act;

(b) the expression "merger reference" included a reference under this section;

(c) in the said section 70, references to the Secretary of State were references to the Director and the reference to three months were a reference to six months;

(d) in paragraph 11 of the said Schedule 3, the reference to section 71 of the 1973 Act were a reference to subsection (2) above; and

(e) paragraph 16(2) of that Schedule were omitted.

(8) For the purposes of references under this section, there shall be not less than eight additional members of the Monopolies Commission appointed from time to time by the Secretary of State; and, if any functions of that Commission in relation to any such reference are performed through a group—

(a) the chairman of that Commission shall select one or more of those additional members to be members of the group; and

(b) the number of regular members to be selected by him under paragraph 10 of Schedule 3 to the 1973 Act shall be reduced by the number of additional members selected.

**15.**—(1) In making a report on a reference under section 14 above, the Monopolies Commission—

(a) shall include in the report definite conclusions on the questions comprised in the reference together with such an account of their reasons for those conclusions as, in their opinion, is expedient for facilitating a proper understanding of those questions and of their conclusions;

(b) where they conclude that any of the matters specified in the reference operate, or may be expected to operate, against the public interest, shall specify in the report the effects adverse to the public interest which those matters have or may be expected to have; and

(c) where they conclude that any adverse effects so specified could be remedied or prevented by modifications of the conditions of a company's appointment under this Chapter, shall specify in the report modifications by which those effects could be remedied or prevented.

(2) Where, on a reference under section 14 above, the Monopolies Commission conclude that a company holding an appointment under this Chapter is a party to an agreement to which the Restrictive Trade Practices Act 1976 applies, the Commission, in making their report on that reference, shall exclude from their consideration the question whether the provisions of that agreement, in so far as they are provisions by virtue of which it is an agreement to which that Act applies, operate, or may be expected to operate, against the public interest; and paragraph (b) of subsection (1) above shall have effect subject to the provisions of this subsection.

(3) Section 82 of the 1973 Act (general provisions as to reports) shall apply in relation to reports of the Monopolies Commission on references under section 14 above as it applies to reports of the Commission under that Act.

(4) A report of the Monopolies Commission on a reference under section 14 above shall be made to the Director.

(5) Subject to subsection (6) below, the Director—

(a) shall, on receiving such a report, send a copy of it to the company to whose appointment under this Chapter the report relates and to the Secretary of State; and

(b) shall, not less than fourteen days after that copy is received by the Secretary of State, publish another copy of that report in such manner as he considers appropriate for bringing the report to the attention of persons likely to be affected by it.

(6) If it appears to the Secretary of State that the publication of any matter in such a report would be against the public interest or the commercial interests of any person, he may, before the end of the period of fourteen days mentioned in paragraph (b) of subsection (5) above, direct the Director to exclude that matter from every copy of the report to be published by virtue of that paragraph; and the Director shall comply with any such direction.

Modification following report.

**16.**—(1) Where a report of the Monopolies Commission on a reference under section 14 above—

(a) includes conclusions to the effect that any of the matters specified in the reference operate, or may be expected to operate, against the public interest;

(b) specifies effects adverse to the public interest which those matters have or may be expected to have;

(c) includes conclusions to the effect that those effects could be remedied or prevented by modifications of the conditions of a company's appointment under this Chapter; and

(d) specifies modifications by which those effects could be remedied or prevented,

the Director shall, subject to the following provisions of this section, make such modifications of the conditions of that appointment as appear to him requisite for the purpose of remedying or preventing the adverse effects specified in the report.

(2) Before making modifications under this section, the Director shall have regard to the modifications specified in the report.

(3) Before making modifications under this section, the Director shall give notice—

(a) stating that he proposes to make the modifications and setting out their effect;

(b) stating the reasons why he proposes to make the modifications; and

(c) specifying the period (not being less than twenty-eight days from the date of publication of the notice) within which representations or objections with respect to the proposed modifications may be made,

and shall consider any representations or objections which are duly made and not withdrawn.

(4) A notice under subsection (3) above shall be given—

(a) by publishing the notice in such manner as the Director considers appropriate for the purpose of bringing the matters to which the notice relates to the attention of persons likely to be affected by the making of the modifications; and

(b) by serving a copy of the notice on the company whose appointment it is proposed to modify.

(5) The Director shall not under this section make any modification of any provisions of a company's appointment under this Chapter which—

    (a) are contained in that appointment for the purposes of section 7(4)(c) above; or

    (b) being provisions relating to the disposal of, or of interests or rights in or over, a company's protected land, are stated in the appointment to be provisions which cannot be modified.

**17.**—(1) Subject to subsection (3) below, where in the circumstances mentioned in subsection (2) below the Secretary of State by order exercises any of the powers specified in—

    (a) Parts I and II of Schedule 8 to the 1973 Act; or

    (b) section 10(2)(a) of the 1980 Act,

the order may also provide for the modification of the conditions of a company's appointment under this Chapter to such extent as may appear to him to be requisite or expedient for the purpose of giving effect to, or taking account of, any provision made by the order.

(2) Subsection (1) above shall have effect where—

    (a) the circumstances are as mentioned in section 56(1) of the 1973 Act (order on report on monopoly reference) and the monopoly situation exists in relation to the carrying out of any of the functions of a relevant undertaker;

    (b) the circumstances are as mentioned in section 73(1) of that Act (order on report on merger reference) and the two or more enterprises which ceased to be distinct enterprises were both engaged in carrying out functions of a relevant undertaker; or

    (c) the circumstances are as mentioned in section 10(1) of the 1980 Act (order on report on competition reference) and the anti-competitive practice relates to the carrying out of any of the functions of a relevant undertaker.

(3) No modification shall be made by virtue of this section of any provisions of a company's appointment under this Chapter which—

    (a) are contained in that appointment for the purposes of section 7(4)(c) above; or

    (b) being provisions relating to the disposal of, or of interests or rights in or over, a company's protected land, are stated in the appointment to be provisions which cannot be modified.

(4) Expressions used in this section and in the 1973 Act or the 1980 Act have the same meanings in this section as in that Act.

## CHAPTER II

### ENFORCEMENT AND INSOLVENCY

#### *Enforcement orders*

**18.**—(1) Subject to subsection (2) and sections 19 and 20 below, where in the case of any company holding an appointment under Chapter I of this Part the Secretary of State or the Director is satisfied—

    (a) that that company is contravening—

        (i) any condition of the company's appointment in relation to which he is the enforcement authority; or

(ii) any statutory or other requirement which is enforceable under this section and in relation to which he is the enforcement authority;

or

(b) that that company has contravened any such condition or requirement and is likely to do so again,

he shall by a final enforcement order make such provision as is requisite for the purpose of securing compliance with that condition or requirement.

(2) Subject to section 19 below, where in the case of any company holding an appointment under Chapter I of this Part—

(a) it appears to the Secretary of State or the Director as mentioned in paragraph (a) or (b) of subsection (1) above; and

(b) it appears to him that it is requisite that a provisional enforcement order be made,

he may (instead of taking steps towards the making of a final order) by a provisional enforcement order make such provision as appears to him requisite for the purpose of securing compliance with the condition or requirement in question.

(3) In determining for the purposes of subsection (2)(b) above whether it is requisite that a provisional enforcement order be made, the Secretary of State or, as the case may be, the Director shall have regard, in particular, to the extent to which any person is likely to sustain loss or damage in consequence of anything which, in contravention of any condition or of any statutory or other requirement enforceable under this section, is likely to be done, or omitted to be done, before a final enforcement order may be made.

(4) Subject to sections 19 and 20 below, where the Secretary of State or the Director has made a provisional enforcement order, he shall confirm it, with or without modifications, if—

(a) he is satisfied that the company to which the order relates—

(i) is contravening any condition or statutory or other requirement in relation to which he is the enforcement authority; or

(ii) has contravened any such condition or requirement and is likely to do so again;

and

(b) the provision made by the order (with any modifications) is requisite for the purpose of securing compliance with that condition or requirement.

(5) An enforcement order—

(a) shall require the company to which it relates (according to the circumstances of the case) to do, or not to do, such things as are specified in the order or are of a description so specified;

(b) shall take effect at such time, being the earliest practicable time, as is determined by or under the order; and

(c) may be revoked at any time by the enforcement authority who made it.

(6) For the purposes of this section and the following provisions of this Act—

   (a) the statutory and other requirements which shall be enforceable under this section in relation to a company holding an appointment under Chapter I of this Part shall be such of the requirements of any enactment or of any subordinate legislation as—

      (i) are imposed in consequence of that appointment; and

      (ii) are made so enforceable by that enactment or subordinate legislation;

   (b) the Director shall be the enforcement authority in relation to the conditions of an appointment under Chapter I of this Part; and

   (c) the enforcement authority in relation to each of the statutory and other requirements enforceable under this section shall be the Secretary of State, the Director or either of them, according to whatever provision is made by the enactment or subordinate legislation by which the requirement is made so enforceable.

(7) In this section and the following provisions of this Chapter—

"enforcement order" means a final enforcement order or a provisional enforcement order;

"final enforcement order" means an order under this section other than a provisional enforcement order;

"provisional enforcement order" means an order under this section which, if not previously confirmed in accordance with subsection (4) above, will cease to have effect at the end of such period (not exceeding three months) as is determined by or under the order.

(8) Where any act or omission constitutes a contravention of a condition of an appointment under Chapter I of this Part or of a statutory or other requirement enforceable under this section, the only remedies for that contravention, apart from those available by virtue of this section, shall be those for which express provision is made by or under any enactment and those that are available in respect of that act or omission otherwise than by virtue of its constituting such a contravention.

**19.**—(1) Neither the Secretary of State nor the Director shall be required to make an enforcement order in relation to any company, or to confirm a provisional enforcement order so made, if he is satisfied—

   (a) that the contraventions were, or the apprehended contraventions are, of a trivial nature;

   (b) that the company has given, and is complying with, an undertaking to take all such steps as it appears to him for the time being to be appropriate for the company to take for the purpose of securing or facilitating compliance with the condition or requirement in question; or

   (c) that the duties imposed on him by Part I of this Act preclude the making or, as the case may be, the confirmation of the order.

(2) The requirement to comply with an undertaking given for the purposes of subsection (1)(b) above shall be treated as a statutory requirement enforceable under section 18 above—

(a) by the Secretary of State; or

(b) with the consent of or in accordance with a general authorisation given by the Secretary of State, by the Director.

(3) Where the Secretary of State or the Director, having notified a company that he is considering the making in relation to the company of an enforcement order or the confirmation of a provisional enforcement order so made, is satisfied as mentioned in paragraph (a), (b) or (c) of subsection (1) above, he shall—

(a) serve notice that he is so satisfied on the company;

(b) publish a copy of the notice in such manner as he considers appropriate for the purpose of bringing the matters to which the notice relates to the attention of persons likely to be affected by them; and

(c) in a case where the Secretary of State is satisfied as mentioned in the said paragraph (b), serve a copy of the notice and of the undertaking given for the purposes of that paragraph on the Director.

(4) The requirements of subsection (3) above shall not apply, in the case of any proposed order or confirmation in respect of a direction under section 208 below, to the extent that the Secretary of State directs that they should not be complied with in the interests of national security.

Procedure for
enforcement
orders.

**20.**—(1) Before making a final enforcement order or confirming a provisional enforcement order, the Secretary of State or the Director shall give notice—

(a) stating that he proposes to make or confirm the order and setting out the effect of the order;

(b) setting out—

(i) the condition or requirement for the purpose of securing compliance with which the order is to be made or confirmed;

(ii) the acts or omissions which, in his opinion, constitute or would constitute contraventions of that condition or requirement; and

(iii) the other facts which, in his opinion, justify the making or confirmation of the order;

and

(c) specifying the period (not being less than twenty-eight days from the date of publication of the notice) within which representations or objections with respect to the proposed order or proposed confirmation may be made,

and shall consider any representations or objections which are duly made and not withdrawn.

(2) A notice under subsection (1) above shall be given—

(a) by publishing the notice in such manner as the Secretary of State or, as the case may be, the Director considers appropriate for the purpose of bringing the matters to which the notice relates to the attention of persons likely to be affected by them; and

(b) by serving a copy of the notice, and a copy of the proposed order or of the order proposed to be confirmed, on the company to which the order relates and, where the notice is given by the Secretary of State, on the Director.

(3) Neither the Secretary of State nor the Director shall make a final enforcement order with modifications, or confirm a provisional enforcement order with modifications, except—

(a) with the consent to the modifications of the company to which the order relates; or

(b) after complying with the requirements of subsection (4) below.

(4) The requirements mentioned in subsection (3) above are that the Secretary of State or, as the case may be, the Director shall—

(a) serve on the company to which the order relates such notice as appears to him to be requisite of his proposal to make or confirm the order with modifications;

(b) in that notice specify the period (not being less than twenty-eight days from the date of the service of the notice) within which representations or objections with respect to the proposed modifications may be made; and

(c) consider any representations or objections which are duly made and not withdrawn.

(5) As soon as practicable after making an enforcement order or confirming a provisional enforcement order, the Secretary of State or, as the case may be, the Director shall—

(a) serve a copy of the order on the company to which the order relates and, where this subsection applies in the case of an order made or confirmed by Secretary of State, on the Director; and

(b) publish such a copy in such manner as he considers appropriate for the purpose of bringing the order to the attention of persons likely to be affected by it.

(6) Before revoking an enforcement order, other than an unconfirmed provisional order, the Secretary of State or the Director shall give notice—

(a) stating that he proposes to revoke the order and setting out its effect; and

(b) specifying the period (not being less than twenty-eight days from the date of publication of the notice) within which representations or objections with respect to the proposed revocation may be made,

and shall consider any representations or objections which are duly made and not withdrawn.

(7) If, after giving a notice under subsection (6) above, the Secretary of State or the Director decides not to revoke the order to which the notice relates, he shall give notice of that decision.

(8) A notice under subsection (6) or (7) above shall be given—

(a) by publishing the notice in such manner as the Secretary of State or, as the case may be, the Director considers appropriate for the purpose of bringing the matters to which the notice relates to the attention of persons likely to be affected by them; and

(b) by serving a copy of the notice on the company to which the order relates and, where the notice is given by the Secretary of State, on the Director.

(9) The requirements of the preceding provisions of this section shall not apply, in the case of any order in respect of a contravention of a direction under section 208 below, to the extent that the Secretary of State directs that they should not be complied with in the interests of national security.

Validity of enforcement orders.

**21.**—(1) If the company to which an enforcement order relates is aggrieved by the order and desires to question its validity on the ground—

(a) that its making or confirmation was not within the powers of section 18 above; or

(b) that any of the requirements of section 20 above have not been complied with in relation to it,

the company may, within forty-two days from the date of service on it of a copy of the order, make an application to the High Court under this section.

(2) On any such application the High Court may, if satisfied that the making or confirmation of the order was not within those powers or that the interests of the company have been substantially prejudiced by a failure to comply with those requirements, quash the order or any provision of the order.

(3) Except as provided by this section, the validity of an enforcement order shall not be questioned in any legal proceedings whatsoever.

Effect of enforcement order.

**22.**—(1) The obligation to comply with an enforcement order shall be a duty owed to any person who may be affected by a contravention of the order.

(2) Where a duty is owed by virtue of subsection (1) above to any person, any breach of the duty which causes that person to sustain loss or damage shall be actionable at the suit of that person.

(3) In any proceedings brought against any company in pursuance of subsection (2) above, other than proceedings in respect of so much of a contravention of any order as consists in a breach of the duty imposed by virtue of section 68(1)(a) below, it shall be a defence for the company to show that it took all reasonable steps and exercised all due diligence to avoid contravening the order.

(4) Without prejudice to any right which any person may have by virtue of subsection (1) above to bring civil proceedings in respect of any contravention or apprehended contravention of an enforcement order, compliance with any such order shall be enforceable by civil proceedings by the relevant enforcement authority for an injunction or for any other appropriate relief.

(5) In subsection (4) above "the relevant enforcement authority", in relation to any enforcement order, means the Secretary of State or the Director or either of them according to who is the enforcement authority in relation to the condition or requirement compliance with which was to be secured by the order.

*Special administration orders*

**23.**—(1) A special administration order is an order of the High Court made in accordance with section 24 or 25 below in relation to a company holding an appointment under Chapter I of this Part and directing that, during the period for which the order is in force, the affairs, business and property of the company shall be managed, by a person appointed by the High Court—

Meaning and effect of special administration order.

(a) for the achievement of the purposes of such an order; and

(b) in a manner which protects the respective interests of the members and creditors of the company.

(2) The purposes of a special administration order made in relation to any company shall be-

(a) the transfer to another company, or (as respects different parts of the area to which the company's appointment relates, or different parts of its undertaking) to two or more different companies, as a going concern, of so much of the company's undertaking as it is necessary to transfer in order to ensure that the functions which have been vested in the company by virtue of its appointment may be properly carried out; and

(b) the carrying out of those functions pending the making of the transfer and the vesting of those functions in the other company or companies (whether by virtue of the transfer or of an appointment or variation which replaces the former company as a relevant undertaker).

(3) Schedule 3 to this Act shall have effect for applying provisions of the Insolvency Act 1986 where a special administration order is made.

1986 c. 45.

(4) Schedule 2 to this Act shall have effect for enabling provision to be made with respect to cases in which a company is replaced by another as a relevant undertaker, without an appointment or variation under Chapter I of this Part, in pursuance of a special administration order.

(5) In this section "business" and "property" have the same meanings as in the Insolvency Act 1986.

1986 c. 45.

**24.**—(1) If, on an application made to the High Court by petition presented—

Special administration orders made on special petitions.

(a) by the Secretary of State; or

(b) with the consent of the Secretary of State, by the Director,

that Court is satisfied in relation to any company which holds an appointment under Chapter I of this Part that any one or more of the grounds specified in subsection (2) below is satisfied in relation to that company, that Court may make a special administration order in relation to that company.

(2) The grounds mentioned in subsection (1) above are, in relation to any company—

(a) that there has been, is or is likely to be such a contravention by the company of any principal duty, not being a contravention in respect of which a notice has been served under subsection (3) of section 19 above, as is serious enough to make it inappropriate for the company to continue to hold its appointment;

(b) that there has been, is or is likely to be such a contravention by the company of the provisions of any enforcement order which—

(i) is not for the time being the subject-matter of proceedings brought by virtue of section 21(1) above; and

(ii) if it is a provisional enforcement order, has been confirmed,

as is serious enough to make it inappropriate for the company to continue to hold its appointment;

(c) that the company is or is likely to be unable to pay its debts;

1985 c. 6.

(d) that, in a case in which the Secretary of State has certified that it would be appropriate, but for section 25 below, for him to petition for the winding up of the company under section 440 of the Companies Act 1985 (petition by the Secretary of State following inspectors' report etc.), it would be just and equitable, as mentioned in that section, for the company to be wound up if it did not hold an appointment under Chapter I of this Part; or

(e) that the company is unable or unwilling adequately to participate in arrangements certified by the Secretary of State or the Director to be necessary by reason of, or in connection with, a proposal for the making by virtue of section 7(4)(c) above of any appointment or variation replacing a company as a relevant undertaker.

(3) Notice of any petition under this section for a special administration order shall be given forthwith to such persons and in such manner as may be prescribed by rules made under section 411 of the Insolvency Act 1986 ("the 1986 Act"); and no such petition shall be withdrawn except with the leave of the High Court.

1986 c. 45.

(4) Subsections (4) and (5) of section 9 of the 1986 Act (powers on application for administration order) shall apply on the hearing of the petition for a special administration order in relation to any company as they apply on the hearing of a petition for an administration order.

(5) Subsections (1), (2) and (4) of section 10 of the 1986 Act (effect of petition) shall apply in the case of a petition for a special administration order in relation to any company as if—

(a) the reference in subsection (1) to an administration order were a reference to a special administration order;

(b) paragraph (b) of that subsection did require the leave of the court for the taking of any of the steps mentioned in paragraphs (b) and (c) of subsection (2) (appointment of, and exercise of functions by, administrative receiver); and

(c) the reference in paragraph (c) of subsection (1) to proceedings included a reference to any proceedings under or for the purposes of section 18 above.

(6) For the purposes of this section a company is unable to pay its debts if—

(a) it is a limited company which is deemed to be so unable under section 123 of the 1986 Act (definition of inability to pay debts); or

(b) it is an unregistered company which is deemed, by virtue of any of sections 222 to 224 of that Act, to be so unable for the purposes of section 221 of that Act (winding up of unregistered companies).

(7) In this section "principal duty", in relation to a company, means a requirement imposed on the company by section 37 or 94 below.

**25.** On an application made to any court for the winding up of a company which holds an appointment under Chapter I of this Part—

(a) the court shall not make a winding-up order in relation to the company; but

(b) if the court is satisfied that it would be appropriate to make such an order if the company were not a company holding such an appointment, it shall, instead, make a special administration order in relation to the company.

Power to make special administration order on winding-up petition.

*Restrictions on voluntary winding up and insolvency proceedings*

**26.**—(1) Where a company holds an appointment under Chapter I of this Part—

(a) the company shall not be wound up voluntarily;

(b) no administration order shall be made in relation to the company under Part II of the Insolvency Act 1986; and

(c) no step shall be taken by any person to enforce any security over the company's property except where that person has served fourteen days' notice of his intention to take that step on the Secretary of State and on the Director.

Restrictions on voluntary winding up and insolvency proceedings.

1986 c. 45.

(2) In this section "security" and "property" have the same meanings as in Parts I to VII of the Insolvency Act 1986.

1986 c. 45.

## CHAPTER III

### PROTECTION OF CUSTOMERS ETC.

#### *General provisions*

**27.**—(1) It shall be the duty of the Director, so far as it appears to him practicable from time to time to do so, to keep under review the carrying on both in England and Wales and elsewhere of activities connected with the matters in relation to which water undertakers or sewerage undertakers carry out functions.

General duty of Director to keep matters under review.

(2) It shall also be the duty of the Director, so far as it appears to him practicable from time to time to do so, to collect information with respect to—

(a) the carrying out by companies appointed under Chapter I of this Part of the functions of relevant undertakers; or

(b) any such company,

with a view to his becoming aware of, and ascertaining the circumstances relating to, matters with respect to which any power or duty is conferred or imposed on him by or under any enactment.

(3) The Secretary of State may give general directions indicating—

(a) considerations to which the Director should have particular regard in determining the order of priority in which matters are to be brought under review in performing his duty under subsection (1) or (2) above; and

(b) considerations to which, in cases where it appears to the Director that any of his powers under Parts II to V and VII of this Act are exercisable, he should have particular regard in determining whether to exercise those powers;

and it shall be the duty of the Director to comply with any such directions.

(4) It shall be the duty of the Director, where either he considers it expedient or he is requested by the Secretary of State or the Director General of Fair Trading to do so, to give information, advice and assistance to the Secretary of State or that Director with respect to any matter relating to—

(a) the functions of either description of relevant undertaker; or

(b) the carrying out of any such functions by a company holding an appointment under Chapter I of this Part.

Customer service committees.

**28.**—(1) Every company holding an appointment under Chapter I of this Part shall be allocated by the Director to a committee established and maintained by him for the purpose, in relation to such companies as may be allocated to it, of carrying out—

(a) the functions assigned by this Act to such a committee; and

(b) such other functions as the committees maintained under this section may be required to carry out by the Director.

(2) The committees maintained under this section shall be known as customer service committees.

(3) There shall not at any time be more than ten customer service committees, but it shall be the duty of the Director so to exercise his powers under this section to establish and maintain customer service committees and to allocate companies to those committees as to secure that at all times—

(a) such customer service committees are maintained; and

(b) such allocations under subsection (1) above are in force,

as he considers appropriate for ensuring that the interests of the customers and potential customers of the companies for the time being holding appointments under Chapter I of this Part are effectively represented.

(4) A customer service committee shall consist of—

(a) a chairman appointed by the Director after consultation with the Secretary of State; and

(b) such number (not less than ten nor more than twenty) of other members appointed by the Director as the Director may determine.

(5) In appointing persons to be members of a customer service committee the Director shall have regard to—

    (a) the desirability of the persons appointed being persons who have experience of, and have shown capacity in, some matter relevant to—

        (i) the functions of a water undertaker or sewerage undertaker; or

        (ii) the carrying out of those functions in relation to any area by a company which the Director has allocated, or is proposing to allocate, to that committee;

    and

    (b) the desirability of—

        (i) the committee including one or more persons with experience of work among, and the special needs of, disabled persons; and

        (ii) persons appointed by virtue of this paragraph including disabled persons.

(6) An appointment of a person to hold office as the chairman of a customer service committee shall be for a term not exceeding four years.

(7) Subject to subsection (6) above, the chairman and other members of a customer service committee shall hold and vacate office in accordance with the terms of their appointments and, notwithstanding that subsection, shall on ceasing to hold office be eligible for re-appointment.

(8) The provisions of Schedule 4 to this Act shall have effect with respect to customer service committees.

**29.**—(1) It shall be the duty of a customer service committee—

    (a) to keep under review all matters appearing to the committee to affect the interests of the persons who are customers or potential customers of the companies allocated to the committee;

    (b) to consult each company so allocated about such of those matters as appear to affect the interests of the customers or potential customers of that company; and

    (c) to make to a company so allocated all such representations about any such matter as the committee considers appropriate.

*Duties of customer service committees.*

(2) Subject to subsection (3) below, it shall be the duty of a customer service committee to investigate any complaint which—

    (a) is made to the committee by any person who is a customer or potential customer of a company allocated to the committee or is referred to the committee by the Director under section 30 below;

    (b) does not appear to the committee to be vexatious or frivolous; and

    (c) relates to the carrying out by that company of any of the functions of a relevant undertaker.

(3) It shall be the duty of a customer service committee to refer to the Director every complaint which is made to the committee by any person in relation to a company allocated to the committee and consists in or amounts to—

    (a) an assertion that the company is contravening or has contravened any condition of the company's appointment under Chapter I of this Part or any statutory or other requirement enforceable under section 18 above; or

    (b) a complaint which the Director would be required to investigate under section 181 below.

(4) It shall be the duty of a customer service committee, where the committee considers it appropriate to do so in connection with any such complaint as is mentioned in subsection (2) above, to make representations on behalf of the complainant to the company in question about any matter—

    (a) to which the complaint relates; or

    (b) which appears to the committee to be relevant to the subject-matter of the complaint;

and it shall be the duty of a customer service committee to refer to the Director or, as the case may be, back to the Director any such complaint as is so mentioned which the committee is unable to resolve.

(5) The only remedy for a breach by a customer service committee of a duty imposed on it by this section shall be the making of such a complaint to the Director as the Director is required to consider under section 30(3)(c) below.

(6) It shall be the duty of the Director to make such arrangements as he considers appropriate for facilitating the provision by one customer service committee to another of any such information as that other committee may require for any purpose relating to the carrying out of its functions.

**Duties of Director with respect to complaints**

**30.**—(1) Where a complaint is made to the Director by a customer or potential customer of a company allocated to a customer service committee and the complaint does not consist in or amount to—

    (a) an assertion that the company is contravening or has contravened any condition of the company's appointment under Chapter I of this Part or any statutory or other requirement enforceable under section 18 above; or

    (b) a complaint which the Director is required to investigate under section 181 below,

it shall be the duty of the Director to consider whether the complaint should be referred to that committee, instead of being dealt with by the Director himself.

(2) Where a complaint which does consist in or amount to such an assertion as is mentioned in subsection (2)(a) above—

    (a) is made to the Director by a customer or potential customer of any company allocated to a customer service committee; or

    (b) is referred to him by such a committee,

it shall be the duty of the Director to consider whether the complaint should be referred by him to the Secretary of State.

(3) It shall be the duty of the Director to consider the following complaints, that is to say—

    (a) any complaint to which the duty imposed by subsection (2) above applies and which is not referred by the Director to the Secretary of State;

    (b) any complaint which is referred to the Director under section 29(4) above; and

    (c) any complaint made to the Director by a customer or potential customer of a company allocated to a customer service committee that the committee has failed to perform any duty imposed on it by section 29(1) to (4) above.

(4) It shall be the duty of the Director to take such steps in consequence of his consideration of any matter in pursuance of this section (including, in a case falling within subsection (3)(b) or (c) above, any step which could have been taken by the committee itself) as he considers appropriate.

### *Provisions with respect to competition*

**31.**—(1) If and to the extent that he is requested by the Director General of Fair Trading to do so, it shall be the duty of the Director to exercise the functions of that Director under Part III of the 1973 Act so far as relating to courses of conduct which are or may be detrimental to the interests of persons who are consumers in relation to—

Functions of Director with respect to competition.

    (a) the supply of water by water undertakers; or

    (b) the provision of sewerage services by sewerage undertakers;

and this duty shall apply whether those interests are economic or interests in respect of health, safety or other matters.

(2) The Director shall continue to be entitled, concurrently with the Director General of Fair Trading, to exercise—

    (a) the functions of that Director under sections 44 and 45 of the 1973 Act; and

    (b) the functions of that Director under sections 50, 52, 53, 86 and 88 of that Act,

so far as relating to monopoly situations which exist or may exist in relation to commercial activities connected with the supply of water or the provision of sewerage services.

(3) The Director shall continue to be entitled, concurrently with the Director General of Fair Trading, to exercise the functions of that Director under sections 2 to 10 and 16 of the 1980 Act so far as relating to courses of conduct which have or are intended to have or are likely to have the effect of restricting, distorting, or preventing competition in connection with the supply of water or securing a supply of water or with the provision or securing of sewerage services.

(4) So far as necessary for the purposes of or in connection with the provisions of subsections (1) to (3) above, the references to the Director General of Fair Trading in—

    (a) Parts III and IV of the 1973 Act;

    (b) sections 86, 88 and 133 of the 1973 Act; and

(c) sections 2 to 10, 16 and 19 of the 1980 Act,

shall be construed as if they were or, as the case may require, as if they included references to the Director.

(5) Before either Director first exercises in relation to any matter functions mentioned in paragraph (a) or in paragraph (b) of subsection (2) above or in subsection (3) above, he shall consult the other Director.

(6) Neither Director shall exercise in relation to any matter any functions mentioned in paragraph (a) or in paragraph (b) of subsection (2) above or in subsection (3) above if any of the functions mentioned in that paragraph or, as the case may be, in subsection (3) above have already been exercised in relation to that matter by the other Director.

(7) It shall be the duty of the Director, for the purpose of assisting the Monopolies Commission in carrying out an investigation on a reference made to them by the Director by virtue of subsection (2) or (3) above, to give to the Commission—

> (a) any information which is in his possession and which relates to matters falling within the scope of the investigation, and which is either requested by the Commission for that purpose or is information which in his opinion it would be appropriate for that purpose to give to the Commission without any such request; and

> (b) any other assistance which the Commission may require, and which it is within his power to give, in relation to any such matters;

and the Commission shall, for the purposes of carrying out any such investigation, take into account any information given to them for that purpose under this subsection.

(8) If any question arises as to whether subsection (2) or (3) above applies to any particular case, that question shall be referred to and determined by the Secretary of State; and no objection shall be taken to anything done under—

> (a) Part IV or section 86 or 88 of the 1973 Act; or

> (b) sections 2 to 10 of the 1980 Act,

by or in relation to the Director on the ground that it should have been done by or in relation to the Director General of Fair Trading.

(9) Expressions used in the 1973 Act or the 1980 Act and in this section have the same meanings in this section as in that Act.

Duty to refer merger of water or sewerage undertakings.     **32.**—(1) Subject to the following provisions of this section and to section 33 below, it shall be the duty of the Secretary of State to make a merger reference to the Monopolies Commission if it appears to him that it is or may be the fact—

> (a) that arrangements are in progress which, if carried into effect, will result in a merger of any two or more water enterprises; or

> (b) that such a merger has taken place otherwise than as a result of the carrying into effect of arrangements that have been the subject of a reference by virtue of paragraph (a) above.

(2) The Secretary of State shall not make a merger reference under this section in respect of any actual or prospective merger of two or more water enterprises if it appears to him that the take over from which the merger has resulted or, as the case may be, would result was initiated before 9 a.m. on 11th January 1989.

(3) For the purposes of subsection (2) above a merger of two or more enterprises results from a take over initiated before 9 a.m. on 11th January 1989 if—

(a) the Secretary of State or the Director General of Fair Trading was given notice before that time on that date of the material facts about the proposed arrangements or transactions resulting in the merger; or

(b) the merger results exclusively from the acceptance of offers to acquire shares in a body corporate and those offers—

(i) were all made before that time on that date; or

(ii) in so far as they were not so made, consist in offers made, by the same person and in respect of the same shares, in substitution for offers made before that time on that date.

**33.**—(1) The Secretary of State shall not make a merger reference under section 32 above in respect of any actual or prospective merger of two or more water enterprises if it appears to him—

(a) that the value of the assets taken over does not exceed or, as the case may be, would not exceed the amount for the time being specified in section 64(1)(b) of the 1973 Act (condition of merger reference relating to amount of assets taken over); or

(b) that the only water enterprises already belonging to the person making the take over are enterprises each of which has assets the value of which does not exceed or, as the case may be, would not exceed that amount.

(2) In relation to a merger of two or more water enterprises—

(a) the value of the assets taken over shall, for the purposes of subsection (1) above, be determined in accordance with section 67 of the 1973 Act by reference only to assets employed in or appropriated to a water enterprise; and

(b) the value of the assets of a water enterprise belonging to the person making the take over shall be taken for those purposes to be the value of such assets employed in or appropriated to that enterprise as by virtue of the exceptions in paragraph (a) of subsection (2) of that section are disregarded in determining the value of the assets taken over;

and paragraph (b) of that subsection shall apply for determining the value of the assets referred to in paragraph (b) above as it applies in relation to the assets taken over.

(3) For the purposes of this section and of any determination in accordance with this section—

(a) the assets treated as employed in or appropriated to a water enterprise carried on by a company holding an appointment under Chapter I of this Part shall include all the assets for the time being of that company;

(b) every water enterprise any of whose assets fall to be disregarded as mentioned in subsection (2)(b) above shall be treated as belonging to the person making the take over;

(c) the enterprises mentioned in paragraph (b) above shall be treated as separate enterprises in so far as they are carried on by different companies holding appointments under Chapter I of this Part; and

(d) subsections (3) and (4) of section 67 of the 1973 Act (assets treated as appropriated to an enterprise and mergers over a period) shall apply as they apply for the purposes of, and of any determination in accordance with, subsection (2) of that section.

(4) If the Secretary of State considers that it is appropriate—

(a) for subsection (1) above to have effect with a reference in paragraph (a) to a different amount; or

(b) for the condition set out in that paragraph to be modified in any other respect,

he may, in relation to mergers after the coming into force of the regulations, by regulations make such modifications of that paragraph and, for that purpose, of the other provisions of this section as may be prescribed.

**34.**—(1) Subject to subsections (2) to (4) below, the 1973 Act shall have effect in relation to any reference under section 32 above as if—

(a) any such merger of two or more water enterprises as is required to be the subject of such a reference were a merger situation qualifying for investigation; and

(b) a reference under that section were made under section 64 of that Act or, as the case may be, under section 75 of that Act (references in anticipation of a merger).

(2) Nothing in subsection (1) above shall have the effect in relation to any reference under section 32 above of applying—

(a) so much of Part V of the 1973 Act as requires the Monopolies Commission to consider any of the matters set out in subsection (1) of section 64 of that Act; or

(b) the provisions of sections 69(2) to (4) and 75(3) of that Act (power to restrict matters referred).

(3) In determining on a reference under section 32 above whether any matter operates, or may be expected to operate, against the public interest the Monopolies Commission—

(a) shall have regard to the desirability of giving effect to the principle that the number of water enterprises which are under independent control should not be reduced so as to prejudice the Director's ability, in carrying out his functions by virtue of this Act, to make comparisons between different such water enterprises; and

(b) shall have regard to the desirability of achieving any other purpose so far only as they are satisfied—

(i) that that other purpose can be achieved in a manner that does not conflict with that principle; or

(ii) that the achievement of that other purpose is of substantially greater significance in relation to the public interest than that principle and cannot be brought about except in a manner that conflicts with that principle.

(4) No order shall be made under Part V of the 1973 Act in consequence of any merger reference made under section 32 above in respect of an actual merger unless the reference was made within the period of six months beginning with whichever is the later of—

(a) the day on which the merger took place; and

(b) the day on which the material facts about the transactions which resulted in the merger first came to the notice of the Secretary of State or the Director General of Fair Trading or were made public within the meaning of section 64 of the 1973 Act;

and if on such a reference the Monopolies Commission are satisfied that the reference was not made within that period their report on the reference shall state that fact and nothing else.

**35.**—(1) In this Chapter-

Construction of merger provisions.

"enterprise" has the meaning given for the purposes of sections 64 to 77 of the 1973 Act by section 63(2) of that Act; and

"water enterprise" means an enterprise carried on by a relevant undertaker.

(2) References in this Chapter, in relation to any two or more enterprises, to the merger of those enterprises are references to those enterprises ceasing, within the meaning of Part V of the 1973 Act, to be distinct enterprises; and sections 66 and 66A of that Act (time at which enterprises cease to be distinct) shall have effect for the purposes of this Chapter as they have effect for the purposes of that Part.

(3) The reference in section 34(3) above to the number of water enterprises under independent control is a reference to the number of water enterprises there would be if two or more water enterprises counted as one enterprise wherever they would be treated for the purposes of Part V of the 1973 Act as having ceased to be distinct enterprises.

(4) Nothing in sections 32 to 34 above shall prejudice any power of the Secretary of State, in a case in which he is not required to make a reference under section 32 above, to make a merger reference under Part V of the 1973 Act in respect of any actual or prospective merger of two or more water enterprises.

## CHAPTER IV

### INTERPRETATION OF PART II

**36.**—(1) In this Part—

Interpretation of Part II.<br>1973 c. 41.<br>1980 c. 21.

"the 1973 Act" means the Fair Trading Act 1973; and

"the 1980 Act" means the Competition Act 1980.

(2) References in this Part to an appointment or variation replacing a company as a relevant undertaker are references to the following, that is to say—

(a) the appointment of a company to be the water undertaker or sewerage undertaker for any area which is or includes the whole or any part of any area for which another company already holds an appointment as water undertaker or, as the case may be, sewerage undertaker; or

(b) a variation by virtue of which the area for which a company holds an appointment under Chapter I of this Part is modified so as to include the whole or any part of an area for which another company already holds an appointment as water undertaker or, as the case may be, sewerage undertaker.

(3) For the purposes of this Part premises in a part of an area are served by a company holding an appointment under Chapter I of this Part—

(a) in relation to an appointment or variation by virtue of which that company would be replaced as the water undertaker for that part of that area, if those premises—

(i) are supplied with water by means of a connection with a distribution main of that company; or

(ii) consist in a building or part of a building which is situated within thirty metres of such a main;

and

(b) in relation to an appointment or variation by virtue of which that company would be replaced as the sewerage undertaker for that part of that area, if those premises—

(i) are drained by means of a relevant sewer; or

(ii) consist in a building or part of a building which is situated within thirty metres of such a sewer, not being a storm-water overflow sewer.

(4) In this section—

"distribution main" means a water main that is not a trunk main; and

"relevant sewer", in relation to any appointment or variation which would replace a company as a sewerage undertaker, means any of the following, that is to say—

(a) a public sewer vested in that company;

(b) a sewer in relation to which that company has made a declaration of vesting under section 102 below which has not yet taken effect;

(c) a drain or sewer in relation to which that company has entered into an agreement under section 104 below.

## PART III

### WATER SUPPLY

#### CHAPTER I

##### GENERAL DUTIES OF WATER UNDERTAKERS

General duty to maintain water supply system etc.

**37.**—(1) It shall be the duty of every water undertaker to develop and maintain an efficient and economical system of water supply within its area and to ensure that all such arrangements have been made—

(a) for providing supplies of water to premises in that area and for making such supplies available to persons who demand them; and

(b) for maintaining, improving and extending the water undertaker's water mains and other pipes,

as are necessary for securing that the undertaker is and continues to be able to meet its obligations under this Part.

(2) The duty of a water undertaker under this section shall be enforceable under section 18 above—

(a) by the Secretary of State; or

(b) with the consent of or in accordance with a general authorisation given by the Secretary of State, by the Director.

(3) The obligations imposed on a water undertaker by the following Chapters of this Part, and the remedies available in respect of contraventions of those obligations, shall be in addition to any duty imposed or remedy available by virtue of any provision of this section or section 38 below and shall not be in any way qualified by any such provision.

**38.**—(1) For the purpose-

Standards of performance in connection with water supply.

(a) of facilitating the determination of the extent to which breaches of the obligations imposed by the following provisions of this Part are to amount to breaches of the duty imposed by section 37 above; or

(b) of supplementing that duty by establishing overall standards of performance in relation to that duty,

the Secretary of State may, in accordance with section 39 below, by regulations provide for contraventions of such requirements as may be prescribed to be treated for the purposes of this Act as breaches of that duty.

(2) The Secretary of State may, in accordance with section 39 below, by regulations prescribe such standards of performance in connection with the provision of supplies of water as, in his opinion, ought to be achieved in individual cases.

(3) Regulations under subsection (2) above may provide that if a water undertaker fails to meet a prescribed standard it shall pay such amount as may be prescribed to any person who is affected by the failure and is of a prescribed description.

(4) Without prejudice to the generality of the power conferred by subsection (2) above, regulations under that subsection may—

(a) include in a standard of performance a requirement for a water undertaker, in prescribed circumstances, to inform a person of his rights by virtue of any such regulations;

(b) provide for any dispute under the regulations to be referred by either party to the dispute to the Director;

(c) make provision for the procedure to be followed in connection with any such reference and for the Director's determination on such a reference to be enforceable in such manner as may be prescribed;

(d) prescribe circumstances in which a water undertaker is to be exempted from requirements of the regulations.

Procedure for regulations under section 38.

**39.**—(1) The Secretary of State shall not make any regulations under section 38 above unless—

(a) the Director has made to the Secretary of State a written application complying with subsection (2) below;

(b) the Secretary of State is satisfied that a copy of the application has been served by the Director on every water undertaker specified in the application;

(c) such period as the Secretary of State considers appropriate has been allowed for the making—

(i) by the Director; and

(ii) by any affected water undertaker,

of representations or objections with respect to the Director's proposals and any modifications proposed by the Secretary of State; and

(d) the Secretary of State has considered both the Director's reasons for his proposals and every representation or objection which has been duly made with respect to those proposals, or any proposed modifications of those proposals, and has not been withdrawn.

(2) An application made by the Director to the Secretary of State complies with this subsection if it—

(a) sets out draft provisions proposed by the Director for inclusion in regulations under section 38 above;

(b) specifies the water undertaker or undertakers in relation to which it is proposed those provisions should apply; and

(c) summarises the Director's reasons for his proposals.

(3) The Secretary of State shall not make any regulations under section 38 above except where—

(a) the only provisions of the regulations are the provisions proposed by the Director in his application or those provisions with such modifications as the Secretary of State considers appropriate; and

(b) each of the modifications (if any) of the Director's proposals to which effect is given by the regulations is a modification the proposal to make which has been notified—

(i) to the Director; and

(ii) to any water undertaker appearing to the Secretary of State to be likely to be affected by the modifications.

CHAPTER II

SUPPLY DUTIES

*Major supplies*

**40.**—(1) Where, on the application of a water undertaker— Bulk supplies.

(a) it appears to the Director that it is necessary or expedient for the purposes of this Part that another water undertaker should give a supply of water in bulk to the applicant; and

(b) he is satisfied that the giving and taking of such a supply cannot be secured by agreement,

the Director may by order require the undertakers to give and to take such a supply for such period and on such terms and conditions as may be provided in the order.

(2) An order under this section shall have effect as an agreement between the water undertakers in question but may be varied or revoked by a subsequent order made by the Director on the application of either of those undertakers, as well as by agreement between the undertakers.

(3) The Director shall not make an order under this section which he considers affects the carrying out by the NRA of any of its functions unless he has first consulted the NRA.

(4) In determining what provision to make by an order under this section in respect of the giving of any supply by a water undertaker the Director shall have regard to the desirability of the undertaker's recovering the expenses of complying with its obligations under this section and of securing a reasonable return on its capital.

**41.**—(1) It shall be the duty of a water undertaker (in accordance with Duty to comply section 44 below) to provide a water main to be used for providing such with water main supplies of water to premises in a particular locality in its area as (so far requisition. as those premises are concerned) are sufficient for domestic purposes, if—

(a) the undertaker is required to provide the main by a notice served on the undertaker by one or more of the persons who under subsection (2) below are entitled to require the provision of the main for that locality;

(b) the premises in that locality to which those supplies would be provided by means of that main are—

(i) premises consisting in buildings or parts of buildings; or

(ii) premises which will so consist when proposals made by any person for the erection of buildings or parts of buildings are carried out;

and

(c) the conditions specified in section 42 below are satisfied in relation to that requirement.

(2) Each of the following persons shall be entitled to require the provision of a water main for any locality, that is to say—

(a) the owner of any premises in that locality;

(b) the occupier of any premises in that locality;

(c) any local authority within whose area the whole or any part of that locality is situated;

(d) where the whole or any part of that locality is situated in a new town, within the meaning of the New Towns Act 1981—

    (i) the Commission for the New Towns; and

    (ii) the Development Board for Rural Wales or the development corporation for the new town, according to whether or not the new town is situated within the area for which that Board is for the time being responsible;

and

(e) where the whole or any part of that locality is situated within an area designated as an urban development area under Part XVI of the Local Government, Planning and Land Act 1980, the urban development corporation.

(3) The duty of a water undertaker under this section to provide a water main shall be owed to the person who requires the provision of the main or, as the case may be, to each of the persons who joins in doing so.

(4) Where a duty is owed by virtue of subsection (3) above to any person, any breach of that duty which causes that person to sustain loss or damage shall be actionable at the suit of that person; but, in any proceedings brought against a water undertaker in pursuance of this subsection, it shall be a defence for the undertaker to show that it took all reasonable steps and exercised all due diligence to avoid the breach.

(5) In this section "local authority", in relation to the Inner Temple and the Middle Temple, includes, respectively, the Sub-Treasurer of the Inner Temple and the Under-Treasurer of the Middle Temple.

Financial conditions of compliance.

**42.**—(1) The conditions mentioned in section 41(1)(c) above are satisfied in relation to a requirement for the provision of a water main by a water undertaker if—

(a) such undertakings as the undertaker may have reasonably required in accordance with subsection (2) below have been given by the person or persons who have required the provision of the main; and

(b) such security as the undertaker may have reasonably required has been provided for the discharge of any obligations imposed by those undertakings on any person who, under subsection (3) below, may be required to secure his undertakings.

(2) The undertakings which a water undertaker may require for the purposes of subsection (1) above in respect of any water main are undertakings which—

(a) bind the person or persons mentioned in that subsection to pay to the undertaker, in respect of each of the twelve years following the provision of the main, an amount not exceeding the relevant deficit (if any) for that year on that main; and

(b) in the case of undertakings binding two or more persons, bind them either jointly and severally or with liability to pay apportioned in such manner as they may agree.

(3) For the purposes of subsection (1)(b) above a person may be required to secure his undertakings in relation to the provision of a water main if—

(a) it was by virtue of section 41(2)(a) or (b) above that he required, or joined in requiring, the provision of the main; and

(b) he is not a public authority.

(4) Where for the purposes of subsection (1)(b) above any sums have been deposited with a water undertaker by way of security for the discharge of any obligation, the undertaker shall pay interest at such rate as may be determined either—

(a) by the undertaker with the approval of the Director; or

(b) in default of a determination under paragraph (a) above, by the Director,

on every sum of 50p so deposited for every three months during which it remains in the hands of the undertaker.

(5) An approval or determination given or made by the Director for the purposes of subsection (4) above—

(a) may be given or made in relation to the provision of a particular water main, in relation to the provision of mains of a particular description or in relation to the provision of water mains generally; and

(b) may be revoked at any time.

(6) Any dispute between a water undertaker and any other person as to—

(a) the undertakings or security required by the undertaker for the purposes of this section; or

(b) the amount required to be paid in pursuance of any such undertaking,

shall be referred to the arbitration of a single arbitrator appointed by agreement between the undertaker and that person or, in default of agreement, by the President of the Institution of Civil Engineers.

(7) In this section "relevant deficit" has the meaning given by section 43 below.

**43.**—(1) For the purposes of section 42 above the relevant deficit for any year on a water main is the amount (if any) by which the water charges payable for the use during that year of that main are exceeded by the annual borrowing costs of a loan of the amount required for the provision of that main.

Calculation of "relevant deficit" for the purposes of section 42.

(2) The annual borrowing costs of a loan of the amount required for the provision of a water main is the aggregate amount which would fall to be paid in any year by way of payments of interest and repayments of capital if an amount equal to so much of the costs reasonably incurred in providing that main as were not incurred in the provision of additional capacity had been borrowed, by the water undertaker providing the main, on terms—

(a) requiring interest to be paid and capital to be repaid in twelve equal annual instalments; and

(b) providing for the amount of the interest to be calculated at such rate, and in accordance with such other provision, as may have been determined for the purposes of this subsection.

(3) A determination for the purposes of subsection (2) above shall be made either—

(a) by the undertaker with the approval of the Director; or

(b) in default of such a determination, by the Director.

(4) For the purposes of this section the costs reasonably incurred in providing a water main ("the new main") shall include—

(a) the costs reasonably incurred in providing such other water mains and such tanks, service reservoirs and pumping stations as it is necessary to provide in consequence of the provision of the new main; and

(b) such proportion (if any) as is reasonable of the costs reasonably incurred in providing any such additional capacity in an earlier main as falls to be used in consequence of the provision of the new main.

(5) In subsection (4) above the reference to an earlier main, in relation to the new main, is a reference to any water main which—

(a) has been provided in the period of twelve years immediately before the provision of the new main; and

(b) was so provided in pursuance of a water main requisition.

(6) Any reference in this section to the provision of additional capacity in a water main provided in pursuance of a requirement under any enactment is a reference to such works carried out or other things done in connection with the provision of that main as are carried out or done for the purpose of enabling that main to be used for purposes in addition to those for which it is necessary to provide the main in order to comply with the requirement.

(7) Any reference in this section to the water charges payable for the use during any year of any main provided by a water undertaker is a reference to so much of the aggregate of any charges payable to the water undertaker in respect of services provided in the course of that year as represents charges which—

(a) have been imposed by the undertaker in relation to premises which are connected with that main; and

(b) are reasonably attributable to the provision of a supply of water (whether or not for domestic purposes) to those premises by means of that main.

(8) An approval or determination given or made by the Director for the purposes of subsection (2) above—

(a) may be given or made in relation to the provision of a particular water main, in relation to the provision of mains of a particular description or in relation to the provision of water mains generally; and

(b) may be revoked at any time except in relation to a water main that has already been provided.

(9) In this section "water main requisition" means—

(a) a requirement under section 41 above (including, by virtue of paragraph 1 of Schedule 2 to the Water Consolidation (Consequential Provisions) Act 1991, a requirement under section 40 of the Water Act 1989);

(b) a requirement under the provisions of section 36 or 37 of the Water Act 1945 or of section 29 of Schedule 3 to that Act (water main requisitions); or

(c) a requirement under any local statutory provision corresponding to section 41 above or to any of those provisions of that Act of 1945.

**44.**—(1) A water undertaker shall not be in breach of a duty imposed by section 41 above in relation to any locality unless-

(a) the period of three months beginning with the relevant day has expired; and

(b) the water undertaker has not, before the end of that period, so laid the water main to be provided as to enable service pipes to premises in that locality to connect with the main at the places determined under subsection (3) below.

(2) The period mentioned in subsection (1)(a) above may be extended in any case—

(a) by agreement between the water undertaker and the person or persons who required the provision of the main; or

(b) where there is a dispute as to whether the period should be extended, by an arbitrator on a reference under subsection (4) below.

(3) The places mentioned in subsection (1)(b) above shall be—

(a) such places as are determined by agreement between the water undertaker and the person or persons who required the provision of the water main; or

(b) in default of agreement, such places as are determined by an arbitrator, on a reference under subsection (4) below, to be the places at which it is reasonable, in all the circumstances, for service pipes to premises in the locality in question to connect with the water main.

(4) A reference for the purposes of subsection (2) or (3) above shall be to a single arbitrator appointed—

(a) by agreement between the undertaker and the person or persons who required the provision of the water main; or

(b) in default of agreement, by the President of the Institution of Civil Engineers.

(5) In this section "relevant day", in relation to a requirement to provide a water main for any locality, means the day after whichever is the later of the following, that is to say—

(a) the day on which the conditions specified in section 42 above are satisfied in relation to the requirement; and

(b) the day on which the places where service pipes to premises in that locality will connect with the main are determined under subsection (3) above.

*Domestic connections*

Duty to make
connections with
main.

**45.**—(1) Subject to the following provisions of this section and to sections 46 and 47 below, it shall be the duty of a water undertaker (in accordance with section 51 below) to make a connection under this section where the owner or occupier of any premises in the undertaker's area which—

(a) consist in the whole or any part of a building; or

(b) are premises on which any person is proposing to erect any building or part of a building,

serves a notice on the undertaker requiring it, for the purpose of providing a supply of water for domestic purposes to that building or part of a building, to connect a service pipe to those premises with one of the undertaker's water mains.

(2) Where a notice has been served for the purposes of this section, the duty imposed by subsection (1) above shall be a duty, at the expense of the person serving the notice, to make the connection required by the notice if—

(a) the main with which the service pipe is required to be connected is neither a trunk main nor a water main which is or is to be used solely for the purpose of supplying water otherwise than for domestic purposes; and

(b) such conditions as the undertaker may have imposed under sections 47 to 50 below have been satisfied;

and, subject to section 51 below, that duty shall arise whether or not the service pipe to which the notice relates has been laid when the notice is served.

(3) A notice for the purposes of this section—

(a) shall be accompanied or supplemented by all such information as the undertaker may reasonably require; and

(b) if the notice has effect so that a requirement is imposed on the undertaker by virtue of section 46(4) below, shall set out the matters that have given rise to the imposition of that requirement;

but, subject to section 51(5) below and without prejudice to the effect (if any) of any other contravention of this subsection, a failure to provide information in pursuance of the obligation to supplement such a notice shall not invalidate that notice.

(4) The duty imposed on a water undertaker by this section shall be owed to the person who served the notice by virtue of which the duty arises.

(5) Where a duty is owed by virtue of subsection (4) above to any person, any breach of that duty which causes that person to sustain loss or damage shall be actionable at the suit of that person; but, in any proceedings brought against a water undertaker in pursuance of this subsection, it shall be a defence for the undertaker to show that it took all reasonable steps and exercised all due diligence to avoid the breach.

(6) Where a water undertaker carries out any works which it is its duty under this section to carry out at another person's expense, the undertaker shall be entitled to recover from that person an amount equal to the expenses reasonably incurred by the undertaker in carrying out the works.

(7) Nothing in this section or in sections 46 to 51 below shall impose any duty on a water undertaker to connect a service pipe to any premises with a service pipe to any other premises.

(8) In the following provisions of this Chapter a notice served for the purposes of this section is referred to as a connection notice.

**46.**—(1) Where a water undertaker is required to make a connection in pursuance of any connection notice, it shall also be the duty of the undertaker, at the expense of the person serving the notice, to carry out such of the works to which this section applies as need to be carried out before the connection can be made.

(2) This section applies to the laying of so much of the service pipe to be connected with the water main as it is necessary, for the purpose of making that connection, to lay in a street.

(3) In a case where—

(a) the water main with which the service pipe is to be connected is situated in a street;

(b) the premises consisting in the building or part of a building in question together with any land occupied with it abut on the part of the street where the main is situated; and

(c) the service pipe to those premises will—

(i) enter the premises otherwise than through an outer wall of a building abutting on the street; and

(ii) have a stopcock fitted to it by the undertaker in the premises,

this section applies to the laying of so much of the service pipe as it is necessary, for the purpose of making the required connection, to lay in land between the boundary of the street and that stopcock.

(4) In a case where the connection notice is served in compliance with a requirement imposed by a notice by a local authority under section 80 below, this section applies to the laying of so much of the service pipe to be connected with a water main in pursuance of the connection notice as it is necessary, for the purpose of making the connection, to lay in land owned or occupied by a person who is certified by that authority—

(a) to have unreasonably refused his consent to the laying of the service pipe; or

(b) to have sought to make the giving of his consent subject to unreasonable conditions.

(5) Where a water main is alongside a street and within eighteen metres of the middle of that street, subsections (2) to (4) above shall have effect in relation to the laying, for the purpose of making a connection with that main, of a service pipe to any premises as if the street included so much of the land between the main and the boundary of the street as is not comprised in those premises or in any land occupied with those premises.

(6) It shall be the duty of any water undertaker making a connection in pursuance of a connection notice to ensure that a stopcock belonging to the undertaker is fitted to the service pipe which is connected.

(7) Subsections (4) to (6) of section 45 above shall have effect-

(a) in relation to any duties which, by virtue of a connection notice, are imposed on a water undertaker by this section; and

(b) in relation to any works which, by virtue of the service of such a notice, such an undertaker carries out under this section at another person's expense,

as they have effect by virtue of that notice in relation to the duty which arises under that section or, as the case may be, to works which the undertaker carries out under that section at another person's expense.

(8) Subject to subsection (9) below, a water undertaker may comply with any duty under this section to lay a service pipe by laying a water main instead; but nothing in section 45 above or this section shall impose any duty on a water undertaker to lay a water main where it has no power to lay a service pipe.

(9) Where a water undertaker exercises its power under subsection (8) above to lay a water main instead of a service pipe—

(a) paragraph (a) of section 51(1) below shall have effect as if any additional time reasonably required by reason of the laying of the main instead of the service pipe were included in the time allowed by that paragraph for the laying of the service pipe; but

(b) the expenses recoverable by virtue of section 45(6) and subsection (7) above shall not exceed such amount as it would have been reasonable for the undertaker to have incurred in laying a service pipe instead of the main.

Conditions of connection with water main.

**47.**—(1) Subject to subsection (3) and sections 48 to 50 below, where the owner or occupier of any premises ("the relevant premises") serves a connection notice on a water undertaker, the undertaker may make compliance with one or more of the requirements specified in subsection (2) below a condition of its complying with the duties to which it is subject by virtue of that notice.

(2) The requirements mentioned in subsection (1) above are—

(a) a requirement that such security as the undertaker may reasonably require has been provided for the discharge of any obligations imposed by virtue of section 45(6) or 46(7)(b) above on the person who served the connection notice;

(b) a requirement, in a case where the connection required by the connection notice is necessary as a consequence of a disconnection made by reason of any person's failure to pay any charges, that the person serving the connection notice has paid any amount owed by him to the undertaker—

(i) in respect of a supply of water to the relevant premises; or

(ii) in respect of expenses incurred in the making of the disconnection;

(c) a requirement that a meter for use in determining the amount of any charges which have been or may be fixed in relation to the relevant premises by reference to volume has been installed and connected either—

(i) by the undertaker; or

(ii) in accordance with specifications approved by the undertaker;

(d) a requirement that—

(i) so much of the service pipe to the relevant premises as does not belong to, or fall to be laid by, the undertaker; and

(ii) the plumbing of the premises,

comply with specifications approved by the undertaker for the purpose of ensuring that it will be reasonably practicable for such a meter as is mentioned in paragraph (c) above to be installed and connected as so mentioned;

(e) a requirement that a separate service pipe has been provided—

(i) to each house or building on the relevant premises; or

(ii) where different parts of a building on the relevant premises are separately occupied, to each of those parts or to any of them;

(f) a requirement, in relation to the relevant premises—

(i) that such a requirement as may be imposed under section 66 below has been complied with; or

(ii) in a case where such a requirement could be imposed but for there already being such a cistern as is mentioned in that section, that the cistern and its float-operated valve are in good repair;

(g) a requirement that there is no contravention in relation to the water fittings used or to be used in connection with—

(i) the supply of water to the relevant premises; or

(ii) the use of water in those premises,

of such of the requirements of regulations under section 74 below as are prescribed for the purposes of this paragraph; and

(h) a requirement that every such step has been taken as has been specified in any notice served on any person under section 75 below in relation to the relevant premises.

(3) A condition shall not be imposed by a water undertaker under this section on a person who has served a connection notice except by a counter-notice served on that person before the end of the period of fourteen days beginning with the day after the service of the connection notice.

(4) This section shall be without prejudice to the provisions of sections 233 and 372 of the Insolvency Act 1986 (conditions of supply after insolvency).

1986 c. 45.

**48.**—(1) Where for the purposes of subsection (2)(a) of section 47 above any sums have been deposited with a water undertaker by way of security for the discharge of any obligation, the undertaker shall pay interest at such rate as may be determined either—

Interest on sums deposited in pursuance of the deposit condition.

(a) by the undertaker with the approval of the Director; or

(b) in default of a determination under paragraph (a) above, by the Director,

on every sum of 50p so deposited for every three months during which it remains in the hands of the undertaker.

(2) An approval or determination by the Director for the purposes of this section—

(a) may be given or made in relation to a particular case or description of cases or generally; and

(b) may be revoked at any time.

Supplemental provisions with respect to the metering conditions.

**49.**—(1) The power conferred on a water undertaker to impose conditions under section 47 above for the purposes of metering—

(a) shall be exercisable in relation to any premises even if the undertaker has no immediate intention, when the power is exercised, of fixing charges in relation to those premises by reference to volume; but

(b) shall not be exercisable so as to require the alteration or removal of any pipe laid or plumbing installed before 1st April 1989.

(2) Specifications approved by any water undertaker for the purposes of subsection (2)(c) or (d) of section 47 above may be approved—

(a) in relation to particular premises; or

(b) by being published in such manner as the undertaker considers appropriate, in relation to premises generally or to any description of premises.

(3) Any dispute between a water undertaker and any other person as to the terms of any condition imposed under section 47 above for the purposes of metering shall be referred to the arbitration of a single arbitrator appointed—

(a) by agreement between the undertaker and that person; or

(b) in default of agreement, by the Secretary of State.

(4) References in this section to the imposition of a condition under section 47 above for the purposes of metering are references to the imposition of conditions by virtue of subsection (2)(c) or (d) of that section.

Restriction on imposition of condition requiring separate service pipes.

**50.**—(1) This section applies where the effect of a connection notice served in respect of any house is to require a service pipe to that house to be connected with a water main with which it has previously been connected.

(2) Where this section applies, the water undertaker on which the connection notice is served shall not be entitled to make the reconnection subject to any such condition as, apart from this section, may be imposed by virtue of section 47(2)(e) above unless the undertaker would have been entitled under section 64 below to require the provision of a separate service pipe if the reconnection had already been made.

**51.**—(1) A water undertaker shall not be in breach of a duty imposed by virtue of the service of a connection notice unless—

(a) in the case of a duty to lay any service pipe or to connect any service pipe to which such a duty relates, it has failed to lay that pipe or to make that connection as soon as reasonably practicable after the relevant day;

(b) in the case of a duty to connect a service pipe the whole of which has already been laid when the notice is served on the undertaker, it has failed to make the connection before the end of the period of fourteen days beginning with the relevant day.

(2) In any case in which a water undertaker is subject to any such duty as is mentioned in subsection (1)(a) above, it shall be presumed, unless the contrary is shown in relation to that case, that the period of twenty-one days beginning with the relevant day is the period within which it is reasonably practicable for a water undertaker—

(a) to lay so much of any service pipe; and

(b) to fit such stopcock,

as it is necessary to lay or fit in that case for connecting a water main in a street with a service pipe at the boundary of any premises which abut on the part of the street where the main is situated.

(3) Where—

(a) a connection notice is served in respect of any premises; and

(b) at the time when the notice is served, the customer's part of the service pipe to those premises has not been laid,

the duties of the undertaker under sections 45 and 46 above shall not arise by virtue of that notice until the person serving the notice, having obtained the necessary consents from the owners and occupiers of any affected land, has, at his own expense, laid so much of the service pipe as it is necessary, for the purpose of making the connection, to lay otherwise than in a street or in land mentioned in subsections (3) to (5) of section 46 above.

(4) In subsection (3) above the reference to the customer's part of the service pipe to any premises is a reference to so much of the service pipe to those premises as falls to be laid otherwise than by the water undertaker in pursuance of section 46 above.

(5) Where—

(a) a person who has served a connection notice on a water undertaker has failed to comply with his obligation under section 45(3)(a) above to supplement that notice with information required by the undertaker; and

(b) that requirement was made by the undertaker at such a time before the end of the period within which the undertaker is required to comply with the duties imposed by virtue of the notice as gave that person a reasonable opportunity to provide the required information within that period,

the undertaker may delay its compliance with those duties until a reasonable time after the required information is provided.

(6) In this section "the relevant day", in relation to a duty imposed on a water undertaker by virtue of a connection notice, means the day after whichever is the latest of the following days, that is to say-

(a) the day on which the notice was served on the undertaker;

(b) in a case where it is necessary for the person serving the notice to lay any service pipe after serving the notice, the day on which a notice stating that the pipe has been laid is served on the undertaker;

(c) the day on which all such conditions are satisfied as the undertaker has, under sections 47 to 50 above, made conditions of its compliance with that duty.

### *Domestic supplies*

The domestic supply duty.

**52.**—(1) The domestic supply duty of a water undertaker in relation to any premises is a duty, until there is an interruption of that duty—

(a) to provide to those premises such a supply of water as (so far as those premises are concerned) is sufficient for domestic purposes; and

(b) to maintain the connection between the undertaker's water main and the service pipe by which that supply is provided to those premises.

(2) Subject to the following provisions of this section and to section 53 below, a water undertaker shall owe a domestic supply duty in relation to any premises to which this section applies and which are situated in the area of the undertaker if—

(a) a demand for a supply of water for domestic purposes has been made, in accordance with subsection (5) below, to the undertaker in respect of those premises; or

(b) those premises are premises to which this section applies by reason of a supply of water provided before 1st September 1989,

and there has been no interruption of the domestic supply duty in relation to those premises since that demand was made or, as the case may be, since the beginning of 1st September 1989.

(3) This section applies to any premises if—

(a) they consist in the whole or any part of a building and are connected by means of a service pipe to a water main; and

(b) the requirements of subsection (4) below are satisfied in relation to those premises.

(4) The requirements of this subsection are satisfied in relation to any premises if—

(a) the pipe by means of which the premises are connected to the water main in question was first connected with that main in pursuance of a connection notice served in respect of those premises;

(b) that pipe was the means by which a supply of water from that main was being supplied to those premises for domestic purposes immediately before 1st September 1989;

(c) the condition specified in paragraph (b) above would be satisfied in relation to the premises if any service pipe to those premises had not been temporarily disconnected for the purposes of any necessary works which were being carried out immediately before 1st September 1989; or

(d) the condition specified in any of the preceding paragraphs—

   (i) has been satisfied in relation to the premises at any time on or after 1st September 1989; and

   (ii) would continue to be satisfied in relation to the premises had not the whole or any part of a service pipe to those premises, or the main with which such a pipe had been connected, been renewed (on one or more previous occasions).

(5) For the purposes of this section a demand in respect of any premises is made in accordance with this subsection if it is made—

(a) by the person who is the occupier of the premises at the time when the demand is made; or

(b) by a person who is the owner of the premises at that time and agrees with the undertaker to pay all the undertaker's charges in respect of the supply demanded.

(6) For the purposes of this section—

(a) there is an interruption of the domestic supply duty owed by a water undertaker in relation to any premises if that supply is cut off by anything done by the undertaker in exercise of any of its disconnection powers, other than a disconnection or cutting off for the purposes of the carrying out of any necessary works; and

(b) a domestic supply duty owed in relation to any premises shall not be treated as interrupted by reason only of a change of the occupier or owner of the premises.

(7) Nothing in this section shall impose any duty on a water undertaker—

(a) to provide a supply of water directly from, or maintain any connection with, a water main which is a trunk main or is or is to be used solely for the purpose of supplying water otherwise than for domestic purposes; or

(b) to provide a supply of water to any premises, or maintain the connection between a water main and a service pipe to any premises, during any period during which it is reasonable—

   (i) for the supply of water to those premises to be cut off or reduced; or

   (ii) for the pipe to be disconnected,

for the purposes of the carrying out of any necessary works.

(8) In this section references to the disconnection powers of a water undertaker are references to the powers conferred on the undertaker by any of sections 60 to 62 and 75 below.

**53.**—(1) Where a demand for the purposes of section 52(2) above has been made to a water undertaker in respect of any premises ("the relevant premises"), the undertaker may make compliance with one or more of the requirements specified in subsection (2) below a condition of providing his first supply of water in compliance with that demand.

(2) The requirements mentioned in subsection (1) above are—

    (a) a requirement, in a case where the demand is made as a consequence of a supply having been cut off by reason of any person's failure to pay any charges, that the person making the demand has paid any amount owed by him to the undertaker—

        (i) in respect of a supply of water to the relevant premises; or

        (ii) in respect of expenses incurred in cutting off any such supply;

    (b) a requirement, in relation to the relevant premises

        (i) that such a requirement as may be imposed under section 66 below has been complied with; or

        (ii) in a case where such a requirement could be imposed but for there already being such a cistern as is mentioned in that section, that the cistern and its float-operated valve are in good repair;

    (c) a requirement that there is no contravention in relation to the water fittings used or to be used in connection with—

        (i) the supply of water to the relevant premises; or

        (ii) the use of water in those premises,

    of such of the requirements of regulations under section 74 below as are prescribed for the purposes of this subsection; and

    (d) a requirement that every such step has been taken as has been specified in any notice served on any person under section 75 below in relation to the relevant premises.

(3) This section shall be without prejudice to the provisions of sections 233 and 372 of the Insolvency Act 1986 (conditions of supply after insolvency).

**54.**—(1) A duty imposed on a water undertaker under section 52 above—

    (a) to provide a supply of water to any premises; or

    (b) to maintain a connection between a water main and a service pipe by which such a supply is provided,

shall be owed to the consumer.

(2) Where a duty is owed by virtue of this section to any person, any breach of that duty which causes that person to sustain loss or damage shall be actionable at the suit of that person; but, in any proceedings brought against a water undertaker in pursuance of this subsection, it shall be a defence for the undertaker to show that it took all reasonable steps and exercised all due diligence to avoid the breach.

*Other supplies*

**55.**—(1) This section applies where the owner or occupier of any premises in the area of a water undertaker requests the undertaker to provide a supply of water to those premises and—

(a) the premises are premises which do not consist in the whole or any part of a building; or

(b) the requested supply is for purposes other than domestic purposes.

(2) Where this section applies, it shall be the duty of the water undertaker, in accordance with such terms and conditions as may be determined under section 56 below—

(a) to take any such steps as may be so determined in order to enable the undertaker to provide the requested supply; and

(b) having taken any such steps, to provide that supply.

(3) A water undertaker shall not be required by virtue of this section to provide a new supply to any premises, or to take any steps to enable it to provide such a supply, if the provision of that supply or the taking of those steps would—

(a) require the undertaker, in order to meet all its existing obligations to supply water for domestic or other purposes, together with its probable future obligations to supply buildings and parts of buildings with water for domestic purposes, to incur unreasonable expenditure in carrying out works; or

(b) otherwise put at risk the ability of the undertaker to meet any of the existing or probable future obligations mentioned in paragraph (a) above.

(4) A water undertaker shall not be required by virtue of this section to provide a new supply to any premises, or to take any steps to enable it to provide such a supply, if there is a contravention in relation to the water fittings used or to be used in connection with—

(a) the supply of water to those premises; or

(b) the use of water in those premises,

of such of the requirements of regulations under section 74 below as are prescribed for the purposes of this subsection.

(5) Where—

(a) a request has been made by any person to a water undertaker for the purposes of subsection (2) above; and

(b) the steps which the undertaker is required to take by virtue of that request include steps for the purpose of obtaining any necessary authority for, or agreement to, any exercise by the undertaker of any of its powers or the carrying out by the undertaker of any works,

the failure of the undertaker to acquire the necessary authority or agreement shall not affect any liability of that person, under any term or condition in accordance with which those steps are taken, to re-imburse the undertaker in respect of some or all of the expenses incurred by the undertaker in taking those steps.

(6) Nothing in this section shall impose any duty on a water undertaker to provide a supply of water to any premises during any period during which it is reasonable for the supply of water to those premises to be cut off or reduced for the purposes of the carrying out of any necessary works.

(7) The duty of a water undertaker to supply water under this section at the request of any person, and any terms and conditions determined under section 56 below in default of agreement between the undertaker and that person, shall have effect as if contained in such an agreement.

(8) Except so far as otherwise provided by the terms and conditions determined under section 56 below in relation to any supply, the duties of a water undertaker under this section shall have effect subject to the provisions of sections 60 to 63 and 75 below.

Determinations on requests for non-domestic supplies.

**56.**—(1) Subject to subsection (3) below, any terms or conditions or other matter which falls to be determined for the purposes of a request made by any person to a water undertaker for the purposes of section 55 above shall be determined—

(a) by agreement between that person and the water undertaker; or

(b) in default of agreement, by the Director according to what appears to him to be reasonable.

(2) Subject to subsection (3) below, the Director shall also determine any dispute arising between any person and a water undertaker by virtue of subsection (3) or (4) of section 55 above.

(3) The Director may, instead of himself making a determination under subsection (1) or (2) above, refer any matter submitted to him for determination under that subsection to the arbitration of such person as he may appoint.

(4) For the purposes of any determination under this section by the Director or any person appointed by him it shall be for a water undertaker to show that it should not be required to comply with a request made for the purposes of section 55 above.

(5) The charges in respect of a supply provided in compliance with any request made for the purposes of section 55 above—

(a) shall not be determined by the Director or a person appointed by him, except in so far as, at the time of the request, no provision is in force by virtue of a charges scheme under section 143 below in respect of supplies of the applicable description; and

(b) in so far they do fall to be determined, shall be so determined having regard to the desirability of the undertaker's—

(i) recovering the expenses of complying with its obligations under section 55 above; and

(ii) securing a reasonable return on its capital.

(6) To the extent that subsection (5)(a) above excludes any charges from a determination under this section, those charges shall be fixed from time to time by a charges scheme under section 143 below, but not otherwise.

(7) The determination of any matter under this section shall be without prejudice to the provisions of sections 233 and 372 of the Insolvency Act 1986 (conditions of supply after insolvency).

1986 c. 45.

57.—(1) It shall be the duty of a water undertaker to allow any person to take water for extinguishing fires from any of its water mains or other pipes on which a fire-hydrant is fixed.

(2) Every water undertaker shall, at the request of the fire authority concerned, fix fire-hydrants on its water mains (other than its trunk mains) at such places as may be most convenient for affording a supply of water for extinguishing any fire which may break out within the area of the undertaker.

(3) It shall be the duty of every water undertaker to keep every fire-hydrant fixed on any of its water mains or other pipes in good working order and, for that purpose, to replace any such hydrant when necessary.

(4) It shall be the duty of a water undertaker to ensure that a fire authority has been supplied by the undertaker with all such keys as the authority may require for the fire-hydrants fixed on the water mains or other pipes of the undertaker.

(5) Subject to section 58(3) below, the expenses incurred by a water undertaker in complying with its obligations under subsections (2) to (4) above shall be borne by the fire authority concerned.

(6) Nothing in this section shall require a water undertaker to do anything which it is unable to do by reason of the carrying out of any necessary works.

(7) The obligations of a water undertaker under this section shall be enforceable under section 18 above by the Secretary of State.

(8) In addition, where a water undertaker is in breach of its obligations under this section, the undertaker shall be guilty of an offence and liable—

    (a) on summary conviction, to a fine not exceeding the statutory maximum;

    (b) on conviction on indictment, to a fine.

(9) In any proceedings against any water undertaker for an offence under subsection (8) above it shall be a defence for that undertaker to show that it took all reasonable steps and exercised all due diligence to avoid the commission of the offence.

(10) In this section "fire authority" has the same meaning as in the Fire Services Act 1947.

58.—(1) A water undertaker shall, at the request of the owner or occupier of any factory or place of business, fix a fire-hydrant, to be used for extinguishing fires and not other purposes, at such place on any suitable water main or other pipe of the undertaker as is as near as conveniently possible to that factory or place of business.

(2) For the purposes of subsection (1) above a water main or other pipe is suitable, in relation to a factory or place of business, if—

    (a) it is situated in a street which is in or near to that factory or place of business; and

    (b) it is of sufficient dimensions to carry a hydrant and is not a trunk main.

(3) Subsection (5) of section 57 above shall not apply in relation to expenses incurred in compliance, in relation to a specially requested fire-hydrant, with the obligations under subsections (3) and (4) of that section.

PART III
Duty to provide a supply of water etc. for fire-fighting.

1947 c. 41.

Specially requested fire-hydrants.

C

(4) Any expenses incurred by a water undertaker—

(a) in complying with its obligations under subsection (1) above; or

(b) in complying, in relation to a specially requested fire-hydrant, with its obligations under section 57(3) or (4) above,

shall be borne by the owner or occupier of the factory or place of business in question, according to whether the person who made the original request for the hydrant did so in his capacity as owner or occupier.

(5) Subsections (6) to (9) of section 57 above shall apply in relation to the obligations of a water undertaker under this section as they apply to the obligations of a water undertaker under that section.

(6) In this section—

1961 c. 34.

"factory" has the same meaning as in the Factories Act 1961; and

"specially requested fire-hydrant" means a fire-hydrant which—

(a) is fixed on a water main or other pipe of a water undertaker; and

1989 c. 15.

(b) was fixed on that main or pipe (whether before or after it became such a main or pipe under the Water Act 1989) in pursuance of a request made by the owner or occupier of a factory or place of business.

Supplies for other public purposes.

**59.**—(1) A water undertaker shall, at the request of a sewerage undertaker, highway authority or local authority, provide, from such of its pipes as are of an appropriate capacity, a supply of water for cleansing sewers and drains, for cleansing and watering highways or, as the case may be, for supplying any public pumps, baths or wash-houses.

(2) A supply of water provided by a water undertaker under this section shall be provided upon such terms and conditions as may be reasonable.

(3) A water main or other pipe of a water undertaker shall be treated as of an appropriate capacity for the purposes of this section if and only if it has a fire-hydrant fixed on it.

(4) Nothing in this section shall require a water undertaker to do anything which it is unable to do by reason of the carrying out of any necessary works.

(5) The obligations of a water undertaker under this section shall be enforceable under section 18 above by the Director.

### *Disconnections*

Disconnections for the carrying out of necessary works.

**60.**—(1) Subject to the following provisions of this section, a water undertaker may—

(a) disconnect a service pipe which, for the purposes of providing a supply of water to any premises, is connected with any water main of that undertaker; or

(b) otherwise cut off a supply of water to any premises,

if it is reasonable for the disconnection to be made, or the supply to be cut off, for the purposes of the carrying out of any necessary works.

(2) The power of a water undertaker under this section to cut off a supply of water shall include power to reduce a supply of water.

(3) Except in an emergency or in the case of a reduction which is immaterial, the power of a water undertaker under this section to cut off or reduce a supply shall be exercisable in relation to any premises only after the undertaker has served reasonable notice on the consumer of the proposal for the carrying out of the necessary works.

(4) Where a water undertaker exercises its power under this section to make any disconnection or to cut off or reduce a supply of water to any premises for the purposes of the carrying out of any necessary works, it shall owe a duty to the consumer to secure—

    (a) that those works are carried out with reasonable dispatch; and

    (b) that any supply of water to those premises for domestic purposes is interrupted for more than twenty-four hours for the purposes of the carrying out of those works only if an emergency supply has been made available (whether or not in pipes) within a reasonable distance of the premises.

(5) Any breach by a water undertaker of the duty owed by virtue of subsection (4) above which causes any person to whom it is owed to sustain loss or damage shall be actionable at the suit of that person.

**61.**—(1) Subject to the following provisions of this section, a water undertaker may disconnect a service pipe which for the purposes of providing a supply of water to any premises is connected with any water main of that undertaker, or may otherwise cut off a supply of water to any premises, if the occupier of the premises—

Disconnections for non-payment of charges.

    (a) is liable (whether in his capacity as occupier or under any agreement with the undertaker) to pay charges due to the undertaker in respect of the supply of water to those premises; and

    (b) has failed to do so before the end of the period of seven days beginning with the day after he is served with notice requiring him to do so.

(2) Where—

    (a) a water undertaker has served a notice for the purposes of paragraph (b) of subsection (1) above on a person; and

    (b) within the period of seven days mentioned in that paragraph, that person serves a counter-notice on the undertaker stating that he disputes his liability to pay the charges in question,

the undertaker shall not in respect of that notice exercise his power by virtue of that subsection in relation to any premises except at a time when that person is the occupier of the premises and those charges are enforceable against that person in a manner specified in subsection (3) below.

(3) For the purposes of subsection (2) above charges are enforceable in a manner specified in this subsection against a person if-

    (a) the undertaker is able to enforce a judgment against that person for the payment of the charges; or

    (b) that person is in breach of an agreement entered into, since the service of his counter-notice, for the purpose of avoiding or settling proceedings by the undertaker for the recovery of the charges.

(4) A water undertaker which exercises its power under this section to disconnect any pipe or otherwise to cut off any supply of water may recover, from the person in respect of whose liability the power is exercised, any expenses reasonably incurred by the undertaker in making the disconnection or in otherwise cutting off the supply.

(5) Where—

(a) a water undertaker has power under this section to disconnect any pipe to any premises, or otherwise to cut off any supply to any premises; and

(b) a supply of water is provided to those premises and to other premises wholly or partly by the same service pipe,

the undertaker may exercise that power so as to cut off the supply to those other premises if and only if the same person is the occupier of the premises in relation to which the charges are due and of the other premises.

**62.**—(1) Subject to the following provisions of this section, a water undertaker may—

(a) disconnect a service pipe which for the purposes of providing a supply of water to any premises is connected with any water main of that undertaker; or

(b) otherwise cut off a supply of water to any premises,

if notice specifying the time after which a supply of water to those premises will no longer be required has been served on the undertaker by a consumer and that time has passed.

(2) No person shall be liable to a water undertaker for any expenses incurred by the undertaker in exercising the power conferred on the undertaker by this section.

**63.**—(1) Where a water undertaker—

(a) disconnects a service pipe to any inhabited house, or otherwise cuts off a supply of water to such a house; and

(b) does so without restoring the supply to that house before the end of the period of twenty-four hours beginning with the time when it is cut off,

the undertaker shall, no later than forty-eight hours after that time, serve notice that it has cut off that supply on the local authority in whose area the house is situated.

(2) A water undertaker which fails, without reasonable excuse, to serve a notice on a local authority as required by subsection (1) above shall be guilty of an offence under this section.

(3) A water undertaker shall be guilty of an offence under this section if—

(a) it disconnects a service pipe to any premises, or otherwise cuts off a supply of water to any premises, in a case in which it has no power to do so under sections 60 to 62 above, section 75 below or any other enactment; or

(b) in disconnecting any such pipe or cutting off any such supply it fails, without reasonable excuse, to comply with any requirement of the provisions in pursuance of which it disconnects the pipe or cuts off the supply.

(4) A water undertaker which is guilty of an offence under this section shall be liable, on summary conviction, to a fine not exceeding level 3 on the standard scale.

### Means of supply

**64.**—(1) Subject to the following provisions of this section, a water undertaker may require the provision of a separate service pipe to any premises within its area which—

(a) consist in a house or any other building or part of a building, being, in the case of a part of a building, a part which is separately occupied; and

(b) are already supplied with water by the undertaker but do not have a separate service pipe.

(2) Where the supply of water to two or more houses was provided to those houses before 15th April 1981 wholly or partly by the same service pipe and continues to be so provided, the water undertaker shall not require the provision of separate service pipes to those houses until—

(a) the service pipe, in so far as it belongs to a person other than the undertaker, becomes so defective as to require renewal or is no longer sufficient to meet the requirements of those houses;

(b) a payment in respect of the supply of water to any of those houses remains unpaid after the end of the period for which it is due;

(c) the houses are, by structural alterations to one or more of them, converted into a larger number of houses;

(d) the owner or occupier of any of those houses has interfered with, or allowed another person to interfere with, the existing service pipe and thereby caused the supply of water to any house to be interfered with; or

(e) the undertaker has reasonable grounds for believing that such interference as is mentioned in paragraph (d) above is likely to take place.

(3) If, in the case of any such premises as are described in subsection (1) above, the water undertaker which provides a supply of water to those premises serves notice on the consumer requiring the provision of a separate service pipe and setting out the power of the undertaker under subsection (4) below—

(a) that consumer shall, within three months after the service of the notice, lay so much of the required pipe as the undertaker is not under a duty to lay by virtue of paragraph (b) below;

(b) sections 45 to 51 above shall apply as if that consumer had by a connection notice required the undertaker to connect the separate service pipe to those premises with the undertaker's water main;

(c) that consumer shall be presumed, without prejudice to his power to make further demands and requests—

> > (i) in so far as those premises were provided before the service of the notice with a supply of water for domestic purposes, to have made a demand for the purposes of section 52 above that such a supply is provided by means of the separate service pipe; and
>
> > (ii) in so far as those premises were provided before the service of the notice with a supply of water for other purposes, to have requested the undertaker to provide the same supply by means of that pipe as was provided before the service of the notice;
>
> and
>
> (d) on providing a supply of water to those premises by means of the separate service pipe, the undertaker may cut off any supply replaced by that supply and may make such disconnections of pipes by which the replaced supply was provided as it thinks fit.

(4) If a person upon whom a notice has been served for the purposes of subsection (3) above fails to comply with the notice, the water undertaker may—

> (a) itself carry out the works which that person was required to carry out; and
>
> (b) recover the expenses reasonably incurred by the undertaker in doing so from that person.

(5) Without prejudice—

> (a) to the power of a water undertaker by virtue of paragraph (b) of subsection (3) above to impose conditions under section 47 above; or
>
> (b) to the power conferred by virtue of paragraph (d) of that subsection,

any works carried out by a water undertaker by virtue of the provisions of the said paragraph (b) or of subsection (4) above shall be necessary works for the purposes of this Chapter.

Duties of undertakers as respects constancy and pressure.

**65.**—(1) Subject to the following provisions of this section, it shall be the duty of a water undertaker to cause the water in such of its water mains and other pipes as—

> (a) are used for providing supplies of water for domestic purposes; or
>
> (b) have fire-hydrants fixed on them,

to be laid on constantly and at such a pressure as will cause the water to reach to the top of the top-most storey of every building within the undertaker's area.

(2) Nothing in subsection (1) above shall require a water undertaker to provide a supply of water at a height greater than that to which it will flow by gravitation through its water mains from the service reservoir or tank from which that supply is taken.

(3) For the purposes of this section a water undertaker shall be entitled to choose the service reservoir or tank from which any supply is to be taken.

(4) Nothing in subsection (1) above shall impose any duty on a water undertaker to maintain the constancy or pressure of any supply of water during any period during which it is reasonable for that supply to be cut off or reduced for the purposes of the carrying out of any necessary works.

(5) The Secretary of State may by order modify the application of the preceding provisions of this section in relation to any water undertaker.

(6) The Secretary of State shall not make an order under subsection (5) above except—

    (a) in accordance with Schedule 5 to this Act; and

    (b) on an application made in accordance with that Schedule by the Director or by the water undertaker in relation to which the order is made.

(7) Subject to subsection (6) above, the power of the Secretary of State to make an order under subsection (5) above shall be exercisable by statutory instrument subject to annulment in pursuance of a resolution of either House of Parliament

(8) An order under subsection (5) above may—

    (a) require the payment of compensation by a water undertaker to persons affected by the order;

    (b) make different provision for different cases, including different provision in relation to different persons, circumstances or localities; and

    (c) contain such supplemental, consequential and transitional provision as the Secretary of State considers appropriate.

(9) The obligations of a water undertaker under this section shall be enforceable under section 18 above by the Secretary of State.

(10) In addition, where a water undertaker is in breach of a duty under this section, the undertaker shall be guilty of an offence and liable—

    (a) on summary conviction, to a fine not exceeding the statutory maximum;

    (b) on conviction on indictment, to a fine.

(11) In any proceedings against any water undertaker for an offence under subsection (10) above it shall be a defence for that undertaker to show that it took all reasonable steps and exercised all due diligence to avoid the commission of the offence.

**66.**—(1) A water undertaker may require that any premises consisting in—

Requirements by undertaker for maintaining pressure.

    (a) any building or part of a building the supply of water to which need not, in accordance with provision contained in or made under this Act, be constantly laid on under pressure; or

    (b) any relevant house to which water is required to be delivered at a height greater than a point 10.5 metres below the draw-off level of the service reservoir or tank from which a supply of water is being provided by the undertaker to those premises,

shall be provided with a cistern which has a float-operated valve and is fitted on the pipe by means of which water is supplied to those premises.

(2) A water undertaker may, in the case of such a house as is mentioned in paragraph (b) of subsection (1) above, require that a cistern the provision of which is required under that subsection shall be capable of holding sufficient water to provide an adequate supply to the house for a period of twenty-four hours.

(3) If, where a water undertaker provides a supply of water to any premises, the consumer, after having been required to do so by notice served on him by the undertaker, fails before the end of the period specified in the notice—

(a) to provide a cistern in accordance with a requirement under this section; or

(b) to put any such cistern and its float-operated valve into good repair,

the water undertaker may itself provide a cistern, or carry out any repairs necessary to prevent waste of water.

(4) The period specified for the purposes of subsection (3) above in a notice under this section shall be a period of not less than twenty-eight days beginning with the day after the service of the notice.

(5) Where a water undertaker provides a cistern or carries out any repairs under subsection (3) above, it may recover the expenses reasonably incurred by it in doing so from the owner of the premises in question.

(6) In this section—

"pre-transfer supplier", in relation to a house, means the person who was supplying water to that house immediately before 1st September 1989; and

"relevant house" means any house other than a house in relation to which the following two conditions are satisfied, that is to say—

(i) the erection of the house was commenced before 1st September 1989; and

(ii) no such requirement as is mentioned in subsection (1) or (2) above could have been imposed in relation to the house under any enactment having effect immediately before that date in relation to the pre-transfer supplier.

### CHAPTER III

#### QUALITY AND SUFFICIENCY OF SUPPLIES

*Standards of wholesomeness*

Standards of wholesomeness.

**67.**—(1) The Secretary of State may by regulations make provision that water that is supplied to any premises is or is not to be regarded as wholesome for the purposes of this Chapter if it satisfies or, as the case may be, fails to satisfy such requirements as may be prescribed.

(2) Without prejudice to the generality of subsection (1) above, regulations under this section may, for the purpose of determining the wholesomeness of any water—

(a) prescribe general requirements as to the purposes for which the water is to be suitable;

(b) prescribe specific requirements as to the substances that are to be present in or absent from the water and as to the concentrations of substances which are or are required to be present in the water;

(c) prescribe specific requirements as to other characteristics of the water;

(d) provide that the question whether prescribed requirements are satisfied may be determined by reference to such samples as may be prescribed;

(e) enable the Secretary of State to authorise such relaxations of and departures from the prescribed requirements (or from any of them) as may be prescribed, to make any such authorisation subject to such conditions as may be prescribed and to modify or revoke any such authorisation or condition; and

(f) enable the Secretary of State to authorise a local authority (either instead of the Secretary of State or concurrently with him) to exercise in relation to a private supply any power conferred on the Secretary of State by regulations made by virtue of paragraph (e) above.

### General obligations of undertakers

**68.**—(1) It shall be the duty of a water undertaker—

Duties of water undertakers with respect to water quality.

(a) when supplying water to any premises for domestic or food production purposes to supply only water which is wholesome at the time of supply; and

(b) so far as reasonably practicable, to ensure, in relation to each source or combination of sources from which that undertaker supplies water to premises for domestic or food production purposes, that there is, in general, no deterioration in the quality of the water which is supplied from time to time from that source or combination of sources.

(2) For the purposes of this section and section 69 below and subject to subsection (3) below, water supplied by a water undertaker to any premises shall not be regarded as unwholesome at the time of supply where it has ceased to be wholesome only after leaving the undertaker's pipes.

(3) For the purposes of this section where water supplied by a water undertaker to any premises would not otherwise be regarded as unwholesome at the time of supply, that water shall be regarded as unwholesome at that time if—

(a) it has ceased to be wholesome after leaving the undertaker's pipes but while in a pipe which is subject to water pressure from a water main or which would be so subject but for the closing of some valve; and

(b) it has so ceased in consequence of the failure of the undertaker, before supplying the water, to take such steps as may be prescribed for the purpose of securing the elimination, or reduction to a minimum, of any prescribed risk that the water would cease to be wholesome after leaving the undertaker's pipes.

(4) The provisions of this section shall apply in relation to water which is supplied by a water undertaker whether or not the water is water which the undertaker is required to supply by virtue of any provision of this Act.

(5) The duties of a water undertaker under this section shall be enforceable under section 18 above by the Secretary of State.

Regulations for preserving water quality.

**69.**—(1) The Secretary of State may by regulations require a water undertaker to take all such steps as may be prescribed for the purpose of securing compliance with section 68 above.

(2) Without prejudice to the generality of the power conferred by subsection (1) above, regulations under that subsection may impose an obligation on a water undertaker—

(a) to take all such steps as may be prescribed for monitoring and recording whether the water which that undertaker supplies to premises for domestic or food production purposes is wholesome at the time of supply;

(b) to take all such steps as may be prescribed for monitoring and recording the quality of the water from any source, or combination of sources, which that undertaker uses or is proposing to use for supplying water to any premises for domestic or food production purposes;

(c) to ensure that a source which that undertaker is using or proposing to use for supplying water for domestic or food production purposes is not so used until prescribed requirements for establishing the quality of water which may be supplied from that source have been complied with;

(d) to keep records of the localities within which all the premises supplied with water for domestic or food production purposes by that undertaker are normally supplied from the same source or combination of sources;

(e) to comply with prescribed requirements with respect to the analysis of water samples or with respect to internal reporting or organisational arrangements.

(3) Without prejudice to subsections (1) and (2) above, the Secretary of State may by regulations make provision with respect to the use by water undertakers, for the purposes of or in connection with the carrying out of their functions—

(a) of such processes and substances; and

(b) of products that contain or are made with such substances or materials,

as he considers might affect the quality of any water.

(4) Without prejudice to the generality of the power conferrred by subsection (3) above, regulations under that subsection may—

(a) forbid the use by water undertakers of processes, substances and products which have not been approved under the regulations or which contravene the regulations;

(b) for the purposes of provision made by virtue of paragraph (a) above, require processes, substances and products used by water undertakers to conform to such standards as may be prescribed by or approved under the regulations;

(c) impose such other requirements as may be prescribed with respect to the use by water undertakers of prescribed processes, substances and products;

(d) provide for the giving, refusal and revocation, by prescribed persons, of approvals required for the purposes of the regulations, for such approvals to be capable of being made subject to such conditions as may be prescribed and for the modification and revocation of any such condition;

(e) impose obligations to furnish prescribed persons with information reasonably required by those persons for the purpose of carrying out functions under the regulations;

(f) provide for a contravention of the regulations to constitute—

(i) a summary offence punishable, on summary conviction, by a fine not exceeding level 5 on the standard scale or such smaller sum as may be prescribed; or

(ii) an offence triable either way and punishable, on summary conviction, by a fine not exceeding the statutory maximum and, on conviction on indictment, by a fine;

and

(g) require prescribed charges to be paid to persons carrying out functions under the regulations.

(5) The Secretary of State may by regulations require a water undertaker—

(a) to publish information about the quality of water supplied for domestic or food production purposes to any premises by that undertaker; and

(b) to provide information to prescribed persons about the quality of water so supplied.

(6) Regulations under subsection (5) above—

(a) shall prescribe both the information which is to be published or provided in pursuance of the regulations and the manner and circumstances in which it is to be published or provided;

(b) may require the provision of information by a water undertaker to any person to be free of charge or may authorise it to be subject to the payment by that person to the undertaker of a prescribed charge; and

(c) may impose such other conditions on the provision of information by a water undertaker to any person as may be prescribed.

**70.**—(1) Subject to subsection (3) below, where a water undertaker supplies water by means of pipes to any premises and that water is unfit for human consumption, the undertaker shall be guilty of an offence and liable—

Offence of supplying water unfit for human consumption.

(a) on summary conviction, to a fine not exceeding the statutory maximum;

(b) on conviction on indictment, to a fine.

(2) For the purposes of section 210 below and any other enactment under which an individual is guilty of an offence by virtue of subsection (1) above the penalty on conviction on indictment of an offence under this section shall be deemed to include imprisonment (in addition to or instead of a fine) for a term not exceeding two years.

(3) In any proceedings against any water undertaker for an offence under this section it shall be a defence for that undertaker to show that it—

    (a) had no reasonable grounds for suspecting that the water would be used for human consumption; or

    (b) took all reasonable steps and exercised all due diligence for securing that the water was fit for human consumption on leaving its pipes or was not used for human consumption.

(4) Proceedings for an offence under this section shall not be instituted except by the Secretary of State or the Director of Public Prosecutions.

*Waste, contamination, misuse etc.*

Waste from water sources.

**71.**—(1) Subject to subsections (2) and (3) below, a person shall be guilty of an offence under this section if—

    (a) he causes or allows any underground water to run to waste from any well, borehole or other work; or

    (b) he abstracts from any well, borehole or other work water in excess of his reasonable requirements.

(2) A person shall not be guilty of an offence by virtue of subsection (1)(a) above in respect of anything done for the purpose—

    (a) of testing the extent or quality of the supply; or

    (b) of cleaning, sterilising, examining or repairing the well, borehole or other work in question.

(3) Where underground water interferes or threatens to interfere with the carrying out or operation of any underground works (whether waterworks or not), it shall not be an offence under this section, if no other method of disposing of the water is reasonably practicable, to cause or allow the water to run to waste so far as may be necessary for enabling the works to be carried out or operated.

(4) A person who is guilty of an offence under this section shall be liable, on summary conviction, to a fine not exceeding level 3 on the standard scale.

(5) On the conviction of a person under this section, the court may—

    (a) order that the well, borehole or other work to which the offence relates shall be effectively sealed; or

    (b) make such other order as appears to the court to be necessary to prevent waste of water.

(6) If any person fails to comply with an order under subsection (5) above, then, without prejudice to any penalty for contempt of court, the court may, on the application of the NRA, authorise the NRA to take such steps as may be necessary to execute the order; and any expenses incurred in taking any such steps shall be recoverable summarily as a civil debt from the person convicted.

(7) Any person designated for the purpose by the NRA shall, on producing some duly authenticated document showing his authority, have a right at all reasonable times—

    (a) to enter any premises for the purpose of ascertaining whether there is, or has been, any contravention of the provisions of this section on or in connection with the premises;

    (b) to enter any premises for the purpose of executing any order of the court under this section which the NRA has been authorised to execute in those premises.

(8) Part I of Schedule 6 to this Act shall apply to the rights of entry conferred by subsection (7) above.

**72.**—(1) Subject to subsections (2) and (3) below, a person is guilty of an offence under this section if he is guilty of any act or neglect whereby the water in any waterworks which is used or likely to be used—

    (a) for human consumption or domestic purposes; or

    (b) for manufacturing food or drink for human consumption,

is polluted or likely to be polluted.

    *Contamination of water sources.*

(2) Nothing in this section shall be construed as restricting or prohibiting any method of cultivation of land which is in accordance with the principles of good husbandry.

(3) Nothing in this section shall be construed as restricting or prohibiting the reasonable use of oil or tar on any highway maintainable at public expense so long as the highway authority take all reasonable steps for preventing—

    (a) the oil or tar; and

    (b) any liquid or matter resulting from the use of the oil or tar,

from polluting the water in any waterworks.

(4) A person who is guilty of an offence under this section shall be liable—

    (a) on summary conviction, to a fine not exceeding the statutory maximum and, in the case of a continuing offence, to a further fine not exceeding £50 for every day during which the offence is continued after conviction;

    (b) on conviction on indictment, to imprisonment for a term not exceeding two years or to a fine or to both.

(5) In this section "waterworks" includes—

    (a) any spring, well, adit, borehole, service reservoir or tank; and

    (b) any main or other pipe or conduit of a water undertaker.

**73.**—(1) If any person who is the owner or occupier of any premises to which a supply of water is provided by a water undertaker intentionally or negligently causes or suffers any water fitting for which he is responsible to be or remain so out of order, so in need of repair or so constructed or adapted, or to be so used—

    *Offences of contaminating, wasting and misusing water etc.*

(a) that water in a water main or other pipe of a water undertaker, or in a pipe connected with such a water main or pipe, is or is likely to be contaminated by the return of any substance from those premises to that main or pipe;

(b) that water that has been supplied by the undertaker to those premises is or is likely to be contaminated before it is used; or

(c) that water so supplied is or is likely to be wasted or, having regard to the purposes for which it is supplied, misused or unduly consumed,

that person shall be guilty of an offence and liable, on summary conviction, to a fine not exceeding level 3 on the standard scale.

(2) Any person who uses any water supplied to any premises by a water undertaker for a purpose other than one for which it is supplied to those premises shall, unless the other purpose is the extinguishment of a fire, be guilty of an offence and liable, on summary conviction, to a fine not exceeding level 3 on the standard scale.

(3) Where a person has committed an offence under subsection (2) above, the water undertaker in question shall be entitled to recover from that person such amount as may be reasonable in respect of any water wasted, misused or improperly consumed in consequence of the commission of the offence.

(4) For the purposes of this section the owner or occupier of any premises shall be regarded as responsible for every water fitting on the premises which is not a water fitting which a person other than the owner or, as the case may be, occupier is liable to maintain.

Regulations for preventing contamination, waste etc. and with respect to water fittings.

**74.**—(1) The Secretary of State may by regulations make such provision as he considers appropriate for any of the following purposes, that is to say—

(a) for securing—

(i) that water in a water main or other pipe of a water undertaker is not contaminated; and

(ii) that its quality and suitability for particular purposes is not prejudiced,

by the return of any substance from any premises to that main or pipe;

(b) for securing that water which is in any pipe connected with any such main or other pipe or which has been supplied to any premises by a water undertaker is not contaminated, and that its quality and suitability for particular purposes is not prejudiced, before it is used;

(c) for preventing the waste, undue consumption and misuse of any water at any time after it has left the pipes of a water undertaker for the purpose of being supplied by that undertaker to any premises; and

(d) for securing that water fittings installed and used by persons to whom water is or is to be supplied by a water undertaker are safe and do not cause or contribute to the erroneous measurement of any water or the reverberation of any pipes.

(2) Without prejudice to the generality of subsection (1) above, regulations under this section may, for any of the purposes specified in that subsection, make provision in relation to such water fittings as may be prescribed—

(a) for forbidding the installation, connection or use of the fittings if they have not been approved under the regulations or if they contravene the regulations;

(b) for requiring the fittings, for the purposes of provision made by virtue of paragraph (a) above, to be of such a size, nature, strength or workmanship, to be made of such materials or in such a manner or to conform to such standards as may be prescribed by or approved under the regulations;

(c) for imposing such other requirements as may be prescribed with respect to the installation, arrangement, connection, testing, disconnection, alteration and repair of the fittings and with respect to the materials used in their manufacture;

(d) for the giving, refusal and revocation, by prescribed persons, of approvals required for the purposes of the regulations; and

(e) for such approvals to be capable of being made subject to such conditions as may be prescribed and for the modification and revocation of any such condition.

(3) Without prejudice as aforesaid, regulations under this section may—

(a) impose separate or concurrent duties with respect to the enforcement of the regulations on water undertakers, local authorities and such other persons as may be prescribed;

(b) confer powers on a water undertaker or local authority to carry out works and take other steps, in prescribed circumstances, for remedying any contravention of the regulations;

(c) provide for the recovery by a water undertaker or local authority of expenses reasonably incurred by the undertaker or authority in the exercise of any power conferred by virtue of paragraph (b) above;

(d) repeal or modify the provisions of section 73 above or section 75 below;

(e) provide for a contravention of the regulations to constitute a summary offence punishable, on summary conviction, by a fine not exceeding level 5 on the standard scale or such smaller sum as may be prescribed;

(f) require prescribed charges to be paid to persons carrying out functions under the regulations;

(g) enable the Secretary of State to authorise such relaxations of and departures from such of the requirements of the regulations as may be prescribed, to make any such authorisation subject to such conditions as may be prescribed and to modify or revoke any such authorisation or condition;

(h) enable the Secretary of State to authorise a water undertaker or local authority (either instead of the Secretary of State or concurrently with him) to exercise any power conferred on the Secretary of State by regulations made by virtue of paragraph (g) above; and

     (i) require disputes arising under the regulations to be referred to arbitration and for determinations under the regulations to be subject to such rights of appeal as may be prescribed.

(4) Without prejudice to sections 84 and 170 below, any person designated in writing for the purposes of this subsection in such manner as may be prescribed may—

     (a) enter any premises for the purpose of—

          (i) ascertaining whether any provision contained in or made or having effect under this Act with respect to any water fittings or with respect to the waste or misuse of water is being or has been contravened;

          (ii) determining whether, and if so in what manner, any power or duty conferred or imposed on any person by regulations under this section should be exercised or performed; or

          (iii) exercising any such power or performing any such duty;

     or

     (b) carry out such inspections, measurements and tests on premises entered by that person or on water fittings or other articles found on any such premises, and take away such samples of water or of any land and such water fittings and other articles, as that person has been authorised to carry out or take away in accordance with regulations under this section.

(5) Part II of Schedule 6 to this Act shall apply to the rights and powers conferred by subsection (4) above.

(6) The power of the Secretary of State under this section to make regulations with respect to the matters specified in the preceding provisions of this section shall include power, by regulations under this section—

1991 c. 60.

1945 c. 42.

1989 c. 15.

     (a) to modify the operation of Schedule 2 to the Water Consolidation (Consequential Provisions) Act 1991 in relation to any byelaws made under section 17 of the Water Act 1945 which have effect by virtue of paragraph 19 of Schedule 26 to the Water Act 1989 and that Schedule 2; and

     (b) to revoke or amend any such byelaws;

but, so long as any such byelaws so have effect, the references in sections 47(2)(g), 53(2)(c) and 55(4) above to such regulations under this section as are prescribed shall have effect as including references to those byelaws.

(7) Any sums received by the Secretary of State in consequence of the provisions of any regulations under this section shall be paid into the Consolidated Fund.

1987 c. 43.

(8) In this section "safe" has the same meaning as in Part II of the Consumer Protection Act 1987.

**Power to prevent damage and to take steps to prevent contamination, waste etc.**

**75.**—(1) Without prejudice to any power conferred on water undertakers by regulations under section 74 above, where a water undertaker which provides a supply of water to any premises has reason for believing—

(a) that damage to persons or property is being or is likely to be caused by any damage to, or defect in, any water fitting used in connection with the supply of water to those premises which is not a service pipe belonging to the undertaker;

(b) that water in a water main or other pipe of the undertaker is being or is likely to be contaminated by the return of any substance from those premises to that main or pipe;

(c) that water which is in any pipe connected with any such main or other pipe or which has been supplied by the undertaker to those premises is being or is likely to be contaminated before it is used; or

(d) that water which has been or is to be so supplied is being or is likely to be wasted or, having regard to the purposes for which it is supplied, misused or unduly consumed,

the undertaker may exercise the power conferred by subsection (2) below in relation to those premises.

(2) The power conferred by this subsection in relation to any premises is—

(a) where the case constitutes an emergency, power to disconnect the service pipe or otherwise to cut off the supply of water to those premises; and

(b) in any other case, power to serve notice on the consumer requiring him to take such steps as may be specified in the notice as necessary to secure that the damage, contamination, waste, misuse or undue consumption ceases or, as the case may be, does not occur.

(3) Where a water undertaker, in exercise of the power conferred by virtue of subsection (2)(a) above, disconnects a service pipe to any premises or otherwise cuts off any supply of water to any premises, the undertaker shall, as soon as reasonably practicable after the supply is disconnected or cut off, serve a notice on the consumer specifying the steps which that person is required to take before the undertaker will restore the supply.

(4) The steps specified in a notice under subsection (3) above shall be the steps necessary to secure that, as the case may be—

(a) the damage, contamination, waste, misuse or undue consumption; or

(b) the likelihood of damage, contamination, waste, misuse or undue consumption,

would not recur if the supply were restored.

(5) A water undertaker which fails, without reasonable excuse, to serve a notice in accordance with subsection (3) above shall be guilty of an offence and liable, on summary conviction, to a fine not exceeding level 3 on the standard scale.

(6) A notice served for the purposes of subsection (2)(b) above shall—

(a) specify the period, not being less than the period of seven days beginning with the day after the service of the notice, within which the steps specified in the notice are to be taken; and

(b) set out the powers of the undertaker under subsections (7) to (9) below.

(7) Where a water undertaker has served a notice for the purposes of subsection (2)(b) above in relation to any premises and—

(a) the case becomes an emergency; or

(b) the premises appear to be unoccupied and the steps specified in the notice are not taken before the end of the period so specified,

the undertaker may disconnect the service pipe to those premises or otherwise cut off the supply of water to those premises.

(8) Subsections (3) to (5) above shall apply where a water undertaker exercises its power under subsection (7) above as they apply where such an undertaker exercises its power by virtue of subsection (2)(a) above.

(9) Where, in a case not falling within subsection (7)(a) or (b) above, any steps specified in a notice served by a water undertaker for the purposes of subsection (2)(b) above have not been taken by the end of the period so specified, the water undertaker shall have power—

(a) to take those steps itself; and

(b) subject to subsection (10) below, to recover any expenses reasonably incurred by the undertaker in taking those steps from the person on whom the notice was served;

and any steps taken by a water undertaker by virtue of paragraph (a) above shall be necessary works for the purposes of Chapter II of this Part.

(10) Where any steps are taken by virtue of this section and it is shown that, in the circumstances of the case, those steps were not necessary as mentioned in subsection (2) or, as the case may be, (4) above, the water undertaker in question-

(a) shall not be entitled to recover any expenses incurred by it in taking those steps; and

(b) shall be liable to pay to any other person who took any of those steps an amount equal to any expenses reasonably incurred by that person in taking any of those steps.

Temporary hosepipe bans.

**76.**—(1) If a water undertaker is of the opinion that a serious deficiency of water available for distribution by that undertaker exists or is threatened, that undertaker may, for such period as it thinks necessary, prohibit or restrict, as respects the whole or any part of its area, the use for the purpose of—

(a) watering private gardens; or

(b) washing private motor cars,

of any water supplied by that undertaker and drawn through a hosepipe or similar apparatus.

(2) A water undertaker imposing a prohibition or restriction under this section shall, before it comes into force, give public notice of it, and of the date on which it will come into force, in two or more newspapers circulating in the locality affected by the prohibition or restriction.

(3) Any person who, at a time when a prohibition or restriction under this section is in force, contravenes its provisions shall be guilty of an offence and liable, on summary conviction, to a fine not exceeding level 3 on the standard scale.

(4) Where a prohibition or restriction is imposed by a water undertaker under this section, charges made by the undertaker for the use of a hosepipe or similar apparatus shall be subject to a reasonable reduction and, in the case of a charge paid in advance, the undertaker shall make any necessary repayment or adjustment.

(5) In this section "private motor car" means any mechanically propelled vehicle intended or adapted for use on roads other than—

    (a) a public service vehicle, within the meaning of the Public Passenger Vehicles Act 1981; or

    

    (b) a goods vehicle within the meaning of the Road Traffic Act 1988,

    

and includes any vehicle drawn by a private motor car.

### Local authority functions

**77.**—(1) It shall be the duty of every local authority to take all such steps as they consider appropriate for keeping themselves informed about the wholesomeness and sufficiency of water supplies provided to premises in their area, including every private supply to any such premises.

General functions of local authorities in relation to water quality.

(2) It shall be the duty of a local authority to comply with any direction given by the Secretary of State to that authority, to authorities of a description applicable to that authority or to local authorities generally as to—

    (a) the cases and circumstances in which they are or are not to exercise any of the powers conferred on them by this Chapter in relation to private supplies; and

    (b) the manner in which those powers are to be exercised.

(3) The Secretary of State may by regulations make such provision, supplementing the provisions of this section and of sections 78 and 79(2) below, as he considers appropriate for—

    (a) imposing duties and conferring powers on local authorities with respect to the acquisition of information about the quality and sufficiency of water supplies provided to premises in their areas; and

    (b) regulating the performance of any duty imposed by or under any of those provisions.

(4) Without prejudice to the generality of subsection (3) above, regulations under that subsection may—

    (a) prescribe the matters to be taken into account by a local authority in determining, for the purposes of subsection (1) above, what is appropriate;

    (b) provide, for the purposes of the exercise or performance of any power or duty conferred or imposed on a local authority by or under any of the provisions mentioned in subsection (3) above, for such samples of water to be taken and analysed at such times and in such manner as may be prescribed;

    (c) authorise local authorities to exercise or perform any such power or duty through prescribed persons;

(d) provide for the recovery by a local authority from prescribed persons of such amounts as may be prescribed in respect of expenses reasonably incurred by the authority in the exercise of any such power or the performance of any such duty.

Local authority functions in relation to undertakers' supplies.

**78.**—(1) It shall be the duty of a local authority to notify any water undertaker of anything appearing to the authority to suggest—

(a) that any supply by that undertaker of water for domestic or food production purposes to any premises in the area of that authority is, has been or is likely to become unwholesome or (so far as any such premises are concerned) insufficient for domestic purposes;

(b) that the unwholesomeness or insufficiency of any such supply is, was or is likely to be such as to cause a danger to life or health; or

(c) that the duty imposed on that undertaker by virtue of section 68(1)(b) above is being, has been or is likely to be so contravened as to affect any supply of water to premises in that area.

(2) Where a local authority have notified a water undertaker of any such matter as is mentioned in subsection (1) above, it shall be the duty of that authority, if they are not satisfied that all such remedial action as is appropriate will be taken by the undertaker, to inform the Secretary of State about the contents of the notification.

Local authority functions where piped supplies insufficient or unwholesome.

**79.**—(1) This section applies to a case in which it is not practicable at reasonable cost for a water undertaker, by supplying water in pipes, to provide or maintain such a supply of wholesome water to any particular premises in its area as (so far as those premises are concerned) is sufficient for domestic purposes.

(2) In any case to which this section applies, it shall be the duty of the local authority in whose area the premises in question are situated, if they are satisfied—

(a) that the insufficiency or unwholesomeness of the supply of water for domestic purposes to those premises is such as to cause a danger to life or health; and

(b) that it is practicable at reasonable cost for the water undertaker, by providing it otherwise than in pipes, to provide to those premises such a supply of wholesome water as is sufficient for those purposes,

to require the undertaker, under subsection (3) below, to provide a supply of water to those premises otherwise than in pipes.

(3) Where, in a case to which this section applies—

(a) the insufficiency or unwholesomeness of the supply of water for domestic purposes to the premises in question is such as to cause a danger to life or health;

(b) it is practicable at reasonable cost for the water undertaker, by providing it otherwise than in pipes, to provide to those premises such a supply of wholesome water as (so far as those premises are concerned) is sufficient for domestic purposes; and

(c) the local authority in whose area those premises are situated notify the undertaker of the danger to life or health and require the undertaker to provide a supply otherwise than in pipes,

it shall be the duty of the undertaker, for such period as may be required by that local authority, to provide any supply to those premises which it is practicable at reasonable cost to provide otherwise than in pipes and which it is required to provide by that authority.

(4) Where under this section a local authority require the provision by a water undertaker of a supply of water to any premises, that authority—

(a) shall be liable to the undertaker for any charges payable by virtue of Chapter I of Part V of this Act in respect of the provision of that supply; but

(b) shall have power to recover the whole or any part of any charges paid by virtue of this subsection from the owner or occupier of the premises to which the supply is provided.

(5) In this section references to the provision of a supply of water to any premises otherwise than in pipes shall have effect, in a case in which it is practicable at reasonable cost to provide a supply (whether or not in pipes) to a place within a reasonable distance of those premises, as including references to the provision of a supply to that place.

(6) The duty of a water undertaker under subsection (3) above shall be enforceable under section 18 above by the Secretary of State.

**80.**—(1) Subject to the following provisions of this section, where a local authority are satisfied in relation to any premises in their area which are supplied with water for domestic or food production purposes by means of a private supply—

Remedial powers of local authorities in relation to private supplies.

(a) that any water which is being, has been or is likely to be supplied for those purposes to those premises by means of that private supply is not, was not or, as the case may be, is likely not to be wholesome; or

(b) that that private supply is failing, has failed or is likely to fail to provide to any house on those premises such a supply of wholesome water as (so far as that house is concerned) is sufficient for domestic purposes,

the authority may serve a notice in relation to that private supply on one or more of the relevant persons.

(2) A notice under this section in relation to a private supply of water to any premises shall-

(a) give particulars of the matters mentioned in subsection (1) above in respect of which the notice is served;

(b) specify the steps which, in the opinion of the authority serving the notice, are required to be taken for ensuring that there is a supply of water to those premises which is both wholesome and (so far as any house on those premises is concerned) sufficient for domestic purposes;

(c) specify a period, ending not less than twenty-eight days after the day on which the notice is served, within which any representations or objections with respect to the notice must be received by that authority; and

    (d) state the effect in relation to that notice of section 81(2) and (3) below.

(3) Subject to sections 81 and 82 below, where a local authority serve a notice under this section on any relevant person they may do one or more of the following, that is to say—

    (a) by that notice designate as steps to be taken by the authority themselves such of the steps specified in the notice as they consider it appropriate so to designate;

    (b) by that notice require that person, within such reasonable period as may be specified in the notice, to take one or more of the steps so specified;

    (c) by that notice require that person, at such times as may be determined in accordance with provision contained in the notice, to make to another relevant person or to that authority such payments as may be so determined in respect of expenses reasonably incurred by that other person or that authority in taking any step specified in the notice;

    (d) by that notice undertake from time to time to make such payments to that person as may be so determined in respect of expenses reasonably incurred by that person in taking any step specified in the notice.

(4) The power of a local authority to serve a notice under this section specifying the steps which are required to be taken in relation to any source from which a private supply is provided both to premises in the area of that authority and to premises in the area of another local authority shall be exercisable only where—

    (a) the other authority consent to the service of the notice; or

    (b) the authorities act jointly in exercising their respective powers under this section in relation to that source.

(5) The powers conferred by this section and sections 81 and 82 below shall be so exercised in relation to a private supply of water to any premises where there is no house as to secure that no local authority are required to bear any of the expenses incurred (whether by the authority or by any other person) in taking any of the steps for ensuring that the supply is wholesome which are specified in a notice under this section.

(6) The steps that a relevant person may be required by a notice under this section to take in relation to any premises shall include—

    (a) requiring a supply of water to be provided to those premises by a water undertaker or by any other person; and

    (b) taking such steps for the purpose of securing that such a requirement is complied with, and of enabling such a supply to be so provided, as may be specified in the notice.

(7) For the purposes of this section and sections 81 to 83 below the relevant persons, in relation to a private supply of water to any premises in the area of a local authority, are—

    (a) the owners and occupiers of those premises; and

(b) whether or not the source of the private supply is in that authority's area, the owners and occupiers of the premises where that source is situated and any other person who exercises powers of management or control in relation to that source;

and in sections 81 to 83 below a notice under this section is referred to as a private supply notice.

**81.**—(1) Subject to subsection (2) below, a private supply notice served by a local authority shall not take effect until the end of the period specified in the notice as the period within which representations or objections with respect to the notice must be received by that authority.

(2) Where any written representation or objection with respect to a private supply notice served by a local authority is received by the authority, before the end of the period specified in the notice, from a person on whom the notice was served, that notice shall not take effect unless—

(a) the notice is submitted by the authority to the Secretary of State and is confirmed by him either with or without modifications; or

(b) the representation or objection is withdrawn.

(3) If a local authority submit a private supply notice to the Secretary of State for confirmation, the Secretary of State—

(a) shall consider whether the notice should be confirmed and whether, if it is confirmed, it should be confirmed with or without modifications;

(b) may, with respect to the matters specified in the notice or any proposed modification of it, direct the local authority to serve a private supply notice, in such terms as may be specified in the direction, on any relevant person who has not previously been served with such a notice;

(c) may, for the purposes of paragraph (a) or (b) above cause a local inquiry to be held or afford—

(i) to the local authority; and

(ii) to every person who has made representations or objections with respect to the notice or any proposed direction under paragraph (b) above,

an opportunity of appearing before and being heard by a person appointed by the Secretary of State for the purpose; and

(d) if he is satisfied that the person on whom any notice to be served in pursuance of a direction under paragraph (b) above has had a proper opportunity of having his representations or objections with respect to the proposal for the direction considered, may dispense, in relation to the notice so served, with the provisions of subsections (1) and (2) above and of section 80(2)(c) and (d) above.

(4) Where the Secretary of State confirms a private supply notice (whether with or without modifications)—

(a) he, or if he so directs, the local authority concerned shall serve notice of that confirmation on every person originally served with the notice under section 80 above; and

(b) that notice shall take effect, with any modifications made by the Secretary of State, at such time as may be specified in the notice served under this subsection.

Enforcement and variation of private supply notice.

**82.**—(1) Where any relevant person who is required by virtue of a private supply notice to take any step in relation to any premises fails to take that step within the period specified in the notice, the authority which served the notice may, in accordance with any applicable provision having effect by virtue of section 83 or 84 below, take that step themselves.

(2) Where any step is taken by a local authority in relation to any premises by virtue of subsection (1) above—

(a) the authority may recover from the person who failed to take that step within the specified period any expenses reasonably incurred by the authority in taking that step; and

(b) for the purposes of any requirement under which payments are required to be made to that person by any person other than the authority, sums paid by virtue of paragraph (a) above in respect of the taking of any step shall be deemed to be expenses incurred in the taking of that step by the person who failed to take it.

(3) Nothing in this Act shall confer any right of action on any person in respect of any loss or damage sustained by that person in consequence of the failure by any other person to take any step specified in a private supply notice.

(4) Any sum required to be paid to any person by virtue of any requirement or undertaking contained in a private supply notice shall be recoverable by that person from the person who is required to pay it.

(5) Any requirement which—

(a) is imposed by virtue of a private supply notice on the owner or occupier of any premises; and

(b) is expressed to bind those premises in relation to the owners or occupiers from time to time,

shall bind successive owners or, as the case may be, occupiers of those premises and shall be a local land charge.

(6) Subject to subsection (7) below, a local authority may by notice served on any person modify or revoke the effect in relation to that person of any private supply notice or notice under this subsection (including a notice which has been confirmed, with or without modifications, by the Secretary of State).

(7) Sections 80(2)(c) and (d) and 81 above shall apply, as they apply in relation to a private supply notice, in relation to any notice served by a local authority on any person under subsection (6) above except where the notice—

(a) extends the period within which any step is required to be taken by that person; or

(b) discharges, postpones or abates any obligation of that person to make a payment to the local authority.

Application of certain powers to local authorities in relation to private supplies.

**83.**—(1) For the purposes of the taking of any steps falling to be taken by a local authority by virtue of a designation under subsection (3)(a) of section 80 above the provisions of Part VI of this Act shall have effect—

(a) as if the relevant works powers, so far as conferred on a water undertaker for the purpose of carrying out its functions, were also conferred on a local authority for the purpose of ensuring that a supply of water provided by means of a private supply to any premises in the authority's area is both wholesome and (so far as any house on those premises is concerned) sufficient for domestic purposes;

(b) as if any such power, so far as it is conferred on a water undertaker in relation to things belonging to or operated or used by the undertaker for the purposes of its functions, were conferred by virtue of paragraph (a) above on a local authority in relation to things belonging to or operated or used by that authority, or a relevant person, in connection with the provision of water by means of a private supply;

(c) as if references to a water undertaker in any provision of Part VI of this Act relating to a relevant works power, except the references in sections 181 and 182 below, included references to a local authority; and

(d) as if the making by any person in pursuance of a private supply notice of any payment in respect of sums incurred in the laying of any pipe entitled that person, for the purposes of section 179(1) below, to an interest in the pipe.

(2) Where by virtue of this Act a local authority have power under Part VII of the Local Government Act 1972 (miscellaneous powers of a local authority) to acquire (whether compulsorily or otherwise) any land or right over land for the purpose of ensuring that private supplies of water to premises in their area are both wholesome and (so far as houses on those premises are concerned) sufficient for domestic purposes, that power shall include power to acquire land or any interest or right in or over land in order, for that purpose, to dispose of the land or the interest or right to a person who is a relevant person in relation to such a private supply.

(3) In this section "relevant works powers" means the powers conferred on water undertakers by sections 158, 159, 161, 163 and 165 below.

**84.**—(1) Any person designated for the purpose by a local authority within whose area any waterworks are situated shall, on producing some duly authenticated document showing his authority, have a right at all reasonable hours to enter any premises for the purpose of ascertaining whether there is or has been any contravention of section 72 above in relation to those waterworks.

(2) Any person designated in writing for the purpose by a local authority may—

(a) enter any premises for the purpose of—

(i) ascertaining whether any provision contained in or made or having effect under this Act with respect to any water fittings, or with respect to the waste or misuse of water, is being or has been contravened;

(ii) determining whether, and if so in what manner, any power or duty conferred or imposed on any person by regulations under section 74 above should be exercised or performed; or

(iii) exercising any such power or performing any such duty;

or

(b) carry out such inspections, measurements and tests on premises entered by that person or on water fittings or other articles found on any such premises, and take away such samples of water or of any land and such water fittings and other articles, as that person has been authorised to carry out or take away in accordance with regulations under that section.

(3) Any person designated in writing for the purpose by any local authority may—

(a) enter any premises for the purpose, in relation to any private supply, of—

(i) determining whether, and if so in what manner, any power or duty conferred or imposed on that authority by or under any of sections 77 to 82 above should be exercised or performed; or

(ii) exercising any such power or performing any such duty;

(b) enter any premises to which a supply of water is provided by a water undertaker for the purpose, in relation to a supply so provided of—

(i) determining whether, and if so in what manner, any such power should be exercised or any such duty performed; or

(ii) exercising any such power or performing any such duty;

or

(c) carry out such inspections, measurements and tests on premises entered by that person or of articles found on any such premises, and take away such samples of water or of any land or articles, as the local authority—

(i) consider appropriate for the purposes of any such power or duty; and

(ii) have authorised that person to carry out or take away.

(4) Part I of Schedule 6 to this Act shall apply to the right of entry conferred by subsection (1) above; but nothing in that subsection or in that Part of that Schedule shall entitle any person designated for the purposes of that subsection by a local authority to have access to any waterworks belonging to a water undertaker.

(5) Part II of Schedule 6 to this Act shall apply to the rights and powers conferred by subsections (2) and (3) above.

(6) In subsection (1) above the reference to a local authority includes a reference to a county council and to the Sub-Treasurer of the Inner Temple and the Under-Treasurer of the Middle Temple; and any expenses incurred by the Common Council of the City of London in the exercise of their functions under that subsection shall be defrayed as part of their general expenses.

(7) In this section "waterworks" has the same meaning as in section 72 above.

**85.**—(1) Subject to subsection (2) below, a local authority may serve on any person a notice requiring him to furnish that authority, within a period or at times specified in the notice and in a form and manner so specified, with such information as is reasonably required by that authority for the purpose of exercising or performing any power or duty conferred or imposed on that authority by or under any of sections 77 to 82 above.

(2) The Secretary of State may by regulations make provision for restricting the information which may be required under subsection (1) above and for determining the form in which the information is to be so required.

(3) A person who fails without reasonable excuse to comply with the requirements of a notice served on him under subsection (1) above shall be guilty of an offence and liable, on summary conviction, to a fine not exceeding level 5 on the standard scale.

*Assessors for the enforcement of water quality*

**86.**—(1) The Secretary of State may for the purposes of this section appoint persons to act on his behalf as technical assessors in relation to some or all of—

(a) the powers and duties conferred or imposed on him by or under sections 67 to 70 and 77 to 82 above; and

(b) such other powers and duties in relation to the quality and sufficiency of water supplied by a water undertaker as are conferred or imposed on him by or under any other enactments.

(2) A person appointed under this section shall—

(a) carry out such investigations as the Secretary of State may require him to carry out for the purpose of—

(i) ascertaining whether any duty or other requirement imposed on that undertaker by or under any of sections 68 to 70 or section 79 above is being, has been or is likely to be contravened; or

(ii) advising the Secretary of State as to whether, and if so in what manner, any of the powers of the Secretary of State in relation to such a contravention, or any of the powers (including the powers to make regulations) which are conferred on him by or under any of sections 67 to 70 and 77 to 82 above should be exercised;

and

(b) make such reports to the Secretary of State with respect to any such investigation as the Secretary of State may require.

(3) Without prejudice to the powers conferred by subsection (4) below, it shall be the duty of a water undertaker—

(a) to give a person appointed under this section all such assistance; and

(b) to provide a person so appointed with all such information,

as that person may reasonably require for the purpose of carrying out any such investigation as is mentioned in subsection (2) above.

(4) Any person appointed under this section who is designated in writing for the purpose by the Secretary of State may—

(a) enter any premises for the purpose of carrying out any such investigation as is mentioned in subsection (2) above;

(b) carry out such inspections, measurements and tests on premises entered by that person or of articles or records found on any such premises, and take away such samples of water or of any land or articles, as that person considers appropriate for the purpose of enabling him to carry out any such investigation; or

(c) at any reasonable time require any water undertaker to supply him with copies of, or of extracts from, the contents of any records kept for the purpose of complying with any duty or other requirement imposed on that undertaker by or under any of sections 68 to 70 or section 79 above.

(5) Part II of Schedule 6 to this Act shall apply to the rights and powers conferred by subsection (4) above.

(6) Any water undertaker which fails to comply with the duty imposed on it by virtue of subsection (3) above shall be guilty of an offence and liable, on summary conviction, to a fine not exceeding level 5 on the standard scale.

## CHAPTER IV

### FLUORIDATION

Fluoridation of water supplies at request of health authorities.

**87.**—(1) Where a District Health Authority have applied in writing to a water undertaker for the water supplied within an area specified in the application to be fluoridated, that undertaker may, while the application remains in force, increase the fluoride content of the water supplied by the undertaker within that area.

(2) For the purposes of subsection (1) above an application under this section shall remain in force until the Health Authority, after giving reasonable notice to the water undertaker, withdraw it.

(3) The area specified in an application under this section may be the whole, or any part of, the district of the authority making the application.

(4) Where in exercise of the power conferred by this section, the fluoride content of any water is increased, the increase may be effected only by the addition of one or more of the following compounds of fluorine, that is to say—

hexafluorosilicic acid ($H_2SiF_6$);

disodium hexafluorosilicate ($Na_2SiF_6$).

(5) Any District Health Authority making arrangements with a water undertaker in pursuance of an application under this section shall ensure that those arrangements include provisions designed to secure that the concentration of fluoride in the water supplied to consumers in the area in question is, so far as reasonably practicable, maintained at one milligram per litre.

(6) Water to which fluoride has been added by a water undertaker in exercise of the power conferred by this section (with a view to its supply in any area) may be supplied by that or any other undertaker to consumers in any other area if the undertaker or undertakers concerned consider that it is necessary to do so—

(a) for the purpose of dealing with any serious deficiency in supply; or

(b) in connection with the carrying out of any works (including cleaning and maintenance) by the undertaker concerned or, as the case may be, by any of the undertakers concerned.

(7) In subsection (6) above—

(a) the reference to water to which fluoride has been added by a water undertaker in exercise of the power conferred by this section includes a reference to water to which fluoride has been added by a water authority (within the meaning of the Water (Scotland) Act 1980) in exercise of the power conferred by section 1 of the Water (Fluoridation) Act 1985; and

1980 c. 45.

1985 c. 63.

(b) in relation to a supply of such water by a water undertaker, the reference to the water undertakers concerned shall have effect as references to the water undertaker and the water authority concerned.

(8) In this section "serious deficiency in supply" means any existing or threatened serious deficiency in the supply of water (whether in quantity or quality) caused by an exceptional lack of rain or by any accident or unforeseen circumstances.

(9) In this section and the following provisions of this Chapter references to a District Health Authority are references to any such authority within the meaning of the National Health Service Act 1977.

1977 c. 49.

**88.**—(1) The Secretary of State may by order amend section 87(4) above by—

Power to vary permitted fluoridation agents.

(a) adding a reference to another compound of fluorine; or

(b) removing any reference to a compound of fluorine.

(2) The power of the Secretary of State to make orders under this section shall be exercisable by statutory instrument subject to annulment in pursuance of a resolution of either House of Parliament.

**89.**—(1) This section applies where a District Health Authority propose to make or withdraw an application under section 87 above.

Publicity and consultation.

(2) At least three months before implementing their proposal the District Health Authority shall—

(a) publish details of the proposal in one or more newspapers circulating within the area affected by the proposal; and

(b) give notice of the proposal to every local authority whose area falls wholly or partly within that area.

(3) Before implementing the proposal the District Health Authority shall consult each of the local authorities to which they are required, by virtue of subsection (2)(b) above, to give notice of the proposal.

(4) The District Health Authority shall, not earlier than seven days after publishing details of the proposal in the manner required by subsection (2)(a) above, republish them in that manner.

(5) Where a District Health Authority have complied with this section in relation to the proposal they shall, in determining whether or not to proceed, have such regard as they consider appropriate—

(a) to any representations which have been made to them with respect to it; and

(b) to any consultations under subsection (3) above.

(6) The Secretary of State may direct that this section shall not apply in relation to any proposal of a District Health Authority to withdraw an application under section 87 above.

(7) Where, at any meeting of a District Health Authority, consideration is given to the question whether the authority should make or withdraw an application under section 87 above, section 1(2) of the Public Bodies (Admission to Meetings) Act 1960 (which allows the exclusion of the public in certain circumstances) shall not apply to any proceedings on that question.

1960 c. 67.

(8) In this section "local authority" includes a county council.

Indemnities in respect of fluoridation.

**90.** The Secretary of State may, with the consent of the Treasury, agree to indemnify any water undertaker in respect of such of any of the following as he thinks fit, that is to say—

(a) liabilities incurred by the undertaker in connection with anything done by the undertaker for the purpose of increasing the fluoride content of any water supplied by the undertaker;

(b) costs or expenses which are incurred by the undertaker, or for which the undertaker is liable, in connection with any proceedings which have been or may be brought by any person with respect to—

(i) things done for the purpose of increasing the fluoride content of any water; or

(ii) a proposal to increase the fluoride content of any water;

(c) expenditure incurred by the undertaker in complying with an order made in any such proceedings;

1989 c. 15.

(d) liabilities transferred to the undertaker in accordance with a scheme under Schedule 2 to the Water Act 1989 or Schedule 2 to this Act which, in relation to the person from whom they were transferred, were liabilities falling within paragraph (a) above or liabilities in respect of costs, expenses or other expenditure mentioned in sub-paragraph (b) or (c) above.

**91.** Schedule 7 to this Act shall have effect with respect to fluoridation schemes made before the coming into force of the Water (Fluoridation) Act 1985.

PART III
Pre-1985 fluoridation schemes.
1985 c. 63.

### CHAPTER V

### SUPPLEMENTAL PROVISIONS OF PART III

**92.**—(1) Subject to subsection (2) below, the Secretary of State may by regulations provide that the provisions of Chapters I to III of this Part shall have effect with such modifications as may be prescribed for the purpose of enabling Her Majesty's Government in the United Kingdom to give effect—

Power to give effect to international obligations.

(a) to any Community obligations; or

(b) to any international agreement to which the United Kingdom is for the time being a party.

(2) This section shall not authorise any modification of any of sections 71, 72 and 76 above or of any other provisions of this Part so far as they have effect for the purposes of or in relation to those sections.

**93.**—(1) In this Part—

Interpretation of Part III.

"connection notice" shall be construed in accordance with section 45(8) above;

"consumer", in relation to a supply of water provided by a water undertaker to any premises, means (except in Chapter IV) a person who is for the time being the person on whom liability to pay charges to the undertaker in respect of that supply of water would fall;

"food production purposes" means the manufacturing, processing, preserving or marketing purposes with respect to food or drink for which water supplied to food production premises may be used, and for the purposes of this definition "food production premises" means premises used for the purposes of a business of preparing food or drink for consumption otherwise than on the premises;

"necessary works" includes works carried out, in exercise of any power conferred by or under any enactment, by a person other than a water undertaker;

"private supply" means, subject to subsection (2) below, a supply of water provided otherwise than by a water undertaker (including a supply provided for the purposes of the bottling of water), and cognate expressions shall be construed accordingly;

"private supply notice" shall be construed in accordance with section 80(7) above;

"water fittings" includes pipes (other than water mains), taps, cocks, valves, ferrules, meters, cisterns, baths, water closets, soil pans and other similar apparatus used in connection with the supply and use of water;

"wholesome" and cognate expressions shall be construed subject to the provisions of any regulations made under section 67 above.

(2) For the purposes of any reference in this Part to a private supply, or to supplying water by means of a private supply, water shall be treated as supplied to any premises not only where it is supplied from outside those premises, but also where it is abstracted, for the purpose of being used or consumed on those premises, from a source which is situated on the premises themselves; and for the purposes of this subsection water shall be treated as used on any premises where it is bottled on those premises for use or consumption elsewhere.

(3) For the purposes of this Part a service pipe shall be treated as connected with a water main other than a trunk main even if the connection is an indirect connection made by virtue of a connection with another service pipe.

(4) The rights conferred by virtue of this Part as against the owner or occupier of any premises shall be without prejudice to any rights and obligations, as between themselves, of the owner and occupier of the premises.

# PART IV

## SEWERAGE SERVICES

### CHAPTER I

#### GENERAL FUNCTIONS OF SEWERAGE UNDERTAKERS

*Principal duties and standards of performance*

General duty to provide sewerage system.

**94.**—(1) It shall be the duty of every sewerage undertaker—

(a) to provide, improve and extend such a system of public sewers (whether inside its area or elsewhere) and so to cleanse and maintain those sewers as to ensure that that area is and continues to be effectually drained; and

(b) to make provision for the emptying of those sewers and such further provision (whether inside its area or elsewhere) as is necessary from time to time for effectually dealing, by means of sewage disposal works or otherwise, with the contents of those sewers.

(2) It shall be the duty of a sewerage undertaker in performing its duty under subsection (1) above to have regard—

(a) to its existing and likely future obligations to allow for the discharge of trade effluent into its public sewers; and

(b) to the need to provide for the disposal of trade effluent which is so discharged.

(3) The duty of a sewerage undertaker under subsection (1) above shall be enforceable under section 18 above—

(a) by the Secretary of State; or

(b) with the consent of or in accordance with a general authorisation given by the Secretary of State, by the Director.

(4) The obligations imposed on a sewerage undertaker by the following Chapters of this Part, and the remedies available in respect of contraventions of those obligations, shall be in addition to any duty imposed or remedy available by virtue of any provision of this section or section 95 below and shall not be in any way qualified by any such provision.

(5) In this section "trade effluent" has the same meaning as in Chapter III of this Part.

**95.**—(1) For the purpose-

Standards of performance in connection with provision of sewerage services.

    (a) of facilitating the determination of the extent to which breaches of the obligations imposed by virtue of the following provisions of this Part are to amount to breaches of the duty imposed by section 94 above; or

    (b) of supplementing that duty by establishing overall standards of performance in relation to the provision of sewerage services by any sewerage undertaker,

the Secretary of State may, in accordance with section 96 below, by regulations provide for contraventions of such requirements as may be prescribed to be treated for the purposes of this Act as breaches of that duty.

(2) The Secretary of State may, in accordance with section 96 below, by regulations prescribe such standards of performance in connection with the provision of sewerage services as, in his opinion, ought to be achieved in individual cases.

(3) Regulations under subsection (2) above may provide that, if a sewerage undertaker fails to meet a prescribed standard, it shall pay such amount as may be prescribed to any person who is affected by the failure and is of a prescribed description.

(4) Without prejudice to the generality of the power conferred by subsection (2) above, regulations under that subsection may—

    (a) include in a standard of performance a requirement for a sewerage undertaker, in prescribed circumstances, to inform a person of his rights by virtue of any such regulations;

    (b) provide for any dispute under the regulations to be referred by either party to the dispute to the Director;

    (c) make provision for the procedure to be followed in connection with any such reference and for the Director's determination on such a reference to be enforceable in such manner as may be prescribed;

    (d) prescribe circumstances in which a sewerage undertaker is to be exempted from requirements of the regulations.

**96.**—(1) The Secretary of State shall not make any regulations under section 95 above unless—

Procedure for regulations under section 95.

    (a) the Director has made to the Secretary of State a written application complying with subsection (2) below;

    (b) the Secretary of State is satisfied that a copy of the application has been served by the Director on every sewerage undertaker specified in the application;

    (c) such period as the Secretary of State considers appropriate has been allowed for the making—

        (i) by the Director; and

(ii) by any affected sewerage undertaker,

of representations or objections with respect to the Director's proposals and any modifications proposed by the Secretary of State; and

(d) the Secretary of State has considered both the Director's reasons for his proposals and every representation or objection which has been duly made with respect to those proposals, or any proposed modifications of those proposals, and has not been withdrawn.

(2) An application made by the Director to the Secretary of State complies with this subsection if it—

(a) sets out draft provisions proposed by the Director for inclusion in regulations under section 95 above;

(b) specifies the sewerage undertaker or undertakers in relation to which it is proposed those provisions should apply; and

(c) summarises the Director's reasons for his proposals.

(3) The Secretary of State shall not make any regulations under section 95 above except where—

(a) the only provisions of the regulations are the provisions proposed by the Director in his application or those provisions with such modifications as the Secretary of State considers appropriate; and

(b) each of the modifications (if any) of the Director's proposals to which effect is given by the regulations is a modification the proposal to make which has been notified—

(i) to the Director; and

(ii) to any sewerage undertaker appearing to the Secretary of State to be likely to be affected by the modifications.

*Performance of sewerage undertaker's functions by local authorities etc.*

Performance of sewerage undertaker's functions by local authorities etc.

**97.**—(1) A relevant authority may, in accordance with any arrangements which it has entered into for the purpose with any sewerage undertaker, carry out sewerage functions on that undertaker's behalf in relation to such area comprising the whole or any part of that authority's relevant area, together (where that authority are a local authority or an urban development corporation and the arrangements so provide) with parts of any adjacent relevant areas of other relevant authorities, as may be specified in the arrangements.

(2) Arrangements entered into for the purposes of this section may contain any such provision as may be agreed between the relevant authority and the sewerage undertaker but shall not affect the availability to any person, other than the relevant authority, of any remedy against the undertaker in respect of the carrying out of the undertaker's sewerage functions or of any failure to carry them out.

(3) It is hereby declared that, if arrangements entered into for the purposes of this section so provide, a relevant authority shall be entitled to exercise on behalf of a sewerage undertaker any power which by or under any enactment is exercisable by the undertaker for the purposes of, or in connection with, the carrying out of the undertaker's sewerage functions.

(4) Where arrangements entered into for the purposes of this section provide for a local authority to carry out the sewerage functions of a sewerage undertaker on the undertaker's behalf, section 101 of the Local Government Act 1972 (delegation of functions), so far as it relates to the carrying out of functions by a committee, sub-committee or officer of a local authority, shall have effect in relation to those sewerage functions only in so far as the arrangements do not otherwise provide.

(5) In this section—

"new town" has the same meaning as in the New Towns Act 1981;

"relevant area"—

(a) in relation to a local authority, means the area of the authority and the whole of any new town or urban development area any part of which is situated within the area of the authority;

(b) in relation to the Commission for the New Towns, means any new town;

(c) in relation to the development corporation for any new town, means that new town;

(d) in relation to the Development Board for Rural Wales, means any new town situated within the area for which the Board is for the time being responsible; and

(e) in relation to any urban development corporation for any urban development area, means that area;

"relevant authority" means any of the following, that is to say—

(a) a local authority;

(b) the Commission for the New Towns, a development corporation for a new town or the Development Board for Rural Wales;

(c) the urban development corporation for any urban development area;

"sewerage functions", in relation to a sewerage undertaker, means any of the functions of the undertaker by virtue of its appointment under Chapter I of Part II of this Act as a sewerage undertaker, other than its functions relating to sewage disposal and its functions by virtue of Chapter III of this Part;

"urban development area" means any area so designated under Part XVI of the Local Government, Planning and Land Act 1980.

(6) Nothing in the Public Health Act 1875 (Support of Sewers) Amendment Act 1883 shall apply in relation to any sanitary work by virtue of this section; and in this section "sanitary work" has the same meaning as in that Act of 1883.

PART IV

1972 c. 70.

1981 c. 64.

1980 c. 65.

1883 c. 37.

## CHAPTER II

### PROVISION OF SEWERAGE SERVICES

#### *Requisition of public sewer*

**98.**—(1) It shall be the duty of a sewerage undertaker (in accordance with section 101 below) to provide a public sewer to be used for the drainage for domestic purposes of premises in a particular locality in its area if-

Duty to comply with sewer requisition.

(a) the undertaker is required to provide the sewer by a notice served on the undertaker by one or more of the persons who under subsection (2) below are entitled to require the provision of the sewer for that locality;

(b) the premises in that locality the drainage of which would be by means of that sewer are—

(i) premises on which there are buildings; or

(ii) premises on which there will be buildings when proposals made by any person for the erection of any buildings are carried out;

and

(c) the conditions specified in section 99 below are satisfied in relation to that requirement.

(2) Each of the following persons shall be entitled to require the provision of a public sewer for any locality, that is to say—

(a) the owner of any premises in that locality;

(b) the occupier of any premises in that locality;

(c) any local authority within whose area the whole or any part of that locality is situated;

1981 c. 64.

(d) where the whole or any part of that locality is situated in a new town, within the meaning of the New Towns Act 1981—

(i) the Commission for the New Towns; and

(ii) the Development Board for Rural Wales or the development corporation for the new town, according to whether or not the new town is situated within the area for which that Board is for the time being responsible;

and

1980 c. 65.

(e) where the whole or any part of that locality is situated within an area designated as an urban development area under Part XVI of the Local Government, Planning and Land Act 1980, the urban development corporation.

(3) The duty of a sewerage undertaker under this section to provide a public sewer shall be owed to the person who requires the provision of the sewer or, as the case may be, to each of the persons who joins in doing so.

(4) Where a duty is owed by virtue of subsection (3) above to any person, any breach of that duty which causes that person to sustain loss or damage shall be actionable at the suit of that person; but, in any proceedings brought against a water undertaker in pursuance of this subsection, it shall be a defence for the undertaker to show that it took all reasonable steps and exercised all due diligence to avoid the breach.

(5) In this section the reference to domestic purposes, in relation to the drainage of premises in a particular locality to which a requirement under this section relates, is a reference—

(a) where there are buildings on premises in that locality, to such domestic sewerage purposes as are specified in relation to those buildings in the requirement; and

(b) where any person is proposing to erect buildings on premises in the locality, to such domestic sewerage purposes as are so specified in relation to the buildings and to times after the erection of the buildings.

**99.**—(1) The conditions mentioned in section 98(1)(c) above are satisfied in relation to a requirement for the provision of a public sewer by a sewerage undertaker if—

Financial conditions of compliance.

    (a) such undertakings as the undertaker may have reasonably required in accordance with subsection (2) below have been given by the person or persons who have required the provision of the sewer; and

    (b) such security as the undertaker may have reasonably required has been provided for the discharge of any obligations imposed by those undertakings on any person who, under subsection (3) below, may be required to secure his undertakings.

(2) The undertakings which a sewerage undertaker may require for the purposes of subsection (1) above in respect of any public sewer are undertakings which—

    (a) bind the person or persons mentioned in that subsection to pay to the undertaker, in respect of each of the twelve years following the provision of the sewer, an amount not exceeding the relevant deficit (if any) for that year on that sewer; and

    (b) in the case of undertakings binding two or more persons, bind them either jointly and severally or with liability to pay apportioned in such manner as they may agree.

(3) For the purposes of subsection (1)(b) above a person may be required to secure his undertakings in relation to the provision of a public sewer if—

    (a) it was by virtue of section 98(2)(a) or (b) above that he required, or joined in requiring, the provision of the sewer; and

    (b) he is not a public authority.

(4) Where for the purposes of subsection (1)(b) above any sums have been deposited with a sewerage undertaker by way of security for the discharge of any obligation, the undertaker shall pay interest at such rate as may be determined either—

    (a) by the undertaker with the approval of the Director; or

    (b) in default of a determination under paragraph (a) above, by the Director,

on every sum of 50p so deposited for every three months during which it remains in the hands of the undertaker.

(5) An approval or determination given or made by the Director for the purposes of subsection (4) above—

    (a) may be given or made in relation to the provision of a particular public sewer, in relation to the provision of sewers of a particular description or in relation to the provision of public sewers generally; and

    (b) may be revoked at any time.

PART IV

(6) Any dispute between a sewerage undertaker and any other person as to—

    (a) the undertakings or security required by the undertaker for the purposes of this section; or

    (b) the amount required to be paid in pursuance of any such undertaking,

shall be referred to the arbitration of a single arbitrator appointed by agreement between the undertaker and that person or, in default of agreement, by the President of the Institution of Civil Engineers.

(7) In this section "relevant deficit" has the meaning given by section 100 below.

Calculation of "relevant deficit" for the purposes of section 99.

**100.**—(1) For the purposes of section 99 above the relevant deficit for any year on a public sewer is the amount (if any) by which the drainage charges payable for the use during that year of that sewer are exceeded by the annual borrowing costs of a loan of the amount required for the provision of that sewer.

(2) The annual borrowing costs of a loan of the amount required for the provision of a public sewer is the aggregate amount which would fall to be paid in any year by way of payments of interest and repayments of capital if an amount equal to so much of the costs reasonably incurred in providing that sewer as were not incurred in the provision of additional capacity had been borrowed, by the sewerage undertaker providing the sewer, on terms—

    (a) requiring interest to be paid and capital to be repaid in twelve equal annual instalments; and

    (b) providing for the amount of the interest to be calculated at such rate, and in accordance with such other provision, as may have been determined for the purposes of this subsection.

(3) A determination for the purposes of subsection (2) above shall be made either—

    (a) by the undertaker with the approval of the Director; or

    (b) in default of such a determination, by the Director.

(4) For the purposes of this section the costs reasonably incurred in providing a public sewer ("the new sewer") shall include—

    (a) the costs reasonably incurred in providing such other public sewers and such pumping stations as it is necessary to provide in consequence of the provision of the new sewer; and

    (b) such proportion (if any) as is reasonable of the costs reasonably incurred in providing any such additional capacity in an earlier public sewer as falls to be used in consequence of the provision of the new sewer.

(5) In subsection (4) above the reference to an earlier public sewer, in relation to the new sewer, is a reference to any public sewer which—

    (a) has been provided in the period of twelve years immediately before the provision of the new sewer; and

    (b) was so provided in pursuance of a public sewer requisition.

(6) Any reference in this section to the provision of additional capacity in a public sewer provided in pursuance of a requirement under any enactment is a reference to such works carried out or other things done in connection with the provision of that sewer as are carried out or done for the purpose of enabling that sewer to be used for purposes in addition to those for which it is necessary to provide the sewer in order to comply with the requirement.

(7) Any reference in this section to the drainage charges payable for the use during any year of any sewer provided by a sewerage undertaker is a reference to so much of the aggregate of any charges payable to the sewerage undertaker in respect of services provided in the course of that year as represents charges which—

    (a) have been imposed by the undertaker in relation to such of the premises connected with that sewer as are premises where there are buildings; and

    (b) are reasonably attributable to the use of that sewer for the drainage for domestic sewerage purposes of those premises or to the disposal of effluent drained for any such purpose from those premises.

(8) An approval or determination given or made by the Director for the purposes of subsection (2) above—

    (a) may be given or made in relation to the provision of a particular public sewer, in relation to the provision of sewers of a particular description or in relation to the provision of public sewers generally; and

    (b) may be revoked at any time except in relation to a public sewer that has already been provided.

(9) In this section "public sewer requisition" means—

    (a) a requirement under section 98 above (including, by virtue of paragraph 1 of Schedule 2 to the Water Consolidation (Consequential Provisions) Act 1991, a requirement under section 71 of the Water Act 1989);    *1991 c. 60.*

                                                                  *1989 c. 15.*

    (b) a requirement under the provisions of section 16 of the Water Act 1973 (sewer requisitions); or    *1973 c. 37.*

    (c) a requirement under any local statutory provision corresponding to section 98 above or to any of the provisions of that section 16.

**101.**—(1) A sewerage undertaker shall not be in breach of a duty imposed by section 98 above in relation to any locality unless-    Determination of completion date and route for requisitioned sewer.

    (a) the period of six months beginning with the relevant day has expired; and

    (b) the sewerage undertaker has not, before the end of that period, so laid the public sewer to be provided as to enable drains and private sewers to be used for the drainage of premises in that locality to communicate with the public sewer at the places determined under subsection (3) below.

(2) The period mentioned in subsection (1)(a) above may be extended—

    (a) by agreement between the undertaker and the person or persons who required the provision of the public sewer; or

(b) where there is a dispute as to whether the period should be extended, by an arbitrator on a reference under subsection (4) below.

(3) The places mentioned in subsection (1)(b) above shall be—

(a) such places as are determined by agreement between the sewerage undertaker and the person or persons who required the provision of the public sewer; or

(b) in default of agreement, such places as are determined by an arbitrator on a reference under subsection (4) below to be the places at which it is reasonable, in all the circumstances, for drains or private sewers to be used for the drainage of premises in that locality to communicate with the public sewer.

(4) A reference for the purposes of subsection (3) or (4) above shall be to a single arbitrator appointed—

(a) by agreement between the undertaker and the person or persons who required the provision of the public sewer; or

(b) in default of agreement, by the President of the Institution of Civil Engineers.

(5) In this section "relevant day", in relation to a requirement to provide a public sewer for any locality, means the day after whichever is the later of the following, that is to say—

(a) the day on which the conditions specified in section 99 above are satisfied in relation to the requirement; and

(b) the day on which the places where drains or private sewers to be used for the drainage of premises in that locality will communicate with the public sewer are determined under subsection (3) above.

### *Adoption etc. of sewers and disposal works*

Adoption of
sewers and
disposal works.

**102.**—(1) Subject to the following provisions of this section and to sections 103, 105 and 146(3) below, a sewerage undertaker may at any time declare that—

(a) any sewer which is situated within its area or which serves the whole or any part of that area; or

(b) any sewage disposal works which are so situated or which serve the whole or any part of that area,

shall, as from such date as may be specified in the declaration, become vested in the undertaker.

(2) The owner, or any of the owners, of any sewer or sewage disposal works with respect to which a sewerage undertaker might make a declaration under this section may make an application to that undertaker requesting it to make a declaration under this section with respect to the sewer or works.

(3) A declaration or application under this section may be made with respect to a part only of a sewer.

(4) A sewerage undertaker which proposes to make a declaration under this section—

(a) shall give notice of its proposal to the owner or owners of the sewer or works in question; and

(b) shall take no further action in the matter until two months have elapsed without an appeal against the proposal being lodged under section 105 below or, as the case may be, until any appeal so lodged has been determined.

(5) A sewerage undertaker, in deciding whether a declaration should be made under this section, shall have regard to all the circumstances of the case and, in particular, to the following considerations, that is to say—

(a) whether the sewer or works in question is or are adapted to, or required for, any general system of sewerage or sewage disposal which the undertaker has provided, or proposes to provide, for the whole or any part of its area;

(b) whether the sewer is constructed under a highway or under land reserved by a planning scheme for a street;

(c) the number of buildings which the sewer is intended to serve, and whether, regard being had to the proximity of other buildings or the prospect of future development, it is likely to be required to serve additional buildings;

(d) the method of construction and state of repair of the sewer or works; and

(e) in a case where an owner objects, whether the making of the proposed declaration would be seriously detrimental to him.

(6) Any person who immediately before the making of a declaration under this section was entitled to use the sewer in question shall be entitled to use it, or any sewer substituted for it, to the same extent as if the declaration had not been made.

(7) No declaration may be made under this section in respect of any sewer or works the construction of which was completed before 1st October 1937.

**103.**—(1) Where a sewerage undertaker is about to take into consideration the question of making a declaration under section 102 above with respect to—

Adoption of cross-border sewers etc.

(a) any sewer which is situated within the area of another sewerage undertaker or which, though situated within its own area, serves the whole or any part of the area of another sewerage undertaker; or

(b) any sewage disposal works which are situated within the area of another sewerage undertaker or which, though situated within its own area, serve the whole or any part of the area of another sewerage undertaker,

it shall give notice to the other undertaker.

(2) Where a sewerage undertaker is required to give notice under subsection (1) above to another undertaker, no declaration under section 102 above shall be made by the former undertaker until either—

(a) the other undertaker has consented to the declaration; or

(b) the Secretary of State, on an application made to him, has dispensed with the necessity for such consent, either unconditionally or subject to such conditions as he may think fit to impose.

(3) Where—

(a) a sewer or part of a sewer is vested, or any sewage disposal works are vested, in a relevant body; and

(b) in the case of a sewer, part of a sewer or works vested in railway undertakers or dock undertakers, the sewer or part in question is, or the works are, situated in or on land belonging to those undertakers and held or used by them for the purposes of their undertaking,

a sewerage undertaker shall not make a declaration under section 102 above with respect to the sewer or part or, as the case may be, with respect to the works, except on the application of the relevant body concerned.

(4) Where a sewerage undertaker makes a declaration under section 102 above with respect to—

(a) a sewer which is situated within the area of another sewerage undertaker; or

(b) any sewage disposal works which are so situated,

it shall forthwith give notice of the fact to that other undertaker.

(5) In this section "relevant body" means any sewerage undertaker, any local authority or county council or any railway undertakers or dock undertakers.

Agreements to adopt sewer, drain or sewage disposal works, at future date

**104.**—(1) Subject to subsection (7) and section 146(3) below, a sewerage undertaker may agree with any person constructing, or proposing to construct—

(a) any sewer; or

(b) any sewage disposal works,

that, if the sewer or works is or are constructed in accordance with the terms of the agreement, the undertaker will, upon the completion of the work, at some specified date or on the happening of some future event, declare the sewer or works to be vested in that undertaker.

(2) A person constructing or proposing to construct a sewer may make an application to a sewerage undertaker requesting the undertaker to make an agreement under this section.

(3) An application under subsection (2) above shall be accompanied and supplemented by all such information as the undertaker may reasonably require; but, subject to subsection (4) below and without prejudice to the effect (if any) of any other contravention of the requirements of this section in relation to such an application, a failure to provide information in pursuance of the obligation to supplement such an application shall not invalidate the application.

(4) Where—

(a) a person who has made an application to a sewerage undertaker under subsection (2) above has failed to comply with his obligation under this section to supplement that application with information required by the undertaker; and

(b) that requirement was made by the undertaker at such a time before the end of the period within which the undertaker is required, by virtue of section 105 below, to respond to the application as gave that person a reasonable opportunity to provide the required information within that period,

the undertaker may delay its response to the application until a reasonable time after the required information is provided.

(5) Any agreement made under this section by a sewerage undertaker shall be enforceable against the undertaker by the owner or occupier for the time being of any premises served by the sewer or works to which it relates.

(6) The preceding provisions of this section shall apply also in relation to drains as if references to a sewer included references to a drain; but it shall be a condition of any agreement under this section with respect to a drain that a declaration shall not be made before the drain has become a sewer.

(7) A sewerage undertaker shall not make an agreement under this section with respect to a sewer, drain or sewage disposal works situated within the area of another sewerage undertaker, until either—

(a) that other undertaker has consented to the making of the agreement; or

(b) the Secretary of State, on an application made to him, has dispensed with the necessity for such consent, either unconditionally or subject to such conditions as he may think fit to impose.

**105.**—(1) An owner of any sewer or sewage disposal works may appeal to the Secretary of State if—

Appeals with respect to adoption.

(a) he is aggrieved by the proposal of a sewerage undertaker to make a declaration under section 102 above; or

(b) he is aggrieved by the refusal of a sewerage undertaker to make such a declaration.

(2) Subject to section 104(4) above, a person constructing or proposing to construct a drain or sewer or any sewage disposal works may appeal to the Secretary of State where a sewerage undertaker—

(a) has refused an application under section 104 above;

(b) has offered to grant such an application on terms to which that person objects; or

(c) has failed, before the end of two months from the making of such an application, either to refuse the application or to give notice to the applicant of the terms on which it is prepared to grant the application.

(3) The time for the making of an appeal under subsection (1) above by the owner of any sewer or sewage disposal works shall be-

(a) in the case of an appeal by virtue of paragraph (a) of that subsection, any time within two months after notice of the proposal is served on that owner; and

(b) in the case of an appeal by virtue of paragraph (b) of that subsection, any time after receipt of notice of the undertaker's refusal or, if no such notice is given, at any time after the end of two months from the making of the application for the declaration.

(4) On the hearing of an appeal under this section, the Secretary of State may—

(a) in the case of an appeal under subsection (1) above, allow or disallow the proposal of the sewerage undertaker or, as the case may be, make any declaration which the sewerage undertaker might have made; or

(b) in the case of an appeal under subsection (2) above—

(i) uphold the refusal of the undertaker to grant the application or to modify the terms offered; or

(ii) on behalf of the undertaker, refuse the application or enter into any agreement into which the undertaker might have entered on the application;

and any declaration made under paragraph (a) above shall have the same effect as if it had been made by the undertaker in question.

(5) Where the Secretary of State makes a declaration under subsection (4)(a) above, he may, if he thinks fit—

(a) specify conditions, including conditions as to the payment of compensation by the sewerage undertaker; and

(b) direct that his declaration shall not take effect unless any conditions so specified are accepted.

(6) Where the Secretary of State makes an agreement under subsection (4)(b) above on behalf of a sewerage undertaker, he may do so on such terms as he considers reasonable or, as the case may be, on the terms offered by the undertaker subject to such modifications as he considers appropriate for ensuring that the terms of the agreement are reasonable.

(7) The Secretary of State, in deciding, on an appeal under this section, whether any declaration or agreement should be made, shall have regard to all the circumstances of the case and, in particular, to the considerations specified in section 102(5) above; and for the purposes of this subsection, in its application in relation to an appeal under subsection (2) above, paragraphs (a) to (e) of section 102(5) above shall have effect with the necessary modifications.

*Communication of drains and private sewers with public sewers*

**Right to communicate with public sewers.**

**106.**—(1) Subject to the provisions of this section—

(a) the owner or occupier of any premises in the area of a sewerage undertaker; or

(b) the owner of any private sewer draining premises in the area of any such undertaker,

shall be entitled to have his drains or sewer communicate with the public sewers of that undertaker and thereby to discharge foul water and surface water from those premises or that private sewer.

(2) Subject to the provisions of Chapter III of this Part, nothing in subsection (1) above shall entitle any person—

(a) to discharge directly or indirectly into any public sewer—

(i) any liquid from a factory, other than domestic sewage or surface or storm water, or any liquid from a manufacturing process; or

(ii) any liquid or other matter the discharge of which into public sewers is prohibited by or under any enactment; or

(b) where separate public sewers are provided for foul water and for surface water, to discharge directly or indirectly—

(i) foul water into a sewer provided for surface water; or

(ii) except with the approval of the undertaker, surface water into a sewer provided for foul water; or

(c) to have his drains or sewer made to communicate directly with a storm-water overflow sewer.

(3) A person desirous of availing himself of his entitlement under this section shall give notice of his proposals to the sewerage undertaker in question.

(4) At any time within twenty-one days after a sewerage undertaker receives a notice under subsection (3) above, the undertaker may by notice to the person who gave the notice refuse to permit the communication to be made, if it appears to the undertaker that the mode of construction or condition of the drain or sewer is such that the making of the communication would be prejudicial to the undertaker's sewerage system

(5) For the purpose of examining the mode of construction and condition of a drain or sewer to which a notice under subsection (3) above relates a sewerage undertaker may, if necessary, require it to be laid open for inspection.

(6) Any question arising under subsections (3) to (5) above between a sewerage undertaker and a person proposing to make a communication as to—

(a) the reasonableness of the undertaker's refusal to permit a communication to be made; or

(b) as to the reasonableness of any requirement under subsection (5) above,

may, on the application of that person, be determined by a magistrates' court.

(7) Sections 300 to 302 of the Public Health Act 1936 (which relate to the determination of questions by courts of summary jurisdiction and to appeals against such determinations) shall apply for the purposes of and in relation to a determination on an application under subsection (6) above—

1936 c. 49.

(a) as they apply for the purposes of and in relation to a determination by a magistrates' court under that Act; and

(b) in the case of section 302, as if the reference to a decision of a local authority included a reference to a decision of a sewerage undertaker.

(8) Where a person proposes under this section to make a communication between a drain or sewer and such a public sewer in Greater London as is used for the general reception of sewage from other public sewers and is not substantially used for the reception of sewage from private sewers and drains—

(a) the grounds on which a sewerage undertaker may refuse to permit the communication shall be such grounds as the undertaker thinks fit; and

(b) no application to a magistrates' court may be made under subsection (6) above in respect of any refusal under this subsection.

1961 c. 34.

(9) In this section "factory" has the same meaning as in the Factories Act 1961.

Right of sewerage undertaker to undertake the making of communications with public sewers.

**107.**—(1) Where a person gives to a sewerage undertaker notice under section 106 above of his proposal to have his drains or sewer made to communicate with a public sewer of that undertaker, the undertaker may—

(a) within fourteen days after the receipt of the notice; or

(b) if any question arising under the notice requires to be determined by a magistrates' court, within fourteen days after the determination of that question,

give notice to that person that the undertaker intends itself to make the communication.

(2) If, after a notice has been given to any person under subsection (1) above, that person proceeds himself to make the communication, he shall be guilty of an offence and liable, on summary conviction, to a fine not exceeding level 4 on the standard scale.

(3) Where a sewerage undertaker has given a notice under subsection (1) above—

(a) the undertaker shall have all such rights in respect of the making of the communication as the person desiring it to be made would have; but

(b) it shall not be obligatory on the undertaker to make the communication until either—

(i) there has been paid to the sewerage undertaker any such sum, not exceeding the undertaker's reasonable estimate of the cost of the work, as the undertaker may have required to be paid to it; or

(ii) there has been given to the undertaker such security for the payment of the cost of the work as it may reasonably have required.

(4) If any payment made to a sewerage undertaker under subsection (3) above exceeds the expenses reasonably incurred by it in the carrying out of the work in question, the excess shall be repaid by the undertaker; and, if and so far as those expenses are not covered by such a payment, the undertaker may recover the expenses, or the balance of them, from the person for whom the work was done.

(5) Sections 291, 293 and 294 of the Public Health Act 1936 (which provide for the means of, and for limitations on, the recovery of expenses incurred by a local authority) shall apply in relation to the recovery by a sewerage undertaker of any sums under this section as they apply in relation to the recovery of expenses under that Act by a local authority.

(6) For the purposes of this section, the making of the communication between a drain or private sewer and a public sewer includes all such work as involves the breaking open of a street.

**108.**—(1) Where a sewerage undertaker does not under section 107 above elect itself to make a communication to which a person is entitled under section 106 above, the person making it shall—

    (a) before commencing the work, give reasonable notice to any person directed by the undertaker to superintend the carrying out of the work; and

    (b) afford any such person all reasonable facilities for superintending the carrying out of the work.

(2) For the purpose—

    (a) of exercising his rights under section 106 above; or

    (b) of examining, repairing or renewing any drain or private sewer draining his premises into a public sewer,

the owner or occupier of any premises shall be entitled to exercise the same powers as, for the purpose of carrying out its functions, are conferred on a sewerage undertaker by sections 158 and 161(1) below.

(3) The provisions of Part VI of this Act shall apply, with the necessary modifications, in relation to the power conferred by subsection (2) above as they apply in relation to the power conferred by sections 158 and 161(1) below.

**109.**—(1) Any person who causes a drain or sewer to communicate with a public sewer—

    (a) in contravention of any of the provisions of section 106 or 108 above; or

    (b) before the end of the period mentioned in subsection (4) of that section 106,

shall be guilty of an offence and liable, on summary conviction, to a fine not exceeding level 4 on the standard scale.

(2) Whether proceedings have or have not been taken by a sewerage undertaker in respect of an offence under this section, such an undertaker may—

    (a) close any communication made in contravention of any of the provisions of section 106 or 108 above; and

    (b) recover from the offender any expenses reasonably incurred by the undertaker in so doing.

(3) Sections 291, 293 and 294 of the Public Health Act 1936 (which provide for the means of, and for limitations on, the recovery of expenses incurred by a local authority) shall apply in relation to the recovery by a sewerage undertaker of any sums under this section as they apply in relation to the recovery of expenses under that Act by a local authority.

*Connections between public sewers*

Determination of
disputes with
respect to cross
boundary sewers.
1989 c. 15.

**110.**—(1) Where any part of a sewer is vested in a sewerage undertaker by virtue of section 70 of the Water Act 1989 (cross boundary sewers), the terms on which that part of that sewer—

(a) communicates with such parts of that sewer or of any other sewer; or

(b) discharges into any such sewage disposal works,

as immediately before 1st September 1989 were vested in the same water authority as that part of that sewer but, by virtue of that section, are vested in another sewerage undertaker shall be determined, in default of agreement, by the Director.

(2) A determination by the Director under this section shall have effect as an agreement between the sewerage undertakers in question but may be varied or revoked by a subsequent determination made by the Director on the application of either of those undertakers, as well as by agreement between the undertakers.

(3) In making a determination under this section, the Director shall have regard to the desirability of a sewerage undertaker's recovering the costs resulting from its allowing the sewers of other sewerage undertakers to communicate with its sewers or to discharge into its sewage disposal works and of its securing a reasonable return on its capital.

*Provisions protecting sewerage system*

Restrictions on
use of public
sewers.

**111.**—(1) Subject to the provisions of Chapter III of this Part, no person shall throw, empty or turn, or suffer or permit to be thrown or emptied or to pass, into any public sewer, or into any drain or sewer communicating with a public sewer—

(a) any matter likely to injure the sewer or drain, to interfere with the free flow of its contents or to affect prejudicially the treatment and disposal of its contents; or

(b) any such chemical refuse or waste steam, or any such liquid of a temperature higher than one hundred and ten degrees Fahrenheit, as by virtue of subsection (2) below is a prohibited substance; or

(c) any petroleum spirit or carbide of calcium.

(2) For the purposes of subsection (1) above, chemical refuse, waste steam or a liquid of a temperature higher than that mentioned in that subsection is a prohibited substance if (either alone or in combination with the contents of the sewer or drain in question) it is or, in the case of the liquid, is when so heated—

(a) dangerous;

(b) the cause of a nuisance; or

(c) injurious, or likely to cause injury, to health.

(3) A person who contravenes any of the provisions of this section shall be guilty of an offence and liable—

(a) on summary conviction, to a fine not exceeding the statutory maximum and to a further fine not exceeding £50 for each day on which the offence continues after conviction;

(b) on conviction on indictment, to imprisonment for a term not exceeding two years or to a fine or to both.

(4) For the purposes of so much of subsection (3) above as makes provision for the imposition of a daily penalty—

   (a) the court by which a person is convicted of the original offence may fix a reasonable date from the date of conviction for compliance by the defendant with any directions given by the court; and

   (b) where a court has fixed such a period, the daily penalty shall not be imposed in respect of any day before the end of that period.

(5) In this section the expression "petroleum spirit" means any such—

   (a) crude petroleum;

   (b) oil made from petroleum or from coal, shale, peat or other bituminous substances; or

   (c) product of petroleum or mixture containing petroleum,

as, when tested in the manner prescribed by or under the Petroleum (Consolidation) Act 1928, gives off an inflammable vapour at a temperature of less than seventy-three degrees Fahrenheit.

1928 c. 32.

**112.**—(1) Where—

   (a) a person proposes to construct a drain or sewer; and

   (b) a sewerage undertaker considers that the proposed drain or sewer is, or is likely to be, needed to form part of a general sewerage system which that undertaker provides or proposes to provide,

Requirement that proposed drain or sewer be constructed so as to form part of general system.

the undertaker may require that person to construct the drain or sewer in a manner differing, as regards material or size of pipes, depth, fall, direction or outfall or otherwise, from the manner in which that person proposes, or could otherwise be required by the undertaker, to construct it.

(2) If any person on whom requirements are imposed under this section by a sewerage undertaker is aggrieved by the requirements, he may within twenty-eight days appeal to the Secretary of State.

(3) On an appeal under subsection (2) above with respect to any requirements, the Secretary of State may either disallow the requirements or allow them with or without modification.

(4) It shall be the duty of a person on whom requirements are imposed by a sewerage undertaker under this section to comply with those requirements.

(5) The duty of any person by virtue of subsection (4) above to comply with the requirements of a sewerage undertaker shall be owed to the undertaker; and any breach of that duty which causes the undertaker to sustain loss or damage shall be actionable at the suit of the undertaker.

(6) A sewerage undertaker which exercises the powers conferred on it by this section shall—

   (a) repay to the person constructing the drain or sewer the extra expenses reasonably incurred by that person in complying with the undertaker's requirements; and

(b) until the drain or sewer becomes a public sewer, from time to time repay to that person so much of any expenses reasonably incurred by him in repairing or maintaining the drain or sewer as may be attributable to the undertaker's requirements having been imposed and complied with.

(7) Nothing in this section shall apply in relation to so much of any drain or sewer as is proposed to be constructed by any railway undertakers or dock undertakers in or on land which—

(a) belongs to them; and

(b) is held or used by them for the purposes of their undertaking.

Power to alter drainage system of premises in area.

**113.**—(1) Where any premises have a drain or sewer communicating with a public sewer or a cesspool, but that system of drainage, though sufficient for the effectual drainage of the premises—

(a) is not adapted to the general sewerage system of the area; or

(b) is, in the opinion of the sewerage undertaker for the area, otherwise objectionable,

the undertaker may, at its own expense, close the existing drain or sewer and fill up the cesspool, if any, and do any work necessary for that purpose.

(2) The power conferred on a sewerage undertaker by subsection (1) above shall be exercisable on condition only that the undertaker first provides, in a position equally convenient to the owner of the premises in question, a drain or sewer which—

(a) is equally effectual for the drainage of the premises; and

(b) communicates with a public sewer.

(3) A sewerage undertaker which proposes to carry out any work under this section shall give notice of its proposals to the owner of the premises in question.

(4) If the owner of the premises is aggrieved by the proposals, whether as regards the position or the sufficiency of the drain or sewer proposed to be provided for the drainage of the premises, he may appeal to a magistrates' court.

1936 c. 49.

(5) Sections 300 to 302 of the Public Health Act 1936 (which relate to the determination of questions by courts of summary jurisdiction and to appeals against such determinations) shall apply in relation to an appeal under subsection (4) above and to any determination on such an appeal—

(a) as they apply in relation to appeals against any decision of a local authority under that Act and to determinations on any such appeal; and

(b) in the case of section 302, as if the reference to a decision of a local authority included a reference to a decision of a sewerage undertaker.

(6) The Secretary of State may by regulations make provision with respect to consents and the conditions of consents for discharges of trade effluent into the sewer of a sewerage undertaker through a drain or sewer provided in pursuance of this section.

(7) In this section—

"cesspool" includes a settlement tank or other tank for the reception or disposal of foul matter from buildings; and

"trade effluent" has the same meaning as in Chapter III of this Part.

**114.**—(1) Where it appears to a sewerage undertaker that there are reasonable grounds for believing—

Power to investigate defective drain or sewer.

(a) that any drain connecting with a public sewer, or any private sewer so connecting, is in such a condition as to be injurious or likely to cause injury to health or as to be a nuisance; or

(b) that any such drain or private sewer is so defective as to admit subsoil water,

the undertaker may examine the condition of the drain or sewer and, for that purpose, may apply any test, other than a test by water under pressure and, if the undertaker deems it necessary, open the ground.

(2) If on examination the drain or sewer is found to be in proper condition, the undertaker shall, as soon as possible, reinstate any ground which has been opened by it and make good any damage done by the undertaker.

### *Use of pipes for sewerage purposes*

**115.**—(1) Subject to the provisions of this section, a relevant authority and a sewerage undertaker may agree that—

Use of highway drains as sewers and vice versa.

(a) any drain or sewer which is vested in the authority in their capacity as a highway authority may, upon such terms as may be agreed, be used by the undertaker for the purpose of conveying surface water from premises or streets;

(b) any public sewer vested in the undertaker may, upon such terms as may be agreed, be used by the authority for conveying surface water from roads repairable by the authority.

(2) Where a sewer or drain with respect to which a relevant authority and a sewerage undertaker propose to make an agreement under this section discharges, whether directly or indirectly, into the sewers or sewage disposal works of another sewerage undertaker, the agreement shall not be made without the consent of that other undertaker.

(3) Subject to subsection (4) below, a consent given by a sewerage undertaker for the purposes of subsection (2) above may be given on such terms as that undertaker thinks fit.

(4) Neither a relevant authority nor a sewerage undertaker shall—

(a) unreasonably refuse to enter into an agreement for the purposes of this section; or

(b) insist unreasonably upon terms unacceptable to the other party;

and a sewerage undertaker shall not unreasonably refuse to consent to the making of such an agreement or insist unreasonably upon terms unacceptable to either party.

(5) Any question arising under this section as to whether or not any authority or undertaker is acting unreasonably shall be referred to the Secretary of State, whose decision shall be final.

PART IV

(6) The powers by virtue of paragraph (a) of subsection (1) above of a relevant authority and a sewerage undertaker to enter into an agreement shall be exercisable by two relevant authorities as they would be exercisable if one of them were a sewerage undertaker.

1980 c. 66.

(7) Nothing in this section shall be construed as limiting the rights of a relevant authority under section 264 of the Highways Act 1980.

1936 c. 49.

(8) Part XII of the Public Health Act 1936 shall apply for the purposes of the provisions of this section which confer functions on relevant authorities as they apply for the purposes of the provisions of that Act.

(9) In this section "relevant authority" means a county council or any local authority except a non-metropolitan district council.

(10) The provisions of this section are subject to the provisions of section 146(4) below.

Power to close or restrict use of public sewer.

**116.**—(1) Subject to subsection (3) below, a sewerage undertaker may discontinue and prohibit the use of any public sewer which is vested in the undertaker.

(2) A discontinuance or prohibition under this section may be for all purposes, for the purpose of foul water drainage or for the purpose of surface water drainage.

(3) Before any person who is lawfully using a sewer for any purpose is deprived under this section by a sewerage undertaker of the use of the sewer for that purpose, the undertaker shall—

(a) provide a sewer which is equally effective for his use for that purpose; and

(b) at the undertaker's own expense, carry out any work necessary to make that person's drains or sewers communicate with the sewer provided in pursuance of this subsection.

*Interpretation of Chapter II*

Interpretation of Chapter II.

**117.**—(1) In this Chapter, except in so far as the context otherwise requires—

"dock undertakers" means persons authorised by any enactment, or by any order, rule or regulation made under any enactment, to construct, work or carry on any dock, harbour, canal or inland navigation;

"domestic sewerage purposes", in relation to any premises, means any one or more of the following purposes, that is to say—

(a) the removal, from buildings on the premises and from land occupied with and appurtenant to the buildings, of the contents of lavatories;

(b) the removal, from such buildings and from such land, of water which has been used for cooking or washing; and

(c) the removal, from such buildings and such land, of surface water;

but does not, by virtue of paragraph (b) of this definition, include the removal of any water used for the business of a laundry or for a business of preparing food or drink for consumption otherwise than on the premises.

(2) References in this Chapter to the construction of a sewer or of any sewage disposal works include references to the extension of any existing sewer or works.

(3) In this Chapter "local authority", in relation to the Inner Temple and the Middle Temple, includes, respectively, the Sub-Treasurer of the Inner Temple and the Under-Treasurer of the Middle Temple.

(4) Every application made or consent given under this Chapter shall be made or given in writing.

(5) Nothing in sections 102 to 109 above or in sections 111 to 116 above shall be construed as authorising a sewerage undertaker to construct or use any public or other sewer, or any drain or outfall—

    (a) in contravention of any applicable provision of the Water Resources Act 1991; or

    1991 c. 57.

    (b) for the purpose of conveying foul water into any natural or artificial stream, watercourse, canal, pond or lake, without the water having been so treated as not to affect prejudicially the purity and quality of the water in the stream, watercourse, canal, pond or lake.

(6) A sewerage undertaker shall so carry out its functions under sections 102 to 105, 112, 115 and 116 above as not to create a nuisance.

## CHAPTER III

### TRADE EFFLUENT

*Consent for discharge of trade effluent into public sewer*

**118.**—(1) Subject to the following provisions of this Chapter, the occupier of any trade premises in the area of a sewerage undertaker may discharge any trade effluent proceeding from those premises into the undertaker's public sewers if he does so with the undertaker's consent.

Consent required for discharge of trade effluent into public sewer.

(2) Nothing in this Chapter shall authorise the discharge of any effluent into a public sewer otherwise than by means of a drain or sewer.

(3) The following, that is to say—

    (a) the restrictions imposed by paragraphs (a) and (b) of section 106(2) above; and

    (b) section 111 above so far as it relates to anything falling within paragraph (a) or (b) of subsection (1) of that section,

shall not apply to any discharge of trade effluent which is lawfully made by virtue of this Chapter.

(4) Accordingly, subsections (3) to (8) of section 106 above and sections 108 and 109 above shall have effect in relation to communication with a sewer for the purpose of making any discharge which is lawfully made by virtue of this Chapter as they have effect in relation to communication with a sewer for the purpose of making discharges which are authorised by subsection (1) of section 106 above.

(5) If, in the case of any trade premises, any trade effluent is discharged without such consent or other authorisation as is necessary for the purposes of this Chapter, the occupier of the premises shall be guilty of an offence and liable—

    (a) on summary conviction, to a fine not exceeding the statutory maximum; and

    (b) on conviction on indictment, to a fine.

*Consents on an application*

Application for consent.

    **119.**—(1) An application to a sewerage undertaker for a consent to discharge trade effluent from any trade premises into a public sewer of that undertaker shall be by notice served on the undertaker by the owner or occupier of the premises.

    (2) An application under this section with respect to a proposed discharge of any such effluent shall state—

    (a) the nature or composition of the trade effluent;

    (b) the maximum quantity of the trade effluent which it is proposed to discharge on any one day; and

    (c) the highest rate at which it is proposed to discharge the trade effluent.

Applications for the discharge of special category effluent.

    **120.**—(1) Subject to subsection (3) below, where a notice containing an application under section 119 above is served on a sewerage undertaker with respect to discharges of any special category effluent, it shall be the duty of the undertaker to refer to the Secretary of State the questions—

    (a) whether the discharges to which the notice relates should be prohibited; and

    (b) whether, if they are not prohibited, any requirements should be imposed as to the conditions on which they are made.

    (2) Subject to subsection (3) below, a reference which is required to be made by a sewerage undertaker by virtue of subsection (1) above shall be made before the end of the period of two months beginning with the day after the notice containing the application is served on the undertaker.

    (3) There shall be no obligation on a sewerage undertaker to make a reference under this section in respect of any application if, before the end of the period mentioned in subsection (2) above, there is a refusal by the undertaker to give any consent on the application.

    (4) It shall be the duty of a sewerage undertaker where it has made a reference under this section not to give any consent, or enter into any agreement, with respect to the discharges to which the reference relates at any time before the Secretary of State serves notice on the undertaker of his determination on the reference.

    (5) Every reference under this section shall be made in writing and shall be accompanied by a copy of the notice containing the application in respect of which it is made.

    (6) It shall be the duty of a sewerage undertaker, on making a reference under this section, to serve a copy of the reference on the owner or the occupier of the trade premises in question, according to whether the discharges to which the reference relates are to be by the owner or by the occupier.

    (7) Subject to subsection (8) below, the duties of a sewerage undertaker under this section shall be enforceable under section 18 above by the Secretary of State.

PART IV

(8) Where an application is made to the Secretary of State under section 18 above in respect of a failure by a sewerage undertaker to make a reference under this section, the Secretary of State may, instead of making an order under that section, proceed with the matter as if the application were the reference.

**121.**—(1) The power of a sewerage undertaker, on an application under section 119 above, to give a consent with respect to the discharge of any trade effluent shall be a power to give a consent either unconditionally or subject to such conditions as the sewerage undertaker thinks fit to impose with respect to—

> (a) the sewer or sewers into which the trade effluent may be discharged;
>
> (b) the nature or composition of the trade effluent which may be discharged;
>
> (c) the maximum quantity of trade effluent which may be discharged on any one day, either generally or into a particular sewer; and
>
> (d) the highest rate at which trade effluent may be discharged, either generally or into a particular sewer.

Conditions of consent.

(2) Conditions with respect to all or any of the following matters may also be attached under this section to a consent to the discharge of trade effluent from any trade premises—

> (a) the period or periods of the day during which the trade effluent may be discharged from the trade premises into the sewer;
>
> (b) the exclusion from the trade effluent of all condensing water;
>
> (c) the elimination or diminution, in cases falling within subsection (3) below, of any specified constituent of the trade effluent, before it enters the sewer;
>
> (d) the temperature of the trade effluent at the time when it is discharged into the sewer, and its acidity or alkalinity at that time;
>
> (e) the payment by the occupier of the trade premises to the undertaker of charges for the reception of the trade effluent into the sewer and for the disposal of the effluent;
>
> (f) the provision and maintenance of such an inspection chamber or manhole as will enable a person readily to take samples, at any time, of what is passing into the sewer from the trade premises;
>
> (g) the provision, testing and maintenance of such meters as may be required to measure the volume and rate of discharge of any trade effluent being discharged from the trade premises into the sewer;
>
> (h) the provision, testing and maintenance of apparatus for determining the nature and composition of any trade effluent being discharged from the premises into the sewer;
>
> (i) the keeping of records of the volume, rate of discharge, nature and composition of any trade effluent being discharged and, in particular, the keeping of records of readings of meters and other recording apparatus provided in compliance with any other condition attached to the consent; and

(j) the making of returns and giving of other information to the sewerage undertaker concerning the volume, rate of discharge, nature and composition of any trade effluent discharged from the trade premises into the sewer.

(3) A case falls within this subsection where the sewerage undertaker is satisfied that the constituent in question, either alone or in combination with any matter with which it is likely to come into contact while passing through any sewers-

(a) would injure or obstruct those sewers, or make the treatment or disposal of the sewage from those sewers specially difficult or expensive; or

(b) in the case of trade effluent which is to be or is discharged—

(i) into a sewer having an outfall in any harbour or tidal water; or

(ii) into a sewer which connects directly or indirectly with a sewer or sewage disposal works having such an outfall,

would cause or tend to cause injury or obstruction to the navigation on, or the use of, the harbour or tidal water.

(4) In the exercise of the power conferred by virtue of subsection (2)(e) above, regard shall be had—

(a) to the nature and composition and to the volume and rate of discharge of the trade effluent discharged;

(b) to any additional expense incurred or likely to be incurred by a sewerage undertaker in connection with the reception or disposal of the trade effluent; and

(c) to any revenue likely to be derived by the undertaker from the trade effluent.

(5) If, in the case of any trade premises, a condition imposed under this section is contravened, the occupier of the premises shall be guilty of an offence and liable—

(a) on summary conviction, to a fine not exceeding the statutory maximum; and

(b) on conviction on indictment, to a fine.

(6) In this section "harbour" and "tidal water" have the same meanings as in the Merchant Shipping Act 1894.

1894 c. 60.

(7) This section has effect subject to the provisions of sections 133 and 135(3) below.

Appeals to the Director with respect to decisions on applications etc.

**122.**—(1) Any person aggrieved by—

(a) the refusal of a sewerage undertaker to give a consent for which application has been duly made to the undertaker under section 119 above;

(b) the failure of a sewerage undertaker to give such a consent within the period of two months beginning with the day after service of the notice containing the application; or

(c) any condition attached by a sewerage undertaker to such a consent,

may appeal to the Director.

(2) On an appeal under this section in respect of a refusal or failure to give a consent, the Director may give the necessary consent, either unconditionally or subject to such conditions as he thinks fit to impose for determining any of the matters as respects which the undertaker has power to impose conditions under section 121 above.

(3) On an appeal under this section in respect of a condition attached to a consent, the Director may take into review all the conditions attached to the consent, whether appealed against or not, and may—

(a) substitute for them any other set of conditions, whether more or less favourable to the appellant; or

(b) annul any of the conditions.

(4) The Director may, under subsection (3) above, include provision as to the charges to be made in pursuance of any condition attached to a consent for any period before the determination of the appeal.

(5) On any appeal under this section, the Director may give a direction that the trade effluent in question shall not be discharged until a specified date.

(6) Any consent given or conditions imposed by the Director under this section in respect of discharges of trade effluent shall have effect for the purposes of this Chapter as if given or imposed by the sewerage undertaker in question.

(7) The powers of the Director under this section shall be subject to the provisions of sections 123, 128, 133, 135 and 137 below.

**123.**—(1) Where a reference is made to the Secretary of State under section 120 above, the period mentioned in paragraph (b) of subsection (1) of section 122 above shall not begin to run for the purposes of that subsection, in relation to the application to which the reference relates, until the beginning of the day after the Secretary of State serves notice on the sewerage undertaker in question of his determination on the reference.

(2) If, on an appeal under section 122 above, it appears to the Director—

(a) that the case is one in which the sewerage undertaker in question is required to make a reference under section 120 above before giving a consent; and

(b) that the undertaker has not made such a reference, whether because the case falls within subsection (3) of that section or otherwise,

the Director shall not be entitled to determine the appeal, otherwise than by upholding a refusal, except where the conditions set out in subsection (3) below are satisfied.

(3) The conditions mentioned in subsection (2) above are satisfied if the Director—

(a) has himself referred the questions mentioned in section 120(1) above to the Secretary of State; and

(b) has been sent a copy of the notice of the Secretary of State's determination on the reference.

(4) Every reference under this section shall be made in writing and shall be accompanied by a copy of the notice containing the application in respect of which the appeal and reference is made.

(5) It shall be the duty of the Director, on making a reference under this section, to serve a copy of the reference—

(a) on the owner or the occupier of the trade premises in question, according to whether the discharges to which the reference relates are to be by the owner or by the occupier; and

(b) on the sewerage undertaker in question.

Variation of consents.

**124.**—(1) Subject to sections 128, 133 and 135(3) below, a sewerage undertaker may from time to time give a direction varying the conditions which have been attached to any of its consents under this Chapter to the discharge of trade effluent into a public sewer.

(2) Subject to subsections (3) and (4) and section 125 below, no direction shall be given under this section with respect to a consent under this Chapter—

(a) within two years from the date of the consent; or

(b) where a previous direction has been given under this section with respect to that consent, within two years from the date on which notice was given of that direction.

(3) Subsection (2) above shall not prevent a direction being given before the time specified in that subsection if it is given with the consent of the owner and occupier of the trade premises in question.

(4) A direction given with the consent mentioned in subsection (3) above shall not affect the time at which any subsequent direction may be given.

(5) The sewerage undertaker shall give to the owner and occupier of the trade premises to which a consent under this Chapter relates notice of any direction under this section with respect to that consent.

(6) A notice under subsection (5) above shall—

(a) include information as to the right of appeal conferred by subsection (1) of section 126 below; and

(b) state the date, being a date not less than two months after the giving of the notice, on which (subject to subsection (2) of that section) the direction is to take effect.

(7) For the purposes of this section references to the variation of conditions include references to the addition or annulment of a condition and to the attachment of a condition to a consent to which no condition was previously attached.

Variations within time limit.

**125.**—(1) A sewerage undertaker may give a direction under section 124 above before the time specified in subsection (2) of that section and without the consent required by subsection (3) of that section if it considers it necessary to do so in order to provide proper protection for persons likely to be affected by the discharges which could lawfully be made apart from the direction.

(2) Subject to section 134(3) below, where a sewerage undertaker gives a direction by virtue of subsection (1) above, the undertaker shall be liable to pay compensation to the owner and occupier of the trade premises to which the direction relates, unless the undertaker is of the opinion that the direction is required—

    (a) in consequence of a change of circumstances which—

        (i) has occurred since the beginning of the period of two years in question; and

        (ii) could not reasonably have been foreseen at the beginning of that period;

    and

    (b) otherwise than in consequence of consents for discharges given after the beginning of that period.

(3) Where a sewerage undertaker gives a direction by virtue of subsection (1) above and is of the opinion mentioned in subsection (2) above, it shall be the duty of the undertaker to give notice of the reasons for its opinion to the owner and occupier of the premises in question.

(4) For the purposes of this section the circumstances referred to in subsection (2)(a) above may include the information available as to the discharges to which the consent in question relates or as to the interaction of those discharges with other discharges or matter.

(5) The Secretary of State may by regulations make provision as to the manner of determining the amount of any compensation payable under this section, including the factors to be taken into account in determining that amount.

**126.**—(1) The owner or occupier of any trade premises may—

Appeals with respect to variations of consent.

    (a) within two months of the giving to him under subsection (5) of section 124 above of a notice of a direction under that section; or

    (b) with the written permission of the Director, at any later time,

appeal to the Director against the direction.

(2) Subject to subsection (3) below, if an appeal against a direction is brought under subsection (1) above before the date specified under section 124(6)(b) above in the notice of the direction, the direction shall not take effect until the appeal is withdrawn or finally disposed of.

(3) In so far as the direction which is the subject of an appeal relates to the making of charges payable by the occupier of any trade premises, it may take effect on any date after the giving of the notice.

(4) On an appeal under subsection (1) above with respect to a direction, the Director shall have power—

    (a) to annul the direction given by the sewerage undertaker; and

    (b) to substitute for it any other direction, whether more or less favourable to the appellant;

and any direction given by the Director may include provision as to the charges to be made for any period between the giving of the notice by the sewerage undertaker and the determination of the appeal.

(5) A person to whom notice is given in pursuance of section 125(3) above may, in accordance with regulations made by the Secretary of State, appeal to the Director against the notice on the ground that compensation should be paid in consequence of the direction to which the notice relates.

(6) On an appeal under subsection (5) above the Director may direct that section 125 above shall have effect as if the sewerage undertaker in question were not of the opinion to which the notice relates.

(7) Any consent given or conditions imposed by the Director under this section in respect of discharges of trade effluent shall have effect for the purposes of this Chapter as if given or imposed by the sewerage undertaker in question.

(8) The powers of the Director under this section shall be subject to the provisions of sections 133, 135 and 137 below.

Review by the Secretary of State of consents relating to special category effluent.

**127.**—(1) Where any person, as the owner or occupier of any trade premises, is (whether or not in accordance with a notice under section 132 below) for the time being authorised by virtue of a consent under this Chapter to make discharges of any special category effluent from those premises into a sewerage undertaker's public sewer, the Secretary of State may review the questions—

(a) whether the discharges authorised by the consent should be prohibited; and

(b) whether, if they are not prohibited, any requirements should be imposed as to the conditions on which they are made.

(2) Subject to subsection (3) below, the Secretary of State shall not review any question under this section unless—

(a) the consent or variation by virtue of which the discharges in question are made has not previously been the subject-matter of a review and was given or made—

(i) before 1st September 1989; or

(ii) in contravention of section 133 below;

(b) a period of more than two years has elapsed since the time, or last time, when notice of the Secretary of State's determination on any reference or review relating to that consent or the consent to which that variation relates was served under section 132 below on the owner or occupier of the trade premises in question; or

(c) there has, since the time, or last time, when such a notice was so served, been a contravention of any provision which was included in compliance with a requirement of a notice under section 132 below in the consent or variation by virtue of which the discharges in question are made.

(3) Subsection (2) above shall not apply if the review is carried out—

(a) for the purpose of enabling Her Majesty's Government in the United Kingdom to give effect to any Community obligation or to any international agreement to which the United Kingdom is for the time being a party; or

(b) for the protection of public health or of flora and fauna dependent on an aquatic environment.

*Application for variation of time for discharge*

**128.**—(1) If, after a direction has been given under any of the preceding provisions of this Chapter requiring that trade effluent shall not be discharged until a specified date, it appears to the sewerage undertaker in question that in consequence—

(a) of a failure to complete any works required in connection with the reception and disposal of the trade effluent; or

(b) of any other exceptional circumstances,

a later date ought to be substituted for the date so specified in the direction, the undertaker may apply to the Director for such a substitution.

(2) The Director shall have power, on an application under subsection (1) above, to vary the direction so as to extend the period during which the trade effluent may not be discharged until the date specified in the application or, if he thinks fit, any earlier date.

(3) Not less than one month before making an application under subsection (1) above a sewerage undertaker shall give notice of its intention to the owner and occupier of the trade premises from which the trade effluent is to be discharged.

(4) The Director, before varying a direction on an application under subsection (1) above, shall take into account any representations made to him by the owner or occupier of the trade premises in question.

*Agreements with respect the disposal etc. of trade effluent*

**129.**—(1) Subject to sections 130 and 133 below, a sewerage undertaker may enter into and carry into effect—

(a) an agreement with the owner or occupier of any trade premises within its area for the reception and disposal by the undertaker of any trade effluent produced on those premises;

(b) an agreement with the owner or occupier of any such premises under which it undertakes, on such terms as may be specified in the agreement, to remove and dispose of substances produced in the course of treating any trade effluent on or in connection with those premises.

(2) Without prejudice to the generality of subsection (1) above, an agreement such as is mentioned in paragraph (a) of that subsection may, in particular, provide—

(a) for the construction or extension by the sewerage undertaker of such works as may be required for the reception or disposal of the trade effluent; and

(b) for the repayment by the owner or occupier, as the case may be, of the whole or part of the expenses incurred by the undertaker in carrying out its obligations under the agreement.

(3) It is hereby declared that the power of a sewerage undertaker to enter into an agreement under this section includes a power, by that agreement, to authorise such a discharge as apart from the agreement would require a consent under this Chapter.

PART IV
Reference to the
Secretary of State
of agreements
relating to special
category effluent.

**130.**—(1) Where a sewerage undertaker and the owner or occupier of any trade premises are proposing to enter into an agreement under section 129 above with respect to, or to any matter connected with, the reception or disposal of any special category effluent, it shall be the duty of the undertaker to refer to the Secretary of State the questions—

(a) whether the operations which would, for the purposes of or in connection with the reception or disposal of that effluent, be carried out in pursuance of the proposed agreement should be prohibited; and

(b) whether, if they are not prohibited, any requirements should be imposed as to the conditions on which they are carried out.

(2) It shall be the duty of a sewerage undertaker where it has made a reference under this section not to give any consent or enter into any agreement with respect to any such operations as are mentioned in subsection (1)(a) above at any time before the Secretary of State serves notice on the undertaker of his determination on the reference.

(3) Every reference under this section shall be made in writing and shall be accompanied by a copy of the proposed agreement.

(4) It shall be the duty of a sewerage undertaker, on making a reference under this section, to serve a copy of the reference on the owner or the occupier of the trade premises in question, according to whether it is the owner or occupier who is proposing to be a party to the agreement.

(5) Subject to subsection (6) below, the duties of a sewerage undertaker under this section shall be enforceable under section 18 above by the Secretary of State.

(6) Where an application is made to the Secretary of State under section 18 above in respect of a failure by a sewerage undertaker to make a reference under this section, the Secretary of State may, instead of making an order under that section, proceed with the matter as if the application were the reference.

Review by the
Secretary of State
of agreements
relating to special
category effluent.

**131.**—(1) Where any person, as the owner or occupier of any trade premises, is (whether or not in accordance with a notice under section 132 below) for the time being a party to any agreement under section 129 above with respect to, or to any matter connected with, the reception or disposal of special category effluent, the Secretary of State may review the questions—

(a) whether the operations which, for the purposes of or in connection with the reception or disposal of that effluent, are carried out in pursuance of the agreement should be prohibited; and

(b) whether, if they are not prohibited, any requirements should be imposed as to the conditions on which they are carried out.

(2) Subject to subsection (3) below, the Secretary of State shall not review any question under this section unless—

(a) the agreement by virtue of which the operations in question are carried out has not previously been the subject-matter of a review and was entered into—

(i) before 1st September 1989; or

(ii) in contravention of section 133 below;

(b) a period of more than two years has elapsed since the time, or last time, when notice of the Secretary of State's determination on any reference or review relating to that agreement was served under section 132 below on the owner or occupier of the trade premises in question; or

(c) there has, since the time, or last time, when such a notice was so served, been a contravention of any provision which was included in compliance with a requirement of a notice under section 132 below in the agreement by virtue of which the operations in question are carried out.

(3) Subsection (2) above shall not apply if the review is carried out—

(a) for the purpose of enabling Her Majesty's Government in the United Kingdom to give effect to any Community obligation or to any international agreement to which the United Kingdom is for the time being a party; or

(b) for the protection of public health or of flora and fauna dependent on an aquatic environment.

(4) References in this section to an agreement include references to an agreement as varied from time to time by a notice under section 132 below.

*References and reviews relating to special category effluent*

**132.**—(1) This section applies to—

(a) any reference to the Secretary of State under section 120, 123 or 130 above; and

(b) any review by the Secretary of State under section 127 or 131 above.

Powers and procedure on references and reviews.

(2) On a reference or review to which this section applies, it shall be the duty of the Secretary of State, before determining the questions which are the subject-matter of the reference or review—

(a) to give an opportunity of making representations or objections to the Secretary of State—

(i) to the sewerage undertaker in question; and

(ii) to the following person, that is to say, the owner or the occupier of the trade premises in question, according to whether it is the owner or the occupier of those premises who is proposing to be, or is, the person making the discharges or, as the case may be, a party to the agreement;

and

(b) to consider any representations or objections which are duly made to him with respect to those questions by a person to whom he is required to give such an opportunity and which are not withdrawn.

(3) On determining any question on a reference or review to which this section applies, the Secretary of State shall serve notice on the sewerage undertaker in question and on the person specified in subsection (2)(a)(ii) above.

(4) A notice under this section shall state, according to what has been determined-

  (a) that the discharges or operations to which, or to the proposals for which, the reference or review relates, or such of them as are specified in the notice, are to be prohibited; or

  (b) that those discharges or operations, or such of them as are so specified, are to be prohibited except in so far as they are made or carried out in accordance with conditions which consist in or include conditions so specified; or

  (c) that the Secretary of State has no objection to those discharges or operations and does not intend to impose any requirements as to the conditions on which they are made or carried out.

(5) Without prejudice to section 133 below, a notice under this section, in addition to containing such provision as is specified in sub-paragraph (4) above, may do one or both of the following, that is to say—

  (a) vary or revoke the provisions of a previous notice with respect to the discharges or operations in question; and

  (b) for the purpose of giving effect to any prohibition or other requirement contained in the notice, vary or revoke any consent under this Chapter or any agreement under section 129 above.

(6) Nothing in subsection (1) or (2) of section 121 above shall be construed as restricting the power of the Secretary of State, by virtue of subsection (4)(b) above, to specify such conditions as he considers appropriate in a notice under this section.

(7) The Secretary of State shall have the same right of entry and other powers for the purposes of this section and any provision under which any reference or review to which this section applies is made as are conferred on a sewerage undertaker by section 171 below in relation to any other provision of this Chapter; and the provisions of that section accordingly have effect with the necessary modifications in relation to the power conferred by this subsection.

(8) The Secretary of State shall send a copy of every notice served under this section to the Director.

Effect of determination on reference or review.

**133.**—(1) Where a notice under section 132 above has been served on a sewerage undertaker, it shall be the duty—

  (a) of the undertaker; and

  (b) in relation to that undertaker, of the Director,

so to exercise the powers to which this section applies as to secure compliance with the provisions of the notice.

(2) This paragraph applies to the following powers, that is to say-

  (a) in relation to a sewerage undertaker, its power to give a consent under this Chapter, any of its powers under section 121 or 124 above and any power to enter into or vary an agreement under section 129 above; and

  (b) in relation to the Director, any of his powers under this Chapter.

(3) Nothing in subsection (1) or (2) of section 121 above shall be construed as restricting the power of a sewerage undertaker, for the purpose of complying with this section, to impose any condition specified in a notice under section 132 above.

(4) The duties of a sewerage undertaker under this section shall be enforceable under section 18 above by the Secretary of State.

**134.**—(1) Subject to subsection (2) below, the Secretary of State shall be liable to pay compensation to the relevant person in respect of any loss or damage sustained by that person as a result of any notice under section 132 above containing the Secretary of State's determination on a review which—

Compensation in respect of determinations made for the protection of public health etc.

(a) has been carried out for the protection of public health or of flora and fauna dependent on an aquatic environment; and

(b) but for being so carried out would have been prohibited by virtue of section 127(2) or 131(2) above.

(2) The Secretary of State shall not be required to pay any compensation under this section if the determination in question is shown to have been given in consequence of—

(a) a change of circumstances which could not reasonably have been foreseen at the time when the period of two years mentioned in section 127(2) or, as the case may be, section 131(2) above began to run; or

(b) consideration by the Secretary of State of material information which was not reasonably available to him at that time.

(3) No person shall be entitled to any compensation under section 125 above in respect of anything done in pursuance of section 133 above.

(4) In this section "the relevant person", in relation to a review, means the owner or the occupier of the trade premises in question, according to whether it is the owner or the occupier who makes the discharges to which the review relates or, as the case may be, is a party to the agreement to which it relates.

*Supplemental provisions of Chapter III*

**135.**—(1) On any appeal under section 122 or 126(1) above conditions providing for the payment of charges to the sewerage undertaker in question shall not be determined by the Director except in so far as no provision is in force by virtue of a charges scheme under section 143 below in respect of any such receptions, discharges, removals or disposals of effluent or substances as are of the same description as the reception, discharge, removal or disposal which is the subject-matter of the appeal.

Restrictions on power to fix charges under Chapter III.

(2) In so far as any such conditions as are mentioned in subsection (1) above do fall to be determined by the Director, they shall be determined having regard to the desirability of that undertaker's—

(a) recovering the expenses of complying with its obligations in consequence of the consent or agreement to which the conditions relate; and

(b) securing a reasonable return on its capital.

PART IV

(3) To the extent that subsection (1) above excludes any charges from a determination on an appeal those charges shall be fixed from time to time by a charges scheme under section 143 below but not otherwise.

Evidence from meters etc.

**136.** Any meter or apparatus provided in pursuance of this Chapter in any trade premises for the purpose of measuring, recording or determining the volume, rate of discharge, nature or composition of any trade effluent discharged from those premises shall be presumed in any proceedings to register accurately, unless the contrary is shown.

Statement of case on appeal.

**137.**—(1) At any stage of the proceedings on an appeal under section 122 or 126(1) above, the Director may, and if so directed by the High Court shall, state in the form of a special case for the decision of the High Court any question of law arising in those proceedings.

1981 c. 54.

(2) The decision of the High Court on a special case under this section shall be deemed to be a judgment of the Court within the meaning of section 16 of the Supreme Court Act 1981 (which relates to the jurisdiction of the Court of Appeal); but no appeal to the Court of Appeal shall be brought by virtue of this subsection except with the leave of the High Court or of the Court of Appeal.

Meaning of "special category effluent".

**138.**—(1) Subject to subsection (2) below, trade effluent shall be special category effluent for the purposes of this Chapter if—

> (a) such substances as may be prescribed under this Act are present in the effluent or are present in the effluent in prescribed concentrations; or

> (b) the effluent derives from any such process as may be so prescribed or from a process involving the use of prescribed substances or the use of such substances in quantities which exceed the prescribed amounts.

(2) Trade effluent shall not be special category effluent for the purposes of this Chapter if it is produced, or to be produced, in any process which is a prescribed process designated for central control as from the date which is the determination date for that process.

(3) In subsection (2) above "determination date", in relation to a prescribed process, means—

> (a) in the case of a process for which authorisation is granted, the date on which the enforcing authority grants it, whether in pursuance of the application or, on an appeal, of a direction to grant it;

> (b) in the case of a process for which authorisation is refused, the date of refusal or, on appeal, of the affirmation of the refusal.

(4) In this section—

> (a) "authorisation", "enforcing authority" and "prescribed process" have the meanings given by section 1 of the Environmental Protection Act 1990; and

1990 c. 43.

> (b) the references to designation for central control and to an appeal are references, respectively, to designation under section 4 of that Act and to an appeal under section 15 of that Act.

(5) Without prejudice to the power in subsection (3) of section 139 below, nothing in this Chapter shall enable regulations under this section to prescribe as special category effluent any liquid or matter which is not trade effluent but falls to be treated as such for the purposes of this Chapter by virtue of an order under that section.

**139.**—(1) The Secretary of State may by order provide that, subject to section 138(5) above, this Chapter shall apply in relation to liquid or other matter of any description specified in the order which is discharged into public sewers as it applies in relation to trade effluent.

Power to apply Chapter III to other effluents.

(2) An order applying the provisions of this Chapter in relation to liquid or other matter of any description may provide for it to so apply subject to such modifications (if any) as may be specified in the order and, in particular, subject to any such modification of the meaning for the purposes of this Chapter of the expression "trade premises" as may be so specified.

(3) The Secretary of State may include in an order under this section such provisions as appear to him expedient for modifying any enactment relating to sewage as that enactment applies in relation to the discharge into sewers of any liquid or other matter to which any provisions of this Chapter are applied by an order under this section.

(4) The Secretary of State may include in an order under this section such other supplemental, incidental and transitional provision as appears to him to be expedient.

(5) The power to make an order under this section shall be exercisable by statutory instrument; and no order shall be made under this section unless a draft of it has been laid before, and approved by a resolution of, each House of Parliament.

**140.** Schedule 8 to this Act shall have effect (without prejudice to the provisions of the Water Consolidation (Consequential Provisions) Act 1991 or to sections 16 and 17 of the Interpretation Act 1978) for the purpose of making provision in respect of certain cases where trade effluent was discharged in accordance with provision made before the coming into force of the Water Act 1989.

Pre-1989 Act authority for trade effluent discharges etc.
1991 c. 60.
1978 c. 30.
1989 c. 15.

*Interpretation of Chapter III*

**141.**—(1) In this Chapter, except in so far as the context otherwise requires—

Interpretation of Chapter III.

"special category effluent" has the meaning given by section 138 above;

"trade effluent"—

(a) means any liquid, either with or without particles of matter in suspension in the liquid, which is wholly or partly produced in the course of any trade or industry carried on at trade premises; and

(b) in relation to any trade premises, means any such liquid which is so produced in the course of any trade or industry carried on at those premises,

but does not include domestic sewage;

"trade premises" means, subject to subsection (2) below, any premises used or intended to be used for carrying on any trade or industry.

(2) For the purposes of this Chapter any land or premises used or intended for use (in whole or in part and whether or not for profit)—

(a) for agricultural or horticultural purposes or for the purposes of fish farming; or

(b) for scientific research or experiment,

shall be deemed to be premises used for carrying on a trade or industry; and the references to a trade or industry in the definition of "trade effluent" in subsection (1) above shall include references to agriculture, horticulture, fish farming and scientific research or experiment.

(3) Every application or consent made or given under this Chapter shall be made or given in writing.

(4) Nothing in this Chapter shall affect any right with respect to water in a river stream or watercourse, or authorise any infringement of such a right, except in so far as any such right would dispense with the requirements of this Chapter so far as they have effect by virtue of any regulations under section 138 above.

## PART V

### FINANCIAL PROVISIONS

### CHAPTER I

### CHARGES

*Manner of fixing charges*

Powers of undertakers to charge.

**142.**—(1) Subject to the following provisions of this Chapter, the powers of every relevant undertaker shall include power—

(a) to fix charges for any services provided in the course of carrying out its functions and, in the case of a sewerage undertaker, charges to be paid in connection with the carrying out of its trade effluent functions; and

(b) to demand and recover charges fixed under this section from any persons to whom the undertaker provides services or in relation to whom it carries out trade effluent functions.

(2) Subject to subsection (3) below, the powers conferred by subsection (1) above shall be exercisable—

(a) by or in accordance with a charges scheme under section 143 below; or

(b) by or in accordance with agreements with the persons to be charged.

(3) Paragraph (b) of subsection (2) above shall have effect in relation to the exercise of powers with respect to charges in connection with the carrying out of a sewerage undertaker's trade effluent functions only in so far as provision for the fixing, demanding or recovery of such charges may be contained in an agreement entered into in accordance with section 129 above.

(4) Except in so far as this Chapter otherwise provides, a relevant undertaker may fix charges under this section by reference to such matters, and may adopt such methods and principles for the calculation and imposition of the charges, as appear to the undertaker to be appropriate.

(5) The powers in relation to which this section has effect shall not be exercised so as to contravene any local statutory provision which expressly provides that no charge shall be made for a particular service.

(6) Nothing in subsections (1) to (5) above or in any charges scheme under section 143 below shall affect any power of a relevant undertaker to fix charges under any power conferred otherwise than by virtue of this Chapter.

(7) References in this section to a sewerage undertaker's trade effluent functions are references to its functions under Chapter III of Part IV of this Act.

**143.**—(1) A relevant undertaker may make a scheme ("a charges scheme") which does any one or more of the following, that is to say— Charges schemes.

    (a) fixes the charges to be paid for any services provided by the undertaker in the course of carrying out its functions;

    (b) in the case of a sewerage undertaker, requires such charges as may be fixed by the scheme to be paid to the undertaker where, in the circumstances set out in the scheme—

        (i) a notice containing an application for a consent is served on the undertaker under section 119 above;

        (ii) such a consent as is necessary for the purposes of Chapter III of Part IV of this Act is given by the undertaker; or

        (iii) a discharge is made in pursuance of such a consent;

    and

    (c) makes provision with respect to the times and methods of payment of the charges fixed by the scheme.

(2) The persons who may be required by a charges scheme to pay any charge fixed by virtue of subsection (1)(b) above shall be the person who serves the notice, the person to whom the consent is given or, as the case may be, any person who makes a discharge in pursuance of the consent at any time during the period to which, in accordance with the scheme, the charge relates.

(3) A charges scheme which requires the payment of charges where a discharge has been made in pursuance of such a consent as is mentioned in subsection (1)(b) above may impose—

    (a) a single charge in respect of the whole period for which the consent is in force;

    (b) separate charges in respect of different parts of that period; or

    (c) both such a single charge and such separate charges.

(4) A charges scheme may—

    (a) make different provision for different cases, including different provision in relation to different circumstances or localities; and

(b) contain supplemental, consequential and transitional provision for the purposes of the scheme;

and such a scheme may revoke or amend a previous charges scheme.

(5) Nothing in any charges scheme shall affect—

(a) any power of a relevant undertaker to enter into such an agreement with any person in any particular case as determines the charges to be made for the services provided to that person by the undertaker; or

(b) the power of a sewerage undertaker to enter into any agreement under section 129 above on terms that provide for the making of payments to the undertaker.

Liability of occupiers etc. for charges.

**144.**—(1) Subject to the following provisions of this section and except in so far as provision to the contrary is made by any agreement to which the undertaker is a party—

(a) supplies of water provided by a water undertaker shall be treated for the purposes of this Chapter as services provided to the occupiers for the time being of any premises supplied; and

(b) sewerage services provided by a sewerage undertaker shall be treated for the purposes of this Chapter as provided to the occupiers for the time being of any premises which—

(i) are drained by a sewer or drain connecting, either directly or through an intermediate sewer or drain, with such a public sewer of the undertaker as is provided for foul water or surface water or both; or

(ii) are premises the occupiers of which have, in respect of the premises, the benefit of facilities which drain to a sewer or drain so connecting.

(2) Subject to subsection (3) below, charges which, under the preceding provisions of this Chapter, are fixed in relation to any premises by reference to volume may be imposed so that a person is made liable in relation to those premises to pay charges for services provided by a relevant undertaker after that person has ceased to be the occupier of the premises.

(3) A person shall not be made liable by virtue of subsection (2) above for any charges fixed in relation to any premises by any relevant undertaker, except where—

(a) he fails to inform the undertaker of the ending of his occupation of the premises at least two working days before he ceases to occupy them; and

(b) the charges are in respect of a period ending no later than with the first relevant day.

(4) For the purposes of subsection (3) above, "the first relevant day", in relation to a case in which a person has ceased to be the occupier of any premises in relation to which charges are fixed by a relevant undertaker, means whichever of the following first occurs after he ceases to occupy the premises, that is to say—

(a) where that person informs the undertaker of the ending of his occupation of the premises less than two working days before, or at any time after, he ceases to occupy them, the twenty-eighth day after he so informs the undertaker;

(b) any day on which any meter would normally have been read in order for the amount of the charges to be determined;

(c) any day on which any other person informs the undertaker that he has become the new occupier of the premises.

(5) Where—

(a) any person who is the occupier of any premises to which a supply of water is provided by a water undertaker has served notice on the undertaker for the purposes of section 62 above; and

(b) that notice is given otherwise than in connection with that person's ceasing to be the occupier of the premises in a case in which provision is made by virtue of subsection (2) above for a person who has ceased to be the occupier of the premises to be made liable for any charges,

then, notwithstanding that that person continues to be the occupier of those premises, he shall not be liable to the undertaker (otherwise than in pursuance of a demand for a supply made since the service of the notice) for any charges in respect of any supply of water to those premises after the appropriate time.

(6) In subsection (5) above "the appropriate time", in relation to a case in which a notice has been served for the purposes of section 62 above, means whichever is the later of—

(a) the expiry of the notice; and

(b) the end of the period of two working days beginning with the service of the notice.

(7) In this section any reference to two working days is a reference to a period of forty-eight hours calculated after disregarding any time falling on—

(a) a Saturday or Sunday; or

(b) Christmas Day, Good Friday or any day which is a bank holiday in England and Wales under the Banking and Financial Dealings Act 1971.

1971 c. 80.

(8) Where, in the case of any premises—

(a) the person who was liable, immediately before 1st September 1989, to pay charges in respect of a supply of water to those premises was the owner of those premises, rather than the occupier;

(b) that person was so liable (under section 54 of Schedule 3 to the Water Act 1945 or any other local statutory provision) otherwise than by virtue of an agreement; and

1945 c. 42.

(c) the person who was in fact the occupier of the premises on that date has not ceased to be the occupier before the coming into force of this Act,

then the person who is the owner from time to time of those premises shall continue, until the person mentioned in paragraph (c) above does cease to be the occupier of the premises, to be the person liable and, accordingly, shall be treated for the purposes of this section as if he were the occupier of the premises.

### General restrictions on charging

Charging by reference to rateable value.

**145.**—(1) Charges and other amounts to which this section applies shall not, by virtue of anything contained—

(a) in this Chapter;

(b) in any local statutory provision;

(c) in any charges scheme under section 143 above; or

(d) in any agreement entered into on or after 1st September 1989,

be recoverable by a relevant undertaker from any person if they have been fixed wholly or partly by reference to a rating valuation list or are otherwise determined, whether directly or indirectly, by reference to any value or other amount specified at any time in such a list.

(2) This section applies to—

(a) charges in respect of any services provided at any time after the end of 31st March 2000 by a relevant undertaker in the course of carrying out its functions; and

(b) amounts of any other description which such an undertaker, in exercise of any power conferred by or under any enactment, requires any person to pay in respect of any period ending after that date or in respect of anything done after that date.

(3) In this section "rating valuation list" means a list which is or has at any time been maintained, for the purposes of rating, under section 41 or 52 of the Local Government Finance Act 1988, section 67 of the General Rate Act 1967 or any other enactment.

1988 c. 41.
1967 c. 9.

Connection charges etc. and charges for highway drainage.

**146.**—(1) Subject to subsection (2) below, nothing in this Chapter or in any other enactment shall entitle any relevant undertaker to fix, demand or recover an initial charge for its becoming, or for its taking steps for the purpose of becoming—

(a) the person who provides a supply of water for domestic purposes to any premises; or

(b) the person who provides sewerage services for the purposes of the drainage for domestic sewerage purposes of any premises.

(2) Subject to subsection (3) below, nothing in subsection (1) above or in any other enactment shall be construed as prohibiting the fixing, demand or recovery by a relevant undertaker of—

(a) a charge for the connection to a water supply of premises which have never at any previous time (whether before or after the coming into force of the restriction contained in this section) been connected to a supply of water provided for domestic purposes by a water undertaker or by any other authority or body which at that time provided supplies of water in the course of carrying out functions under any enactment; or

(b) a charge for the connection to a public sewer of premises which have never at any previous time (whether before or after the coming into force of the restriction contained in this section) been connected to a sewer used for the drainage for domestic sewerage purposes of those premises by a sewerage undertaker or by any other authority or body which at that time provided sewerage services in the course of carrying out functions under any enactment.

(3) Nothing in this Chapter or in any other enactment or in the terms of any agreement under section 104 above shall authorise a sewerage undertaker to require any payment to be made to the undertaker in respect of the making by the undertaker of any declaration of vesting under Chapter II of Part IV of this Act or in respect of any agreement to make such a declaration.

(4) Nothing in this Chapter or in any other enactment shall authorise a sewerage undertaker to require any payment to be made to the undertaker by a highway authority in respect of the drainage of any highway or the disposal of the contents of any drain or sewer used for draining any highway.

(5) The preceding provisions of this section, so far as they restrict the making of certain charges, shall be without prejudice—

(a) to enactments by virtue of which a relevant undertaker may recover expenses incurred by it in carrying out works; and

(b) to the power of any such undertaker, by virtue of section 142(4) above, to fix the amount of any of its other charges by reference to such matters as it thinks appropriate.

(6) In this section "domestic sewerage purposes" has the same meaning as in Chapter II of Part IV of this Act.

**147.**—(1) Notwithstanding anything in section 142 above or in any charges scheme under section 143 above or in any agreement as to charges in respect of any supply of water, no charge may be made by any water undertaker in respect of—

Charging for emergency use of water.

(a) water taken for the purpose of extinguishing fires or taken by a fire authority for any other emergency purposes;

(b) water taken for the purpose of testing apparatus installed or equipment used for extinguishing fires or for the purpose of training persons for fire-fighting; or

(c) the availability of water for any purpose mentioned in paragraph (a) or (b) above.

(2) This section shall not prevent the making of charges in respect of work carried out at the request of or for the benefit of any person receiving a supply of water for the purposes mentioned in paragraph (a) or (b) of subsection (1) above.

PART V

(3) This section shall not have the effect, where any water is used or made available for any of the purposes mentioned in paragraph (a) or (b) of subsection (1) above, of requiring a reduction in the charges imposed in respect of the provision for other purposes of the supply from which that water is taken.

1947 c. 41.

(4) In this section "fire authority" has the same meaning as in the Fire Services Act 1947.

*Metering*

Restriction on charging for metering works.

**148.**—(1) Subject to subsections (2) to (4) below and section 177 below, where any meter to be used in determining the amount of any charges is installed by or at the request of any relevant undertaker then, notwithstanding the provisions of any enactment or of any agreement to the contrary between the undertaker and any other person, the undertaker shall bear—

(a) the expenses of installing and connecting the meter;

(b) any expenses incurred in maintaining, repairing, disconnecting or removing the meter in accordance with any requirements of the undertaker; and

(c) any expenses incurred in carrying out any works for purposes connected with the installation and connection of the meter or with the maintenance, repair, disconnection or removal of the meter in accordance with any such requirements.

(2) Subject to subsection (3) below, subsection (1) above shall not require any relevant undertaker to bear, or prevent any such undertaker from recovering from any other person—

(a) any expenses incurred for the purpose of enabling a condition imposed by virtue of subsection (2)(c) or (d) of section 47 above to be satisfied;

(b) any sums which it is entitled to recover in pursuance of any terms or conditions determined under section 56 above;

(c) any sums which it is entitled to recover from that person by virtue of section 64(3)(b) above;

(d) any expenses incurred in relation to a meter which is or is to be used in determining the amount of—

(i) any charges which are to be paid in connection with the carrying out of a sewerage undertaker's functions under Chapter III of Part IV of this Act; or

(ii) any charges provision for which is contained in an agreement entered into in accordance with section 129 above;

(e) any expenses incurred in consequence of the exercise by the occupier of any premises of any option to be charged by the undertaker in relation to any premises by reference to volume rather than by reference to other matters.

(3) For the purposes of subsection (2) above the expenses which an undertaker may require someone else to bear, or may recover from another, by virtue of that subsection shall not include any expenses incurred for the purpose of enabling conditions such as are mentioned in paragraph (a) of that subsection to be satisfied in a case in which the conditions could not have been imposed but for the exercise by the

undertaker of its power by virtue of paragraph (a), (b), (d) or (e) of section 64(2) above to require the provision of a separate service pipe to any premises.

(4) The occupier of any premises where any relevant undertaker installs or has installed a meter shall in all cases bear so much of the expenses referred to in subsection (1) above as is attributable to compliance with a request made by him in accordance with any regulations under section 149 below for the positioning, in a place other than that reasonably proposed by the undertaker, either of the meter or of any pipe or apparatus installed for the purpose of facilitating the use of the meter.

(5) Any dispute between a relevant undertaker and any other person (including another such undertaker)—

    (a) as to whether the undertaker or that other person should bear any expenses under this section; or

    (b) as to the amount of any expenses to be borne by any person under this section,

shall be referred to the arbitration of a single arbitrator appointed by agreement between the undertaker and that person or, in default of agreement, by the Director.

**149.**—(1) The Secretary of State may by regulations make such provision, supplementing—

    (a) the provisions of this Chapter; and

    (b) so far as they relate to works for purposes connected with the fixing of charges in relation to any premises by reference to volume, the provisions of Part VI of this Act,

as he considers appropriate with respect to the installation of meters, with respect to the connection, disconnection, use, maintenance, authentication and testing of meters and with respect to any related matters.

*Further provision relating to charging by volume.*

(2) Without prejudice to the generality of subsection (1) above, regulations under that subsection may—

    (a) regulate the positioning, whether inside or outside the building or other premises in relation to which the meter is to be used, of any meter or of any pipes or apparatus appearing to any relevant undertaker to be required for the purpose of facilitating the use of any meter;

    (b) make any other provision which appears to the Secretary of State to be appropriate with respect to any such pipes or apparatus;

    (c) provide for a reading from a meter to be proved in such manner as may be prescribed and for a reading from a meter to be such evidence as may be prescribed of the volume of water supplied to, or of effluent discharged from, any premises;

    (d) fix the method of determining the amount of the charges to be paid where it appears that a meter has given, or may have given, an incorrect reading;

(e) require a person who is not a relevant undertaker to pay the expenses incurred by such an undertaker in doing anything under the regulations or to pay contributions towards those expenses;

(f) provide for the payment of compensation in respect of anything done by a relevant undertaker under the regulations;

(g) require disputes arising under the regulations to be referred to arbitration;

(h) repeal or amend any local statutory provision.

*Charging for services provided with the help of an undertaker*

Fixing maximum charges for services provided with the help of undertakers' services.

**150.**—(1) The Director may from time to time by order fix maximum charges which a person who is not a relevant undertaker may recover from another such person in respect of water supplies or sewerage services provided to that other person with the help of services provided by a relevant undertaker.

(2) For the purposes of this section water supplies or sewerage services are provided to a person with the help of services provided by a relevant undertaker if—

(a) a facility for that person to have access to a supply of water provided by a water undertaker in pipes, or to make use of sewerage services provided by a sewerage undertaker, is made available to that person otherwise than by the undertaker;

(b) that person is provided with a supply of water in pipes by a person to whom the water is supplied, directly or indirectly, by a water undertaker; or

(c) that person is provided with sewerage services by a person who, for the purpose of providing those services, makes use of sewerage services provided, directly or indirectly, by a sewerage undertaker.

(3) It shall be the duty of the Director to publish any order under this section in such manner as he considers appropriate for the purpose of bringing it to the attention of persons likely to be affected by it.

(4) An order under this section may make different provision for different cases, including different provision in relation to different persons, circumstances or localities, and may fix a maximum charge either by specifying the maximum amount of the charge or by specifying a method of calculating that amount.

(5) Where a person pays a charge in respect of anything to which an order under this section relates and the amount paid exceeds the maximum charge fixed by the order, the amount of the excess shall be recoverable by that person from the person to whom he paid the charge.

## Chapter II

### Financial Assistance for Undertakers

Financial contributions to rural services.

**151.**—(1) Subject to subsection (2) below and to such conditions as the Treasury may determine, the Secretary of State, in any case in which it appears to him to be desirable to do so, may undertake to make a contribution out of money provided by Parliament towards the expenses incurred—

   (a) by a water undertaker in providing a supply of water in a rural locality or in improving an existing supply of water in such a locality;

   (b) by a sewerage undertaker in making adequate provision for the sewerage of a rural locality or for the disposal of such a locality's sewage.

(2) The Secretary of State shall not undertake to make a contribution under this section towards the expenses of making provision for the sewerage of a rural locality, or for the disposal of such a locality's sewage, unless he is satisfied that the need for making the provision is due to anything done or proposed to be done—

   (a) to supply water in pipes in that locality; or

   (b) to increase the supply of water in pipes in that locality.

(3) An undertaking given by the Secretary of State under this section shall provide for the making of the contribution in the form of such lump sum payment or payments, or such periodical payments towards revenue expenditure, as may appear to the Secretary of State to be appropriate.

(4) The Secretary of State may withhold, or reduce the amount of, any contribution which he has undertaken to make towards the expenses incurred by a relevant undertaker in respect of any works or transaction, if it appears to him either—

   (a) that any of the works have been carried out in an unsatisfactory manner;

   (b) that—

      (i) the effectiveness of any of the works is substantially less than as estimated in the proposals submitted to him by the relevant undertaker; and

      (ii) the difference is due to any default, for which the undertaker is responsible, in the formulation of the proposals;

     or

   (c) that there has been any default in the carrying out of the transaction.

**152.**—(1) The Secretary of State may, out of money provided by Parliament, make grants to relevant undertakers for the purpose of defraying or contributing towards any losses they may sustain by reason of compliance with directions given under section 208 below in the interests of national security.

*Grants for national security purposes.*

(2) The approval of the Treasury shall be required for the making of grants under this section.

**153.**—(1) Where a special administration order is for the time being in force in relation to a company, the Secretary of State, may, with the consent of the Treasury—

*Government financial assistance where special administration orders made.*

   (a) make to the company grants or loans of such sums as appear to him to be appropriate for the purpose of facilitating the achievement of the purposes of the order;

(b) agree to indemnify the person appointed to achieve the purposes of the order in respect of liabilities incurred and loss or damage sustained by that person in connection with the carrying out of his functions under the order.

(2) The Secretary of State may, with the consent of the Treasury, guarantee, in such manner and on such conditions as he may think fit, the repayment of the principal of, the payment of interest on and the discharge of any other financial obligation in connection with any sum which is borrowed from any person by a company in relation to which a special administration order is in force at the time when the guarantee is given.

(3) Without prejudice to any provision applied in relation to the company by Schedule 3 to this Act—

(a) the terms and conditions on which a grant is made to any company under this section may require the whole or a part of the grant to be repaid to the Secretary of State if there is a contravention of the other terms and conditions on which the grant is made; and

(b) any loans which the Secretary of State makes to a company under this section shall be repaid to him at such times and by such methods, and interest on the loans shall be paid to him at such rates and at such times, as he may, with the consent of the Treasury, from time to time direct.

(4) Any grant or loan made under this section and any sums required to be paid by the Secretary of State in respect of an indemnity given under this section shall be paid out of money provided by Parliament.

(5) Any sums received under subsection (3) above by the Secretary of State shall be paid into the Consolidated Fund.

Guarantees under section 153.

**154.**—(1) This section applies in relation to any guarantee given by the Secretary of State under section 153 above.

(2) Immediately after a guarantee to which this section applies is given, the Secretary of State shall lay a statement of the guarantee before each House of Parliament.

(3) Where any sum is paid out for fulfilling a guarantee to which this section applies, the Secretary of State shall, as soon as possible after the end of each financial year (beginning with that in which the sum is paid out and ending with that in which all liability in respect of the principal of the sum and in respect of the interest thereon is finally discharged), lay before each House of Parliament a statement relating to that sum.

(4) Any sums required by the Secretary of State for fulfilling a guarantee to which this section applies shall be paid out of money provided by Parliament.

(5) Without prejudice to any provision applied in relation to the relevant company by Schedule 3 to this Act, if any sums are paid out in fulfilment of a guarantee to which this section applies, the relevant company shall make to the Secretary of State, at such times and in such manner as the Secretary of State may from time to time direct—

(a) payments of such amounts as the Secretary of State may so direct in or towards repayment of the sums so paid out; and

(b) payments of interest, at such rate as the Secretary of State may so direct, on what is outstanding for the time being in respect of sums so paid out;

and the consent of the Treasury shall be required for the giving of a direction under this subsection.

(6) Any sums received by the Secretary of State under subsection (5) above shall be paid into the Consolidated Fund.

(7) In subsection (5) above "the relevant company" in relation to a guarantee, means the company which borrowed the sums in respect of which the guarantee was given.

## PART VI

### UNDERTAKERS' POWERS AND WORKS

#### CHAPTER I

##### UNDERTAKERS' POWERS

*Powers in relation to land*

**155.**—(1) A relevant undertaker may be authorised by the Secretary of State to purchase compulsorily any land anywhere in England and Wales which is required by the undertaker for the purposes of, or in connection with, the carrying out of its functions.

Compulsory purchase.

(2) The power of the Secretary of State under subsection (1) above shall include power--

(a) to authorise the acquisition of interests in and rights over land by the creation of new interests and rights; and

(b) by authorising the acquisition by a relevant undertaker of any rights over land which is to be or has been acquired by that undertaker, to provide for the extinguishment of those rights.

(3) Without prejudice to the generality of subsection (1) above, the land which a relevant undertaker may be authorised under that subsection to purchase compulsorily shall include land which is or will be required for the purpose of being given in exchange for, or for any right over, any other land which for the purposes of the Acquisition of Land Act 1981 is or forms part of a common, open space or a fuel or field garden allotment.

1981 c. 67.

(4) Subject to section 188 below, the Acquisition of Land Act 1981 shall apply to any compulsory purchase under subsection (1) above of any land by a relevant undertaker; and Schedule 3 to the said Act of 1981 shall apply to the compulsory acquisition under that subsection of rights by the creation of new rights.

(5) Schedule 9 to this Act shall have effect for the purpose of modifying enactments relating to compensation and the provisions of the Compulsory Purchase Act 1965 in their application in relation to the compulsory acquisition under subsection (1) above of a right over land by the creation of a new right.

1965 c. 56.

(6) The provisions of Part I of the Compulsory Purchase Act 1965 (so far as applicable), other than sections 4 to 8, 10, 21, 27(1) and 31 and Schedule 4, shall apply in relation to any power to acquire land by agreement which is conferred (whether by virtue of the memorandum and

articles of the company for the time being carrying out the functions of the undertaker or any enactment or otherwise) on a relevant undertaker, as if—

> (a) any reference in those provisions to the acquiring authority were a reference to that undertaker; and
>
> (b) any reference to land subject to compulsory purchase were a reference to land which may be purchased by agreement under that power.

Restriction on disposals of land.

**156.**—(1) A company holding an appointment under Chapter I of Part II of this Act shall not dispose of any of its protected land, or of any interest or right in or over any of that land, except with the consent of, or in accordance with a general authorisation given by, the Secretary of State.

(2) A consent or authorisation for the purposes of this section—

> (a) shall be set out in a notice served by the Secretary of State on the company which is or may be authorised, by virtue of the provision contained in the notice, to dispose of land or of interests or rights in or over land or, as the case may be, on every such company; and

1991 c. 57.

> (b) in the case of an authorisation, may be combined with an authorisation for the purposes of section 157 of the Water Resources Act 1991.

(3) A consent or authorisation for the purposes of this section may be given on such conditions as the Secretary of State considers appropriate.

(4) Without prejudice to the generality of subsection (3) above and subject to subsection (5) below, the conditions of a consent or authorisation for the purposes of this section may include—

> (a) a requirement that, before there is any disposal, an opportunity of acquiring the land in question, or an interest or right in or over that land, is to be made available, in such manner and on such terms as may be specified in or determined under provision contained in the notice setting out the consent or authorisation, to such person as may be so specified or determined;
>
> (b) a requirement that the company making the disposal has complied with such of the conditions of its appointment under Chapter I of Part II of this Act as relate to the disposal of its protected land or of any interest or right in or over that land;
>
> (c) a requirement that the company, before making a disposal in a case in which the land in question is situated in a National Park, in the Broads or in an area of outstanding natural beauty or special scientific interest, should do one or both of the following, that is to say—
>
> > (i) consult with the Countryside Commission (as respects land in England) or the Countryside Council for Wales (as respects land in Wales) and, in the case of an area of special scientific interest in England, with the Nature Conservancy Council for England; and

(ii) enter into such agreements under section 39 of the Wildlife and Countryside Act 1981 (management agreements) or such covenants under subsection (6) below as the Secretary of State may determine;

(d) provision requiring determinations under or for the purposes of the consent or authorisation to be made, in such cases as are mentioned in paragraph (c) above, either by the Countryside Commission or the Countryside Council for Wales or only after consultation with that Commission or Council.

(5) A consent or authorisation shall not be given on any such condition as is mentioned in subsection (4)(a) above except where the Secretary of State is satisfied that the condition will have effect in relation only to—

(a) land which, or any interest in or right over which, was acquired by the relevant undertaker in question, or any predecessor of that undertaker, either compulsorily or at a time when the undertaker or that predecessor was authorised to acquire it compulsorily; or

(b) land situated in a National Park, in the Broads or in an area of outstanding natural beauty or special scientific interest.

(6) Where a company holding an appointment under Chapter I of Part II of this Act is proposing, in such a case as is mentioned in subsection (4)(c) above, to dispose of, or of any interest or right in or over, any of its protected land, it may enter into a covenant with the Secretary of State by virtue of which it accepts obligations with respect to—

(a) the freedom of access to the land that is to be afforded to members of the public or to persons of any description; or

(b) the use or management of the land;

and a covenant under this subsection shall bind all persons deriving title from or under that company and shall be enforceable by the Secretary of State accordingly.

(7) Section 3 above shall have effect for the purposes of this section as if every proposal which—

(a) is made by a company holding an appointment as a relevant undertaker with respect to land in a National Park, in the Broads or in an area of outstanding natural beauty or special scientific interest, or with respect to any interest or right in or over any such land; and

(b) is a proposal for which the Secretary of State's consent or authorisation is required under this section,

were a proposal relating to the functions of such an undertaker.

(8) In this section—

"area of outstanding natural beauty or special scientific interest" means an area which—

(a) is for the time being designated as an area of outstanding natural beauty for the purposes of the National Parks and Access to the Countryside Act 1949; or

(b) is an area in relation to which a notification given, or having effect as if given, under section 28 of the Wildlife and Countryside Act 1981 (areas of special scientific interest) for the time being has effect;

and the reference in subsection (4)(c) above to an area of special scientific interest shall, accordingly, be construed as a reference to an area such as is mentioned in paragraph (b) of this definition; and

"the Broads" has the same meaning as in the Norfolk and Suffolk Broads Act 1988.

**157.**—(1) Every relevant undertaker shall have power to make such byelaws as are mentioned in subsection (2) below with respect to any waterway owned or managed by that body and with respect to any land held or managed with the waterway.

(2) The byelaws referred to in subsection (1) above in relation to any waterway or to any land held or managed with any such waterway are byelaws for any of the following purposes, that is to say—

(a) the preservation of order on or in any such waterway or land;

(b) the prevention of damage to anything on or in any such waterway or land or to any such land;

(c) securing that persons resorting to any such waterway or land so behave as to avoid undue interference with the enjoyment of the waterway or land by others.

(3) Without prejudice to the generality of any of the paragraphs of subsection (2) above, the byelaws mentioned in that subsection include byelaws—

(a) regulating sailing, boating, bathing and fishing and other forms of recreation;

(b) prohibiting the use of the waterway in question by boats which are not for the time being registered, in such manner as may be required by the byelaws, with the undertaker making the byelaws;

(c) requiring the provision of such sanitary appliances as may be necessary for the purpose of preventing pollution;

(d) providing for a contravention of the byelaws to constitute a summary offence punishable, on summary conviction, by a fine not exceeding level 5 on the standard scale or such smaller sum as may be specified in the byelaws; and

(e) authorising the making of reasonable charges in respect of the registration of boats for the purposes of the byelaws.

(4) Schedule 10 to this Act shall have effect with respect to byelaws under this section.

(5) Byelaws made under this section shall cease to have effect at the end of the period of ten years beginning with the day on which they were made; but the Secretary of State may by order made by statutory instrument make provision in relation to any particular byelaws for those byelaws to continue to have effect for such period after the time when they would otherwise cease to have effect as may be specified in the order.

(6) In this section—

"boat" includes a vessel of any description, and "boating" shall be construed accordingly;

"waterway" has the same meaning as in the National Parks and Access to the Countryside Act 1949.

### *Pipe-laying*

**158.**—(1) Subject to the following provisions of this section, to section 162(9) below and to the provisions of Chapter III of this Part, every relevant undertaker shall, for the purpose of carrying out its functions, have power—

   (a) to lay a relevant pipe in, under or over any street and to keep that pipe there;

   (b) to inspect, maintain, adjust, repair or alter any relevant pipe which is in, under or over any street; and

   (c) to carry out any works requisite for, or incidental to, the purposes of any works falling within paragraph (a) or (b) above, including for those purposes the following kinds of works, that is to say—

      (i) breaking up or opening a street;

      (ii) tunnelling or boring under a street;

      (iii) breaking up or opening a sewer, drain or tunnel;

      (iv) moving or removing earth and other materials.

(2) Without prejudice to the generality of subsection (1)(c) above, every water undertaker shall have power to erect and keep in any street notices indicating the position of such underground accessories for its relevant pipes as may be used for controlling the flow of water in those pipes.

(3) The power conferred by subsection (2) above shall include power to attach any such notice as is mentioned in that subsection to any building, fence or other structure which is comprised in premises abutting on the street in question.

(4) A stopcock fitted to any service pipe in a street shall be situated as near as reasonably practicable to the boundary of the street; and a water undertaker shall consult with the highway authority concerned before determining in accordance with this subsection where to fit a stopcock in a highway.

(5) Where a water undertaker exercises its powers under this section for the purpose of carrying out works of maintenance, repair or renewal in relation to a service pipe belonging to a person other than the undertaker, the undertaker shall be entitled to recover from the occupier of the premises supplied by means of that pipe the expenses reasonably incurred by that undertaker in so exercising that power.

(6) Until the coming into force of its repeal by the New Roads and Street Works Act 1991 section 20 of the Highways Act 1980 (works in special roads) shall have effect as if the reference in that section to a power under any enactment to lay down or erect apparatus included a reference to any power to lay any relevant pipe which is conferred by this section.

(7) Subject to section 161(7) below, in this section references to a relevant pipe shall be construed—

    (a) in relation to a water undertaker, as references to a water main (including a trunk main), resource main, discharge pipe or service pipe; and

    (b) in relation to a sewerage undertaker, as references to any sewer or disposal main.

Power to lay pipes in other land.    **159.**—(1) Subject to the following provisions of this section, to section 162(9) below and to the provisions of Chapter III of this Part, every relevant undertaker shall, for the purpose of carrying out its functions, have power—

    (a) to lay a relevant pipe (whether above or below the surface) in any land which is not in, under or over a street and to keep that pipe there;

    (b) to inspect, maintain, adjust, repair or alter any relevant pipe which is in any such land;

    (c) to carry out any works requisite for, or incidental to, the purposes of any works falling within paragraph (a) or (b) above.

(2) Nothing in subsection (1) above shall authorise a water undertaker to lay a service pipe in, on or over any land except where—

    (a) there is already a service pipe where that pipe is to be laid; or

    (b) the undertaker is required to lay the pipe in, on or over that land by virtue of any of subsections (3) to (5) of section 46 above.

(3) The power conferred by virtue of paragraph (b) of subsection (1) above, and the power conferred in relation to that paragraph by virtue of paragraph (c) of that subsection shall be exercisable in relation to a service pipe irrespective of the person to whom the pipe belongs; but expenses incurred in exercising those powers in relation to any pipe shall be recoverable from the person to whom the pipe belongs only if and to the extent that that person has agreed to pay them.

(4) The powers conferred by this section shall be exercisable only after reasonable notice of the proposed exercise of the power has been given to the owner and to the occupier of the land where the power is to be exercised.

(5) Subject to subsection (6) below, in relation to any exercise of the powers conferred by this section for the purpose of laying or altering a relevant pipe, the minimum period that is capable of constituting reasonable notice for the purposes of subsection (4) above shall be deemed—

    (a) where the power is exercised for the purpose of laying a relevant pipe otherwise than in substitution for an existing pipe of the same description, to be three months; and

    (b) where the power is exercised for the purpose of altering an existing pipe, to be forty-two days.

(6) Subsection (5) above shall not apply in the case of any notice given with respect to the exercise of any power in an emergency or for the purpose of—

(a) laying or altering a service pipe; or

(b) complying with a duty imposed under section 41 or 98 above.

(7) Subject to subsection (2) above, in this section "relevant pipe" has the same meaning as in section 158 above.

### *Other works powers*

**160.**—(1) A sewerage undertaker may, by agreement with the owner or occupier of any premises, carry out at that person's expense—

Power to carry out works for sewerage purposes.

    (a) any work in connection with the construction, laying, alteration or repair of a sewer or drain which that person is entitled to carry out; or

    (b) any work which the undertaker has required that person to carry out under Part IV of this Act;

and for that purpose the undertaker shall have all such rights as that person would have.

(2) Sections 291, 293 and 294 of the Public Health Act 1936 (which provide for the means of, and for limitations on, the recovery of expenses incurred by a local authority) shall apply in relation to the recovery by a sewerage undertaker of any sums under this section as they apply in relation to the recovery of expenses under that Act by a local authority.

1936 c. 49.

**161.**—(1) Subject to the provisions of Chapter III of this Part, every relevant undertaker shall, for the purpose of carrying out its functions, have power—

Power to deal with foul water and pollution.

    (a) to carry out in a street all such works as are requisite for securing that the water in any relevant waterworks is not polluted or otherwise contaminated; and

    (b) to carry out any works requisite for, or incidental to, the purposes of any works falling within paragraph (a) above, including for those purposes the following kinds of works, that is to say—

        (i) breaking up or opening a street;

        (ii) tunnelling or boring under a street;

        (iii) breaking up or opening a sewer, drain or tunnel;

        (iv) moving or removing earth and other materials;

and the provisions of section 158 above shall, so far as applicable, have effect in relation to the powers conferred by this subsection as they have effect in relation to the powers conferred by subsection (1) of that section.

(2) Subject to the provisions of Chapter III of this Part, every relevant undertaker shall, for the purpose of carrying out its functions, have power—

    (a) to carry out on any land which is not in, under or over a street all such works as are requisite for securing that the water in any relevant waterworks is not polluted or otherwise contaminated; and

(b) to carry out any works requisite for, or incidental to, the purposes of any works falling within paragraph (a) above;

and the provisions of section 159 above shall, so far as applicable, have effect in relation to the powers conferred by this subsection as they have effect in relation to the powers conferred by subsection (1) of that section.

(3) Without prejudice to the powers conferred by subsections (1) and (2) above but subject to the provisions of Chapter III of this Part, every water undertaker shall have power, on any land which belongs to that undertaker or over or in which that undertaker has acquired the necessary easements or rights, to construct and maintain drains, sewers, watercourses, catchpits and other works for the purpose—

(a) of intercepting, treating or disposing of any foul water arising or flowing upon that land; or

(b) of otherwise preventing the pollution—

(i) of any waters, whether on the surface or underground, which belong to the NRA or any water undertaker or from which the NRA or any water undertaker is authorised to take water;

(ii) without prejudice to sub-paragraph (i) above, of any reservoir which belongs to or is operated by the NRA or any water undertaker or which the NRA or any water undertaker is proposing to acquire or construct for the purpose of being so operated; or

(iii) of any underground strata from which the NRA or any water undertaker is for the time being authorised to abstract water in pursuance of a licence under Chapter II of Part II of the Water Resources Act 1991.

1991 c. 57.

(4) Where any water undertaker is proposing to carry out any such works as are mentioned in subsection (3) above and the proposed works will affect any watercourse, the undertaker shall consult the NRA before carrying out the works.

(5) Without prejudice to the protective provisions of Chapter III of this Part, nothing in subsection (3) above shall authorise any water undertaker, without the consent of the navigation authority in question, to intercept or take any water which a navigation authority are authorised to take or use for the purposes of their undertaking.

(6) Any dispute as to whether any consent for the purposes of subsection (5) above is being unreasonably withheld shall be referred to the arbitration of a single arbitrator to be appointed by agreement between the parties to the dispute or, in default of agreement, by the President of the Institution of Civil Engineers.

(7) In section 158 above the references to the laying of a relevant pipe shall include references-

(a) to the laying of any drain or sewer for any of the purposes mentioned in subsection (3)(a) and (b) above; and

(b) to the construction of a watercourse for any of those purposes.

(8) In this section—

"the protective provisions of Chapter III of this Part" means the provisions of sections 183 to 191 below;

"relevant waterworks" means any waterworks which contain water which is or may be used by a water undertaker for providing a supply of water to any premises; and

"waterworks" includes any water main, resource main, service pipe or discharge pipe and any spring, well, adit, borehole, service reservoir or tank.

**162.**—(1) Subject to the following provisions of this section, to section 148 above and to the provisions of Chapter III of this Part, where—

> (a) any relevant undertaker has fixed any charges in relation to any premises by reference to volume or has given notice of its intention of so fixing any charges within the period specified in the notice; and

> (b) there is either—

>> (i) a service pipe which is connected with a water undertaker's water main and by which a supply of water is or could be provided to those premises or to any building in which those premises are contained; or

>> (ii) a drain or private sewer which connects those premises with a public sewer,

the undertaker shall have power, in accordance with section 172 below or otherwise, to carry out any works specified in subsection (3) below.

(2) The power under subsection (1) above to carry out works specified in subsection (3) below shall include power to carry out any such works in a street; and the power conferred by virtue of subsection (1)(c) of section 158 above and subsection (6) of that section shall apply in relation to the power conferred by this subsection as they apply in relation to the powers conferred by that section.

(3) The works mentioned in subsections (1) and (2) above are, in relation to any premises—

> (a) works consisting in the installation and connection of any meter for use in determining the amount of any charges which have been or may be fixed in relation to the premises;

> (b) where the premises comprise a house which is one of two or more houses to which the supply of water is wholly or partly by the same service pipe, works consisting in the installation and connection, for any purpose connected with the installation or connection of such a meter, of a separate service pipe for that house;

> (c) works for the purpose of maintaining, repairing, disconnecting or removing—

>> (i) any meter which has been installed for use in determining the amount of any charges which have been or may be fixed in relation to the premises; or

>> (ii) any pipes or apparatus installed in the course of any works specified in this section;

> and

> (d) any other works appearing to the undertaker to be necessary or expedient for any purpose connected with the carrying out of any works specified in paragraph (a), (b) or (c) above, including

the installation and connection of any pipes or other apparatus on the premises and the alteration or removal of any of the plumbing of the premises.

(4) A notice given for the purposes of subsection (1)(a) above may relate to particular premises or to any description of premises and shall be given—

(a) by publishing the notice in the locality in which the premises to which it relates are situated in such a manner as the undertaker considers appropriate for bringing it to the attention of the persons likely to be affected by it; and

(b) by serving a copy of the notice on the Secretary of State.

(5) Subject to subsection (6) below, any works carried out by a water undertaker by virtue of the provisions of this section shall be necessary works for the purposes of Chapter II of Part III of this Act.

(6) Nothing in this section shall prevent the exercise by a water undertaker of its power by virtue of subsection (3)(b) of section 64 above to impose a condition by virtue of subsection (2)(c) or (d) of section 47 above in a case where it has, under the said section 64, required the provision of a separate service pipe to any premises.

(7) Part II of Schedule 6 to this Act shall apply to the powers conferred by this section.

(8) Any dispute between a relevant undertaker and any other person (including another such undertaker) as to the exercise of any power under this section to carry out any works on any premises shall be referred to the arbitration of a single arbitrator appointed—

(a) by agreement between the undertaker and that person; or

(b) in default of agreement, by the Director.

(9) Without prejudice to subsection (2) above, nothing in section 158, 159 or 161 above shall authorise the installation of any apparatus for measuring or showing the volume of water supplied to, or of effluent discharged from, any premises where that apparatus is to be used for the purpose only of determining the amount of any charges fixed, or to be fixed, in relation to those premises wholly or partly by reference to the volume of that water or effluent.

Power to fit stopcocks.

**163.**—(1) Subject to subsection (2) below and without prejudice to section 159 above, a water undertaker shall have power, at its own expense, to fit a stopcock to any service pipe by which a supply of water is or is to be provided to any premises by the undertaker, whether that pipe belongs to the undertaker or to any other person.

(2) A stopcock fitted in private premises by a water undertaker to any service pipe shall be situated as near as practicable to any street from which that pipe enters those premises.

Agreements for works with respect to water sources.

**164.**—(1) A water undertaker may enter into agreements under this section with the owners and occupiers of any land, or with a local authority, with respect to the carrying out and maintenance by any party to the agreement of such works as the undertaker considers necessary—

(a) for the purpose of draining that land; or

(b) for more effectually collecting, conveying or preserving the purity of any water which the undertaker is for the time being authorised to take.

(2) Before entering into an agreement under this section with respect to the carrying out of works the carrying out of which would result in the discharge of any water into a watercourse otherwise than through public sewers, a water undertaker shall consult the NRA and, if the watercourse is subject to the jurisdiction of a navigation authority, that authority.

(3) An agreement under this section with the owner of any land which is expressed to be binding on and enforceable against the owner's successors in title to that land—

(a) may be registered under section 2 of the Land Charges Act 1972 as an obligation affecting land falling within Class D; and

1972 c. 61.

(b) shall be so binding and enforceable unless it is void by reason of a failure so to register it.

(4) In this section the reference to a local authority includes a reference to a county council and to the Sub-Treasurer of the Inner Temple and the Under-Treasurer of the Middle Temple; and any expenses incurred by the Common Council of the City of London in the exercise of their functions under this section shall be defrayed as part of their general expenses.

*Powers to discharge water*

**165.**—(1) Subject to the following provisions of this section and to section 166 below, where any water undertaker—

Discharges for works purposes.

(a) is exercising or about to exercise any power conferred by section 158, 159, 161 or 163 above (other than the power conferred by section 161(3) above); or

(b) is carrying out, or is about to carry out, the construction, alteration, repair, cleaning, or examination of any reservoir, well, borehole, or other work belonging to or used by that undertaker for the purposes of, or in connection with, the carrying out of any of its functions,

the undertaker may cause the water in any relevant pipe or in any such reservoir, well, borehole or other work to be discharged into any available watercourse.

(2) Nothing in this section shall authorise any discharge which—

(a) damages or injuriously affects the works or property of any railway undertakers or navigation authority; or

(b) floods or damages any highway.

(3) If any water undertaker fails to take all necessary steps to secure that any water discharged by it under this section is as free as may be reasonably practicable from—

(a) mud and silt;

(b) solid, polluting, offensive or injurious substances; and

(c) any substances prejudicial to fish or spawn, or to spawning beds or food of fish,

the undertaker shall be guilty of an offence and liable, on summary conviction, to a fine not exceeding level 3 on the standard scale.

(4) In this section "relevant pipe" means any water main (including a trunk main), resource main, discharge pipe or service pipe.

**166.**—(1) Except in an emergency, no discharge through any pipe the diameter of which exceeds two hundred and twenty-nine millimetres shall be made under section 165 above except with the consent of the NRA and of any navigation authority which carries out functions in relation to—

(a) the part of the watercourse where the discharge is made; or

(b) any part of that watercourse which is less than three miles downstream from the place of the discharge.

(2) Where a water undertaker makes an application to any authority for a consent for the purposes of this section—

(a) that application shall be accompanied or supplemented by all such information as that authority may reasonably require; and

(b) the undertaker shall serve a copy of the application, and of any consent given on that application, on every person who—

(i) is registered with the undertaker in respect of any premises which are within three miles of the place where the discharge to which the application relates is proposed to be made and are not upstream from that place; and

(ii) has not agreed in writing that he need not be served with such a copy;

but, subject to subsection (4) below and without prejudice to the effect (if any) of any other contravention of the requirements of this section in relation to such an application, a failure to provide information in pursuance of the obligation to supplement such an application shall not invalidate the application.

(3) Subject to subsection (4) below, an application for a consent for the purposes of this section shall be determined—

(a) in the case of an application with respect to a particular discharge, before the end of the period of seven days beginning with the day after the application is made; and

(b) in any other case, before the end of the period of three months beginning with that day;

and, subject to that subsection, where an application for any consent is required to be determined within the period specified in paragraph (a) above and is not so determined, the consent applied for shall be deemed to have been given unconditionally.

(4) Where—

(a) an undertaker which has made an application to any authority for a consent for the purposes of this section has failed to comply with its obligation under subsection (2)(a) above to supplement that application with information required by that authority; and

(b) that requirement was made by that authority at such a time before the end of the period within which that authority is required to determine the application as gave the undertaker a reasonable opportunity to provide the required information within that period,

that authority may delay his determination of the application until a reasonable time after the required information is provided.

(5) A consent for the purposes of this section may relate to a particular discharge or to discharges of a particular description and may be made subject to such reasonable conditions as may be specified by the person giving it; but a consent for those purposes shall not be unreasonably withheld.

(6) Any dispute as to whether a consent for the purposes of this section should be given or withheld, or as to whether the conditions to which any such consent is made subject are reasonable, shall be referred to the arbitration of a single arbitrator appointed by agreement between the parties to the dispute or, in default of agreement, by the President of the Institution of Civil Engineers.

(7) Where any discharge under section 165 above is made in an emergency without the consent which, if there were no emergency, would be required by virtue of this section, the undertaker which made the discharge shall, as soon as practicable after making the discharge, serve a notice which—

(a) states that the discharge has been made; and

(b) gives such particulars of the discharge and of the emergency as the persons served with the notice might reasonably require,

on every person on whom that undertaker would have been required to serve the application for that consent or any copy of that application.

(8) If any water undertaker contravenes, without reasonable excuse, any of the requirements of this section or any condition of a consent given for the purposes of this section, it shall be guilty of an offence and liable, on summary conviction, to a fine not exceeding level 3 on the standard scale.

(9) Nothing in this section shall require any consent to be obtained, or any notice to be served, in respect of any discharge if the requirements of section 34 of the Water Act 1945 (temporary discharges into watercourses) in relation to that discharge had been satisfied before 1st September 1989.

1945 c. 42.

### Compulsory works orders

167.—(1) Where a water undertaker is proposing, for the purposes of, or in connection with, the carrying out of any of its functions—

(a) to carry out any engineering or building operations; or

(b) to discharge water into any inland waters or underground strata,

the undertaker may apply to the Secretary of State for an order under this section ("a compulsory works order").

Compulsory works orders.

(2) Subject to the following provisions of this section, the Secretary of State may, on an application under subsection (1) above, by order made by statutory instrument—

(a) confer such compulsory powers; and

(b) grant such authority,

as he considers necessary or expedient for the purpose of enabling any engineering or building operations or discharges of water to be carried out or made for the purposes of, or in connection with, the carrying out of the functions with respect to which the application was made.

(3) Schedule 11 to this Act shall have effect with respect to applications for compulsory works orders and with respect to such orders.

(4) Subject to the provisions of Schedule 11 to this Act, a compulsory works order may—

(a) without prejudice to section 155 above, confer power to acquire compulsorily any land, including—

(i) power to acquire interests in and rights over land by the creation of new rights and interests; and

(ii) power, by the compulsory acquisition by any water undertaker of any rights over land which is to be or has been acquired by that undertaker, to extinguish any such rights;

(b) apply for the purposes of the order, either with or without modifications, any of the relevant provisions of this Part of this Act which do not apply for those purposes apart from by virtue of this paragraph;

(c) make any authority granted by the order subject to such conditions as may be specified in the order;

(d) amend or repeal any local statutory provision;

(e) contain such supplemental, consequential and transitional provision as the Secretary of State considers appropriate.

(5) Without prejudice to any duty imposed by virtue of section 191 below, where—

(a) the Secretary of State makes a compulsory works order authorising a water undertaker to carry out works for or in connection with the construction or operation of a reservoir or conferring compulsory powers for that purpose on such an undertaker; and

(b) it appears to him that the works to be carried out may permanently affect the area in which they are situated and are not primarily intended to benefit the inhabitants of that area,

he may include in the order provision with respect to facilities for recreation or other leisure-time occupation for the benefit of those inhabitants.

(6) Nothing in any compulsory works order shall exempt any water undertaker from any restriction imposed by Chapter II of Part II of the Water Resources Act 1991 (abstraction and impounding of water).

1991 c. 57.

(7) It is hereby declared that a compulsory works order may grant authority for discharges of water by a water undertaker where the undertaker has no power to take water, or to require discharges to be made, from the inland waters or other source from which the discharges authorised by the order are intended to be made; but nothing in so much of any such order as grants authority for any discharges of water shall have the effect of conferring any such power.

(8) In this section the reference to the relevant provisions of this Part is a reference to the provisions of this Part except sections 172 and 173, the provisions of Chapter II and any provision of this Part which is one of the relevant sewerage provisions.

### *Entry to land etc. by water undertakers*

**168.**—(1). Any person designated in writing for the purpose by a relevant undertaker may enter any premises for any of the purposes specified in subsection (2) below.

*Entry for works purposes.*

(2) The purposes mentioned in subsection (1) above are—

    (a) the carrying out of any survey or tests for the purpose of determining—

        (i) whether it is appropriate and practicable for the undertaker to exercise any relevant works power; or

        (ii) how any such power should be exercised;

    or

    (b) the exercise of any such power.

(3) The power, by virtue of subsection (1) above, of a person designated by a relevant undertaker to enter any premises for the purposes of carrying out any survey or tests shall include power—

    (a) to carry out experimental borings or other works for the purpose of ascertaining the nature of the sub-soil; and

    (b) to take away and analyse such samples of water or effluent or of any land or articles as the undertaker—

        (i) considers necessary for the purpose of determining either of the matters mentioned in subsection (2)(a) above; and

        (ii) has authorised that person to take away and analyse.

(4) Part II of Schedule 6 to this Act shall apply to the rights and powers conferred by this section.

(5) In this section "relevant works power" means any power conferred by any of the provisions of sections 158, 159, 161, 163 and 165 above, other than section 161(3).

**169.**—(1) Without prejudice to the rights and powers conferred by section 168 above, any person designated in writing under this section by a water undertaker may enter any premises for any of the purposes specified in subsection (2) below.

*Power to carry out surveys and to search for water.*

(2) The purposes mentioned in subsection (1) above are the carrying out of any survey or tests for the purpose of determining—

    (a) whether it would be appropriate for the undertaker to acquire any land, or any interest or right in or over land, for purposes connected with the carrying out of its functions; or

    (b) whether it would be appropriate for the undertaker to apply for a compulsory works order under section 167 above and what compulsory powers it would be appropriate to apply for under that section.

(3) The power by virtue of subsection (1) above of a person designated under this section to enter any premises for the purpose of carrying out any survey or tests shall include power—

    (a) to carry out experimental borings or other works for the purpose of ascertaining the nature of the sub-soil, the presence of underground water in the sub-soil or the quantity or quality of any such water;

    (b) to install and keep monitoring or other apparatus on the premises for the purpose of obtaining the information on which any such determination as is mentioned in subsection (2) above may be made; and

    (c) to take away and analyse such samples of water or of any land or articles as the undertaker considers necessary for any of the purposes so mentioned and has authorised that person to take away and analyse.

(4) The powers conferred by this section shall not be exercised in any case for purposes connected with the determination of—

    (a) whether, where or how a reservoir should be constructed; or

    (b) whether, where or how a borehole should be sunk for the purpose of abstracting water from or discharging water into any underground strata,

unless the Secretary of State has, in accordance with subsection (5) below, given his written authorisation in relation to that case for the exercise of those powers for those purposes.

(5) The Secretary of State shall not give his authorisation for the purposes of subsection (4) above unless—

    (a) he is satisfied that notice of the proposal to apply for the authorisation has been given to the owner and to the occupier of the premises in question; and

    (b) he has considered any representations or objections with respect to the proposed exercise of the powers under this section which—

        (i) have been duly made to him by the owner or occupier of those premises, within the period of fourteen days beginning with the day after the giving of the notice; and

        (ii) have not been withdrawn.

(6) Part II of Schedule 6 to this Act shall apply to the rights and powers conferred by this section.

Entry etc. for other purposes.

**170.**—(1) Any person designated in writing for the purpose by a water undertaker may enter any premises for any of the following purposes, that is to say—

    (a) the carrying out of any survey or tests for the purpose of determining—

        (i) whether it is appropriate and practicable for the undertaker to exercise any power under any provision of Part III of this Act to disconnect any pipe or cut off any supply of water to any premises or to carry out any works which it is authorised to carry out under section 64(4), 66(3) or 75 above; or

(ii) how any such power should be exercised;

(b) the exercise of any such power;

(c) the monitoring and recording of—

(i) whether water supplied to any premises for domestic or food production purposes is wholesome at the time of supply; or

(ii) the quality of the water from any source, or combination of sources, which is or is to be used for supplying water to any premises for those purposes,

and the carrying out of any tests for that purpose.

(2) Any person designated for the purpose—

(a) by any water undertaker within whose area any waterworks are situated; or

(b) by any water undertaker which takes water from any waterworks,

shall, on producing some duly authenticated document showing his authority, have a right at all reasonable hours to enter any premises for the purpose of ascertaining whether there is, or has been, any contravention of section 72 above in relation to those waterworks.

(3) Any person designated in writing for the purpose by a water undertaker may—

(a) enter any premises for the purpose of—

(i) ascertaining whether any provision contained in or made or having effect under this Act with respect to any water fittings or with respect to the waste or misuse of water is being, or has been, contravened;

(ii) determining whether, and if so in what manner, any power or duty conferred or imposed on any person by regulations under section 74 above should be exercised or performed; or

(iii) exercising any such power or performing any such duty;

or

(b) carry out such inspections, measurements and tests on premises entered by that person or on water fittings or other articles found on any such premises, and take away such samples of water or of any land and such water fittings and other articles, as that person has been authorised to carry out or take away in accordance with regulations under that section.

(4) During any period when a prohibition or restriction under section 76 above is in force, any person designated for the purpose by the water undertaker which imposed the prohibition or restriction shall, on producing some duly authenticated document showing his authority, have a right at all reasonable hours to enter any premises to which the prohibition or restriction applies for the purpose of ascertaining whether there is, or has been, any contravention of the prohibition or restriction.

(5) The power by virtue of subsection (1) above of a person designated by a water undertaker to enter any premises for the purpose of carrying out any survey or tests shall include power to take away such samples of water or effluent or of any land or articles as the undertaker—

    (a) considers necessary for the purpose of determining any of the matters mentioned in paragraph (a) or (c) of that subsection; and

    (b) has authorised that person to carry out or take away.

(6) Expressions used in this section and in any provision of Part III of this Act in relation to which this section has effect shall have the same meaning in this section as in that provision; and, without prejudice to the generality of this provision, subsections (2) and (3) of section 68 above and the definitions of "food production purposes" and "wholesome" in section 93(1) above shall apply for the purposes of any power conferred by virtue of subsection (1)(c)(i) above as they apply for the purposes of that section.

(7) Part I of Schedule 6 to this Act shall apply to the rights of entry conferred by subsections (2) and (4) of this section; and Part II of that Schedule shall apply to the rights and powers conferred by the other provisions of this section.

(8) The provisions of this section shall be without prejudice to the other rights and powers conferred by this Part.

Entry for sewerage purposes.

**171.**—(1) Any person designated in writing for the purpose by a sewerage undertaker shall, on producing any duly authenticated document showing his authority, have a right to enter any premises at all reasonable hours-

    (a) for the purpose of ascertaining whether there is or has been, on or in connection with the premises, any contravention of any of the relevant sewerage provisions which it is the function of the undertaker to enforce;

    (b) for the purpose of ascertaining whether or not circumstances exist which would authorise or require the undertaker to take any action or carry out any works under any of the relevant sewerage provisions;

    (c) for the purpose of taking action or carrying out any works authorised by or under any of the relevant sewerage provisions to be taken or carried out by the undertaker;

    (d) generally for the purpose of carrying out the undertaker's functions under the relevant sewerage provisions.

(2) Part I of Schedule 6 to this Act shall apply to the right of entry conferred by subsection (1) above.

(3) Any person designated by a sewerage undertaker under subsection (1) above for the purpose of exercising any power under this section for the purposes of Chapter III of Part IV of this Act may, on any occasion on which he so exercises that power in relation to any premises, obtain and take away any sample of any trade effluent which is passing (either directly or through a private drain or sewer) from those premises into any of the undertaker's public sewers.

(4) The result of any analysis of a sample taken by any designated person under subsection (1) above shall not be admissible as evidence in any legal proceedings under Chapter III of Part IV of this Act unless the requirements of subsection (5) below are satisfied.

(5) The requirements mentioned in subsection (4) above are that the designated person shall-

   (a) forthwith after taking the sample, notify his intention to have it analysed to the occupier of the trade premises in question;

   (b) there and then divide the sample into three parts;

   (c) cause each part to be placed in a suitable container which shall be sealed up and marked; and

   (d) deliver one part to the occupier, retain one part for future comparison and, if he thinks fit to have an analysis made, submit one part to the analyst.

(6) In this section "trade effluent" and "trade premises" have the same meanings as in Chapter III of Part IV of this Act; and, accordingly, section 139 above shall have effect for the purposes of this section as it has effect for the purposes of that Chapter.

**172.**—(1) Where the conditions set out in section 162(1) above are satisfied in relation to any premises, any person designated in writing for the purpose by the relevant undertaker in question may enter those premises, or any land occupied with those premises, for any of the purposes specified in subsection (2) below.

(2) The purposes mentioned in subsection (1) above are—

   (a) the carrying out of any survey or tests for the purpose of determining—

      (i) whether the carrying out of any works by virtue of paragraph (a) or (b) of subsection (3) of section 162 above is practicable;

      (ii) whether it is necessary or expedient for any purpose connected with the carrying out of any works by virtue of either of those paragraphs for any other works to be carried out; or

      (iii) how any works specified in that subsection should be carried out;

   (b) the carrying out of any works so specified;

   (c) the inspection, examination or testing of any meter which is on those premises or of any pipes or apparatus installed in the course of any works which were carried out for any purpose that is connected with the installation, connection, testing, maintenance or repair of any such meter;

   (d) the ascertainment from any meter of the volume of water supplied to, or of effluent discharged from, those premises.

(3) Part II of Schedule 6 to this Act shall apply in relation to the rights and powers conferred by the preceding provisions of this section.

(4) Where any meter or other recording apparatus is provided in any premises in pursuance of Chapter III of Part IV of this Act for the purpose of assessing any charge, a sewerage undertaker may (instead of exercising its powers under this section) for the purpose of reading that meter or apparatus exercise the power conferred by section 171 above as if that purpose were included in the purposes mentioned in subsection (1) of that section.

**173.**—(1) A person who, without having been designated or authorised for the purpose by a relevant undertaker, purports to be entitled to enter any premises or vessel in exercise of a power exercisable in pursuance of any such designation or authorisation shall be guilty of an offence and liable, on summary conviction, to a fine not exceeding level 4 on the standard scale.

(2) For the purposes of this section it shall be immaterial, where a person purports to be entitled to enter any premises or vessel, that the power which that person purports to be entitled to exercise does not exist or would not be exercisable even if that person had been designated or authorised by a relevant undertaker.

## CHAPTER II

### PROTECTION OF UNDERTAKERS' WORKS, APPARATUS ETC.

#### *Protection of apparatus in general*

**174.**—(1) Subject to subsection (2) below, if any person without the consent of the water undertaker—

(a) intentionally or recklessly interferes with any resource main, water main or other pipe vested in any water undertaker or with any structure, installation or apparatus belonging to any water undertaker; or

(b) by any act or omission negligently interferes with any such main or other pipe or with any such structure, installation or apparatus so as to damage it or so as to have an effect on its use or operation,

that person shall be guilty of an offence and liable, on summary conviction, to a fine not exceeding level 3 on the standard scale.

(2) A person shall not be guilty of an offence under subsection (1) above—

(a) by reason of anything done in an emergency to prevent loss or damage to persons or property; or

(b) by reason of his opening or closing the stopcock fitted to a service pipe by means of which water is supplied to any premises by a water undertaker if—

(i) he has obtained the consent of every consumer whose supply is affected by the opening or closing of that stopcock or, as the case may be, of every other consumer whose supply is so affected; and

(ii) in the case of opening a stopcock, the stopcock was closed otherwise than by the undertaker.

(3) Any person who, without the consent of the water undertaker—

(a) attaches any pipe or apparatus—

(i) to any resource main, water main or other pipe vested in a water undertaker; or

(ii) to any service pipe which does not belong to such an undertaker but which is a pipe by means of which water is supplied by such an undertaker to any premises;

(b) makes any alteration in a service pipe by means of which water is so supplied, or in any apparatus attached to any such pipe; or

(c) subject to subsection (4) below, uses any pipe or apparatus which has been attached or altered in contravention of this section,

shall be guilty of an offence and liable, on summary conviction, to a fine not exceeding level 3 on the standard scale.

(4) In proceedings against any person for an offence by virtue of paragraph (c) of subsection (3) above it shall be a defence for that person to show that he did not know, and had no grounds for suspecting, that the pipe or apparatus in question had been attached or altered as mentioned in that subsection.

(5) If any person wilfully or negligently injures or suffers to be injured any water fitting belonging to a water undertaker, he shall be guilty of an offence and liable, on summary conviction, to a fine not exceeding level 1 on the standard scale.

(6) An offence under subsection (1) or (3) above shall constitute a breach of a duty owed to the water undertaker in question; and any such breach of duty which causes the undertaker to sustain loss or damage shall be actionable at the suit of the undertaker.

(7) The amount recoverable by virtue of subsection (6) above from a person who has committed an offence under subsection (3) above shall include such amount as may be reasonable in respect of any water wasted, misused or improperly consumed in consequence of the commission of the offence.

(8) A water undertaker may—

   (a) do all such work as is necessary for repairing any injury done in contravention of subsection (5) above; and

   (b) recover the expenses reasonably incurred by the undertaker in doing so from the offender summarily as a civil debt.

(9) In this section "consumer" and "water fitting" have the same meanings as in Part III of this Act; and in subsection (1) above the references to apparatus belonging to a water undertaker do not include references to any meter which belongs to such an undertaker and is used by it for the purpose of determining the amount of any charges which have been fixed by the undertaker by reference to volume.

*Protection of meters*

175.—(1) If any person—

   (a) so interferes with a meter used by any relevant undertaker in determining the amount of any charges fixed in relation to any premises as intentionally or recklessly to prevent the meter from showing, or from accurately showing, the volume of water supplied to, or of effluent discharged from, those premises; or

   (b) carries out any works which he knows are likely to affect the operation of such a meter or which require the disconnection of such a meter,

he shall be guilty of an offence and liable, on summary conviction, to a fine not exceeding level 3 on the standard scale.

(2) A person shall not be guilty of an offence under this section in respect of anything done by him with the consent under section 176 below of the undertaker which uses the meter.

Offence of tampering with meter.

**176.**—(1) Where an application is made to any relevant undertaker for a consent for the purposes of section 175 above, the undertaker—

(a) shall give notice of its decision with respect to the application as soon as reasonably practicable after receiving it; and

(b) subject to subsection (2) below, may make it a condition of giving any consent that the undertaker itself should carry out so much of any works to which the application relates as is specified in the notice of its decision.

(2) On such an application a relevant undertaker shall not refuse its consent, or impose any such condition as is mentioned in subsection (1)(b) above, unless it is reasonable to do so.

(3) Where any relevant undertaker has given a notice to any person imposing any such condition as is mentioned in subsection (1)(b) above, the undertaker—

(a) shall carry out those works as soon as reasonably practicable after giving the notice; and

(b) may recover from that person any expenses reasonably incurred by it in doing so.

(4) Any dispute between a relevant undertaker and any other person (including another such undertaker)—

(a) as to whether the undertaker or that other person should bear any expenses under subsection (3) above; or

(b) as to the amount of any expenses to be borne by any person under that subsection,

shall be referred to the arbitration of a single arbitrator appointed by agreement between the undertaker and that person or, in default of agreement, by the Director.

(5) Subsection (3) above shall not apply where the person who was given the notice notifies the undertaker that the carrying out of the works to which the condition relates is no longer required.

Financial
obligations with
respect to any
interference with a
meter.

**177.**—(1) A relevant undertaker which carries out any works made necessary by the commission of an offence under section 175 above shall be entitled to recover any expenses reasonably incurred in carrying out those works from the person who committed the offence.

(2) Any person who sustains any loss or damage in consequence of any failure by any relevant undertaker—

(a) to comply with any obligation imposed on it by section 176 above; or

(b) to exercise reasonable care in the performance of the duty imposed by subsection (3)(a) of that section,

shall be entitled to recover compensation from the undertaker.

(3) Any dispute between a relevant undertaker and any other person (including another such undertaker)—

(a) as to whether the undertaker or that other person should bear any expenses under this section;

(b) as to whether the undertaker should pay any compensation under this section; or

(c) as to the amount of any expenses to be borne by any person under this section or as to the amount of any such compensation,

shall be referred to the arbitration of a single arbitrator appointed by agreement between the undertaker and that person or, in default of agreement, by the Director.

### *Obstruction of sewerage works etc.*

**178.**—(1) A person who wilfully obstructs any person acting in the execution of any of the relevant sewerage provisions shall be guilty of an offence and liable, on summary conviction, to a fine not exceeding level 1 on the standard scale.

(2) If on a complaint made by the owner of any premises, it appears to a magistrates' court that the occupier of those premises is preventing the owner of those premises from carrying out any work which he is required to carry out by or under any of the relevant sewerage provisions, the court may order the occupier to permit the carrying out of the work.

(3) Sections 300 to 302 of the Public Health Act 1936 (which relate to the determination of questions by courts of summary jurisdiction and to appeals against such determinations) shall apply for the purposes of and in relation to the determination under subsection (2) above of any matter by a magistrates' court—

(a) as they apply for the purposes of or in relation to a determination by such a court under that Act; and

(b) in the case of section 302, as if the reference to a decision of a local authority included a reference to a decision of a sewerage undertaker.

### CHAPTER III

### SUPPLEMENTAL PROVISIONS WITH RESPECT TO UNDERTAKERS' POWERS

### *Vesting of works in undertaker*

**179.**—(1) Subject to subsection (3) below and to any provision to the contrary contained in an agreement between the relevant undertaker and the person in whom an interest in the pipe or works is or is to be vested—

(a) every relevant pipe which has been laid, in exercise of any power conferred by this Part or otherwise, by a relevant undertaker; and

(b) every sewage disposal works constructed by a sewerage undertaker,

shall vest in the undertaker which laid it or, as the case may be, the undertaker which constructed them.

(2) In addition to the sewers and works which vest in a sewerage undertaker by virtue of subsection (1) above, the following shall also vest in such an undertaker, that is to say—

(a) every sewer or sewage disposal works with respect to which a declaration of vesting made by that undertaker under Chapter II of Part IV of this Act takes effect; and

(b) every sewer which is laid in the area of that undertaker under Part XI of the Highways Act 1980 (making up private streets) and is not a sewer belonging to a road maintained by a highway authority.

(3) Subsection (1) above shall not apply to a service pipe laid in a street other than the street in which the water main with which it connects is situated and shall not apply to a service pipe laid otherwise than in a street where that pipe is laid—

(a) in pursuance of the duty imposed by virtue of section 46(4) above; or

(b) in substitution for a service pipe belonging to a person other than the person who lays the replacement pipe.

(4) If any water fittings let for hire by a water undertaker are suitably marked, they—

(a) shall continue to be the property of and removable by the undertaker, even if they are fixed to some part of the premises in which they are situated or are laid in the soil under any premises; and

(b) shall not be subject to distress or to the landlord's remedy for rent or be liable to be taken in execution under any process of any court or in any proceedings in bankruptcy against a person in whose possession they are;

but nothing in this subsection shall affect the valuation for rating of any rateable hereditament.

(5) It is hereby declared that anything which, in pursuance of any arrangements under section 97 above, is done on behalf of a sewerage undertaker by a relevant authority within the meaning of that section is, subject to any provision to the contrary contained in any such arrangements, to be treated for the purposes of this section as done by the undertaker.

(6) The preceding provisions of this section are without prejudice, in relation to any company appointed to be a relevant undertaker, to the vesting of anything in that company by virtue of any scheme under Schedule 2 to this Act or of the exercise by any relevant undertaker of any power to acquire property by agreement or compulsorily.

(7) In this section—

"relevant pipe"—

(a) in relation to a water undertaker, means any water main (including a trunk main), resource main, discharge pipe or service pipe; and

(b) in relation to a sewerage undertaker, means any sewer or disposal main;

and

"water fittings" has the same meaning as in Part III of this Act;

and water fittings let on hire by a water undertaker shall be treated as suitably marked for the purposes of this section if and only if they bear either such a distinguishing metal plate affixed to them or such a distinguishing brand or other mark conspicuously impressed or made on them as sufficiently indicates the undertaker as the actual owner of the fittings.

*Damage etc. caused by works*

**180.** Schedule 12 to this Act shall have effect for making provision for imposing obligations for the purpose of minimising the damage caused in the exercise of certain powers conferred on undertakers and for imposing obligations as to the payment of compensation.

**181.**—(1) Subject to subsection (2) below, it shall be the duty of the Director to investigate any complaint made or referred to him with respect to the exercise by a relevant undertaker of any powers conferred on that undertaker by or by virtue of section 159 or 161(2) above.

(2) The Director shall not be required to investigate any such complaint as is mentioned in subsection (1) above if—

   (a) the complaint appears to the Director to be vexatious or frivolous;

   (b) the Director is not satisfied that the complaint has been brought by the complainant to the attention of the relevant undertaker in question and that that undertaker has been given a reasonable opportunity of investigating and dealing with it; or

   (c) the complaint was first made to the Director or the appropriate customer service committee more than twelve months, or such longer period as the Director may for special reasons allow, after the matters to which the complaint relates first came to the notice of the complainant.

(3) Where the Director, in pursuance of his duty under this section, investigates a complaint with respect to the exercise of any powers by a relevant undertaker-

   (a) it shall be the duty of that undertaker to provide the Director with all such information and assistance as he may reasonably require for the purposes of his investigation; and

   (b) it shall be the duty of the Director, before giving any direction under subsection (4) below, to consider any representations made to him by the complainant or by that undertaker with respect to the subject-matter of the complaint.

(4) If on a complaint under subsection (1) above with respect to the exercise of any powers by a relevant undertaker, the Director is satisfied that that undertaker—

   (a) has failed adequately to consult the complainant, before and in the course of exercising those powers, about the manner in which they are exercised; or

   (b) by acting unreasonably in the manner of its exercise of those powers, has caused the complainant to sustain loss or damage or to be subjected to inconvenience,

the Director may direct the undertaker to pay to the complainant an amount, not exceeding £5,000, in respect of that failure, loss, damage or inconvenience.

(5) The Director shall not under subsection (4) above direct a relevant undertaker to pay any amount to a complainant in respect of any loss, damage or inconvenience for which compensation is recoverable under any other enactment except in so far as it appears to him appropriate to do so by reason of any failure of the amount of any such compensation to

PART VI

reflect the fact that it was not reasonable for the undertaker to cause the complainant to sustain the loss or damage or to be subjected to the inconvenience.

(6) The duties of a relevant undertaker by virtue of subsection (3)(a) above shall be enforceable under section 18 above by the Director.

(7) A person to whom any amount is required, in pursuance of a direction under subsection (4) above, to be paid by a relevant undertaker shall be entitled to recover that amount from that undertaker by virtue of this section.

(8) The Secretary of State may by regulations substitute a different amount for the amount for the time being specified in subsection (4) above.

Codes of practice
with respect to
work on private
land.

**182.**—(1) For the purposes of section 181 above it shall be the duty of every company holding an appointment under Chapter I of Part II of this Act as a relevant undertaker—

    (a) as soon as reasonably practicable after its appointment takes effect, to submit to the Secretary of State for his approval a code of practice with respect to its exercise of any powers conferred by or by virtue of section 159 or 161(2) above; and

    (b) if required to do so by the Secretary of State at any subsequent time, to submit proposed modifications of that code to the Secretary of State for his approval.

(2) The Secretary of State, if he considers it appropriate to do so for the purpose of promoting what appear to him to be desirable practices with respect to the exercise, by any company holding an appointment under Chapter I of Part II of this Act as a relevant undertaker, of any powers conferred by or by virtue of section 159 or 161(2) above, may at any time by order made by statutory instrument, in relation to that company—

    (a) approve any code of practice with respect to the exercise of those powers which has been submitted to him (whether or not under subsection (1) above) by that company for his approval;

    (b) approve any modifications of such a code which have been so submitted; or

    (c) withdraw his approval for any such code or modification.

(3) A contravention of a code of practice as for the time being approved under this section in relation to a company shall not—

    (a) affect the powers conferred on that company as a relevant undertaker by this Part;

    (b) of itself entitle any person to be paid any amount under subsection (4) of section 181 above; or

    (c) give rise to any criminal or civil liability;

but the Director shall take into account whether there has been any such contravention in determining whether to give a direction under that subsection to that company and in determining the amount to which any such direction relates.

(4) The Secretary of State shall not make an order under subsection (2) above unless he has first consulted all such persons as he considers it appropriate to consult.

(5) The duties of a relevant undertaker under subsection (1) above shall be enforceable under section 18 above by the Secretary of State.

PART VI

### *Protective provisions*

**183.** Schedule 13 to this Act shall have effect for the protection of particular undertakings in connection with the carrying out of works and other activities by relevant undertakers.

Protection for particular undertakings.

**184.**—(1) The NRA or the Civil Aviation Authority or any internal drainage board, dock undertakers, railway undertakers or airport operator may, after giving reasonable notice to the sewerage undertaker concerned, at their own expense and on substituting an equivalent, take up, divert or alter the level of any sewers, drains, culverts or other pipes which—

Power of certain undertakers to alter public sewers etc.

(a) are vested in the undertaker; and

(b) pass under or interfere with, or interfere with the alteration or improvement of, as the case may be—

(i) any watercourse or other works vested in or under the control of the NRA or that internal drainage board;

(ii) any property of the Civil Aviation Authority;

(iii) any river, canal towing path or works forming part of the undertaking of those dock undertakers;

(iv) the railway of the railway undertakers; or

(v) the airport in question.

(2) In subsection (1) above "an equivalent", in relation to any sewers, drains, culverts or pipes means other sewers, drains, culverts or pipes which will be equally effectual and will entail no additional expense for the sewerage undertaker in question.

(3) Any difference of opinion which arises under this section between a sewerage undertaker and any person as to whether any sewers, drains, culverts or pipes substituted or proposed to be substituted for sewers, drains, culverts or pipes of that undertaker—

(a) are or will be equally effectual; or

(b) entail or will entail additional expense for the sewerage undertaker,

may, at the option of the party complaining, be referred to a single arbitrator appointed by agreement between the parties or, in default of agreement, by the President of the Institution of Civil Engineers.

(4) In this section—

"airport operator" means the person who is the airport operator for the purposes of Part V of the Airports Act 1986 in relation to an airport to which that Part of that Act applies; and

1986 c. 31.

"dock undertakers" has the same meaning as in Chapter II of Part IV of this Act.

**185.**—(1) Where any relevant pipe or other apparatus is for the time being kept installed by a relevant undertaker on, under or over any land, any person with an interest in that land or in adjacent land may by notice to the undertaker require the undertaker to alter or remove that pipe or

Duty to move pipes etc. in certain cases.

apparatus on the ground that the alteration or removal of that pipe or apparatus is necessary to enable that person to carry out a proposed improvement of the land in which he has an interest.

(2) Subject to subsections (3) and (4) below, where a notice is served on a relevant undertaker under subsection (1) above, it shall be the duty of the undertaker to comply with the requirement contained in the notice except to the extent that that requirement is unreasonable.

(3) Nothing in this section shall require a relevant undertaker to alter or remove any pipe or apparatus which is kept installed in, under or over any street.

(4) A relevant undertaker may make it a condition of complying with the duty to which it is subject by virtue of a notice served by any person under subsection (1) above that such security as the undertaker may reasonably require has been provided for the discharge of any obligation of that person under subsection (5) below.

(5) Where a relevant undertaker carries out any works under this section by virtue of a notice having been served by any person under subsection (1) above, the undertaker shall be entitled to recover any expenses reasonably incurred in carrying out those works from that person.

(6) Where any sums have been deposited with a relevant undertaker by way of security for the discharge of any obligation under subsection (5) above, the undertaker shall pay interest at such rate as may be determined either—

(a) by the undertaker with the approval of the Director; or

(b) in default of a determination under paragraph (a) above, by the Director,

on every sum of 50p so deposited for every three months during which it remains in the hands of the undertaker.

(7) An approval or determination by the Director for the purposes of subsection (6) above may be given or made in relation to a particular case or description of cases or generally and may be revoked at any time.

(8) The duty of a relevant undertaker under this section shall be enforceable under section 18 above by the Director.

(9) In this section—

"improvement", in relation to any land, includes any development or change of use but does not include an improvement with respect to the supply of water, or the provision of sewerage services, to any premises; and

"relevant pipe" has the same meaning as in section 158 above.

Protective provisions in respect of flood defence works and watercourses etc.

**186.**—(1) Nothing in this Act shall confer power on any person to do anything, except with the consent of the person who so uses them, which interferes—

(a) with any sluices, floodgates, groynes, sea defences or other works used by any person for draining, preserving or improving any land under any local statutory provision; or

(b) with any such works used by any person for irrigating any land.

(2) Without prejudice to the construction of subsection (1) above for the purposes of its application in relation to the other provisions of this Act, that subsection shall have effect in its application in relation to the relevant sewerage provisions as if any use of or injury to any such works as are mentioned in paragraph (a) or (b) of that subsection were such an interference as is mentioned in that subsection.

(3) Nothing in the relevant sewerage provisions shall authorise a sewerage undertaker injuriously to affect—

  (a) any reservoir, canal, watercourse, river or stream, or any feeder thereof; or

  (b) the supply, quality or fall of water contained in, or in any feeder of, any reservoir, canal, watercourse, river or stream,

without the consent of any person who would, apart from this Act, have been entitled by law to prevent, or be relieved against, the injurious affection of, or of the supply, quality or fall of water contained in, that reservoir, canal, watercourse, river, stream or feeder.

(4) Nothing in the relevant sewerage provisions, except sections 113 and 116 above, shall be taken to affect any right of drainage acquired by any person by prescription or otherwise before 1st October 1937.

(5) Where a relevant undertaker proposes, otherwise than in exercise of any compulsory powers, to construct or alter any relevant inland waters in any internal drainage district or to construct or alter any works on or in any such inland waters, the undertaker shall consult the drainage board for that district before doing so.

(6) A consent for the purposes of subsection (1) above may be given subject to reasonable conditions but shall not be unreasonably withheld.

(7) Any dispute—

  (a) as to whether anything done or proposed to be done interferes or will interfere as mentioned in subsection (1) above;

  (b) as to whether any consent for the purposes of this section is being unreasonably withheld;

  (c) as to whether any condition subject to which any such consent has been given was reasonable; or

  (d) as to whether the supply, quality or fall of water in any reservoir, canal, watercourse, river, stream or feeder is injuriously affected by the exercise of powers under the relevant sewerage provisions,

shall be referred (in the case of a dispute falling within paragraph (d) above, at the option of the party complaining) to the arbitration of a single arbitrator to be appointed by agreement between the parties or, in default of agreement, by the President of the Institution of Civil Engineers.

(8) In this section "relevant inland waters" means any inland waters other than any which form part of a main river for the purposes of Part IV of the Water Resources Act 1991.

1991 c. 57.

(9) The provisions of this section shall be without prejudice to the provisions of Schedule 13 to this Act.

PART VI
Works in tidal
lands etc.

**187.**—(1) Nothing in any of the provisions of this Part relating to any relevant works power shall authorise any relevant undertaker to carry out any works at any place below the place to which the tide flows at mean high water springs, except in accordance with such plans and sections, and subject to such restrictions, as may, before the works are commenced, have been approved by the Secretary of State.

(2) An approval for the purposes of subsection (1) above shall be given to a relevant undertaker by the service on that undertaker of a notice containing the approval.

(3) In subsection (1) above the reference to a relevant works power is a reference to a power conferred by any of the relevant sewerage provisions or by any of sections 158, 159, 161, 163 and 165 above, except the power conferred by section 161(3).

Mineral rights.

1981 c. 67.

**188.** Schedule 14 to this Act (which makes provision with respect to the acquisition of mineral rights by relevant undertakers and with respect to the working of mines and minerals where pipes, sewers or other related works are affected) shall have effect and, in the case of the compulsory acquisition of land by virtue of this Act, shall have effect instead of Schedule 2 to the Acquisition of Land Act 1981 (mineral rights etc. in relation to compulsory purchase orders).

Power to sell
minerals deriving
from sewerage
works.

**189.**—(1) A sewerage undertaker may sell any materials which—

(a) have been removed by that undertaker from any premises, including any street, when carrying out works under, or otherwise carrying into effect the provisions of, the relevant sewerage provisions; and

(b) are not before the end of three days from the date of their removal claimed by the owner and taken away by him.

(2) Where a sewerage undertaker sells any materials under this section, they shall pay the proceeds to the person to whom the materials belonged after deducting the amount of any expenses recoverable by the undertaker from him.

(3) This section is subject to any rights conferred by virtue of paragraph 1 of Schedule 14 to this Act, does not apply to refuse removed by a sewerage undertaker and is not to be taken as prejudicing the determination of the rights and liabilities of a relevant undertaker when exercising a power in any case to which the preceding provisions of this section do not apply.

Saving for
planning controls.
1990 c. 8.

1989 c. 15.

**190.** Without prejudice to the operation of section 90 of the Town and Country Planning Act 1990 (planning permission deemed to be granted in certain cases) in relation to any provision made by or under this Act or any other enactment which by virtue of this Act or the Water Act 1989 relates to the functions of a relevant undertaker, nothing in this Act or in any such enactment shall be construed as authorising the carrying out of any development (within the meaning of that Act of 1990) without the grant of such planning permission as may be required by that Act of 1990.

Duties to make
recreational
facilities available
when building
reservoirs in
Wales.

**191.**—(1) Where a water undertaker carries out any works for or in connection with the construction or operation of a reservoir in Wales which—

(a) permanently affect one or more communities; and

(b) are not primarily intended by that undertaker to benefit the inhabitants of that or those communities,

it shall be the duty of that undertaker to make available facilities for recreation or other leisure-time occupation for the benefit of those inhabitants or to assist others to make such facilities available.

(2) It shall be the duty of every water undertaker, in performing its duty under subsection (1) above, to consult—

(a) the community councils of the communities affected, in the case of communities having such councils; and

(b) in any case, the council of any district in which any community affected is situated.

(3) The duties of a water undertaker under this section shall be enforceable under section 18 above by the Secretary of State.

### *Interpretation of Part VI*

**192.**—(1) In this Part "discharge pipe" means a pipe from which discharges are or are to be made under section 165 above.

Interpretation of Part VI.

(2) In this Part references to maintaining a pipe include references to cleansing it and references to altering a pipe include references to altering its size or course, to moving or removing it and to replacing it with a pipe which is of the same description of relevant pipe (within the meaning of section 158 above) as the pipe replaced.

(3) The powers conferred by this Part on a relevant undertaker shall be exercisable both inside and outside the undertaker's area.

(4) In so far as any powers conferred by this Part on a relevant undertaker authorise the removal of any pipe or the alteration of its size or course, those powers shall be subject to such obligations by virtue of which the undertaker is required—

(a) to maintain a pipe or a connection with it; or

(b) to alter a pipe only where certain conditions are satisfied,

as are imposed on the undertaker by or under any enactment.

(5) The powers conferred by virtue of this Part are without prejudice to any power conferred by virtue of any agreement and are cumulative.

### PART VII

#### INFORMATION PROVISIONS

##### *Reports*

**193.**—(1) The Director shall, as soon as practicable after 31st December each year, make to the Secretary of State a report on—

Reports by Director.

(a) his activities during that year; and

(b) the Monopolies Commission's activities during that year so far as relating to references made by him.

(2) Every such report shall—

 (a) include a general survey of developments, during the year to which it relates, in respect of matters falling within the scope of the Director's functions; and

 (b) set out any general directions given to the Director during that year under section 27(3) above.

(3) The Secretary of State shall lay a copy of every report made by the Director under subsection (1) above before each House of Parliament and shall arrange for copies of every such report to be published in such manner as he considers appropriate.

(4) The Director may also prepare such other reports as appear to him to be expedient with respect to any matters falling within the scope of his functions.

(5) The Director may arrange for copies of any report prepared under subsection (4) above to be published in such manner as he considers appropriate.

(6) In making or preparing any report under this section the Director shall have regard to the need for excluding, so far as that is practicable—

 (a) any matter which relates to the affairs of an individual, where the publication of that matter would or might, in the opinion of the Director, seriously and prejudicially affect the interests of that individual; and

 (b) any matter which relates specifically to the affairs of a particular body of persons, whether corporate or unincorporate, where publication of that matter would or might, in the opinion of the Director, seriously and prejudicially affect the interests of that body.

Reports by customer service committees.

**194.**—(1) A customer service committee —

 (a) shall prepare a report on any such matter as the Director may require; and

 (b) may prepare a report concerning any matter which appears to the customer service committee to affect the interests of the customers or potential customers of a company allocated to the committee,

and, as soon as reasonably practicable after preparing a report under this subsection, a customer service committee shall send a copy of the report to the Director.

(2) As soon as reasonably practicable after the end of each financial year, a customer service committee shall prepare a report on its activities during that year and shall send a copy of that report to the Director.

(3) The Director may arrange for any report which has been sent to him by virtue of this section to be published in such manner as he considers appropriate.

(4) In publishing any report under this section the Director shall have regard to the need for excluding, so far as that is practicable, any such matters as are specified in section 193(6)(a) and (b) above.

*Registers, maps etc.*

**195.**—(1) The Director shall, at such premises and in such form as he may determine, maintain a register for the purposes of Part II of this Act.

The Director's register.

(2) Subject to any direction given under subsection (3) below, the Director shall cause to be entered in the register the provisions of—

(a) every appointment under Chapter I of Part II of this Act, every termination or transfer of any such appointment, every variation of the area for which any company holds any such appointment and every modification of the conditions of any such appointment;

(b) every direction, consent or determination given or made under any such appointment by the Secretary of State, the Monopolies Commission or the Director himself;

(c) every final enforcement order made under section 18 above, every provisional enforcement order made or confirmed under that section and every revocation of such a final or provisional enforcement order;

(d) every undertaking given to and accepted by the Secretary of State or the Director for the purposes of subsection (1)(b) of section 19 above and every notice under subsection (3) of that section; and

(e) every special administration order and every discharge of such an order.

(3) If it appears to the Secretary of State that the entry of any provision in the register would be against the public interest, he may direct the Director not to enter that provision in the register; and the Director shall comply with any such direction.

(4) The contents of the register shall be available for inspection by the public at such times, and subject to the payment of such charges, as may be specified in an order made by the Secretary of State.

(5) Any person may, on the payment of such fee as may be specified in an order so made, require the Director to supply him with a copy of, or extract from, the contents of any part of the register, being a copy or extract which is certified by the Director to be a true copy or extract.

(6) The power to make an order under subsection (4) or (5) above shall be exercisable by statutory instrument subject to annulment in pursuance of a resolution of either House of Parliament.

(7) Any sums received by the Director under this section shall be paid into the Consolidated Fund.

**196.**—(1) It shall be the duty of every sewerage undertaker to secure that copies of—

Trade effluent registers.

(a) every consent given or having effect as if given by the undertaker under Chapter III of Part IV of this Act;

(b) every direction given or having effect as if given by the undertaker under that Chapter;

(c) every agreement entered into or having effect as if entered into by the undertaker under section 129 above; and

(e) every notice served on the undertaker under section 132 above,

are kept available, at all reasonable times, for inspection by the public free of charge at the offices of the undertaker.

(2) It shall be the duty of every sewerage undertaker, on the payment of such sum as may be reasonable, to furnish a person who requests it with a copy of, or of an extract from, anything kept available for inspection under this section.

(3) The duties of a sewerage undertaker under this section shall be enforceable under section 18 above by the Director.

Register for the purposes of works discharges.

**197.**—(1) Every water undertaker shall keep a register of persons and premises for the purposes of section 166 above.

(2) A water undertaker shall enter the name and address of a person in that register in respect of any premises which abut on any watercourse if that person has requested to be so registered and is either—

(a) the owner or occupier of those premises; or

(b) an officer of an association of owners or occupiers of premises which abut on that watercourse and include those premises.

(3) If any water undertaker contravenes, without reasonable excuse, any of the requirements of this section, it shall be guilty of an offence and liable, on summary conviction, to a fine not exceeding level 3 on the standard scale.

Maps of waterworks.

**198.**—(1) Subject to subsections (4) and (5) below, it shall be the duty of every water undertaker to keep records of the location of—

(a) every resource main, water main or discharge pipe which is for the time being vested in that undertaker; and

(b) any other underground works, other than a service pipe, which are for the time being vested in that undertaker.

(2) It shall be the duty of every water undertaker to secure that the contents of any records for the time being kept by it under this section are available, at all reasonable times, for inspection by the public free of charge at an office of the undertaker.

(3) Any information which is required under this section to be made available by a water undertaker for inspection by the public shall be so made available in the form of a map.

(4) For the purpose of determining whether any failure to make a modification of any records kept under this section constitutes a breach of the duty imposed by subsection (1) above, that duty shall be taken to require any modification of the records to be made as soon as reasonably practicable after the completion of the works which make the modification necessary; and, where records kept under this section are modified, the date of the modification and of the completion of the works making the modification necessary shall be incorporated in the records.

(5) Nothing in this section shall require a water undertaker, at any time before 1st September 1999, to keep records of—

(a) any pipe which was laid before 1st September 1989; or

(b) any underground works which were completed before 1st September 1989,

unless those particulars were shown on 31st August 1989 on a map kept by a water authority or statutory water company under section 12 of Schedule 3 to the Water Act 1945 (maps of underground works).

(6) The reference in subsection (5) above to section 12 of Schedule 3 to the Water Act 1945 shall have effect, without prejudice to section 20(2) of the Interpretation Act 1978 (references to enactments to include references to enactments as amended, extended or applied), as including a reference to that section as applied, with or without modifications, by any local statutory provision.

(7) The duties of a water undertaker under this section shall be enforceable under section 18 above by the Secretary of State.

(8) In this section "discharge pipe" has the same meaning as in Part VI of this Act.

**199.**—(1) Subject to subsections (6) to (8) below, it shall be the duty of every sewerage undertaker to keep records of the location and other relevant particulars—

(a) of every public sewer or disposal main which is vested in the undertaker;

(b) of every sewer in relation to which a declaration of vesting has been made by the undertaker under Chapter II of Part IV of this Act but has not taken effect; and

(c) of every drain or sewer which is the subject of any agreement to make such a declaration which has been entered into by the undertaker under section 104 above.

(2) For the purposes of this section the relevant particulars of a drain, sewer or disposal main are (in addition to its location) particulars—

(a) of whether it is a drain, sewer or disposal main and of the descriptions of effluent for the conveyance of which it is or is to be used; and

(b) of whether it is vested in the undertaker or, if it is not, of whether it is a sewer in relation to which a declaration has been made under Chapter II of Part IV of this Act or a drain or sewer which is the subject of an agreement under section 104 above.

(3) The records kept by a sewerage undertaker under this section shall be kept separately in relation to the area of each local authority within whose area there is any drain, sewer or disposal main of which that undertaker is required to keep records and to whom the undertaker is required under section 200 below to provide copies of the contents of those records.

(4) It shall be the duty of every sewerage undertaker to secure that the contents of all the records for the time being kept by it under this section are available, at all reasonable times, for inspection by the public free of charge at an office of the undertaker.

(5) Any information which is required under this section to be made available by a sewerage undertaker for inspection by the public shall be so made available in the form of a map.

(6) For the purpose of determining whether any failure to make a modification of any records kept under this section constitutes a breach of the duty imposed by subsection (1) above, that duty shall be taken to require any modification of the records to be made as soon as reasonably practicable after the completion of the works which make the modification necessary; and, where records kept under this section are modified, the date of the modification and of the completion of the works making the modification necessary shall be incorporated in the records.

(7) Nothing in this section shall require a sewerage undertaker to keep records of any particulars of a drain, sewer or disposal main laid before 1st September 1989 if—

(a) the undertaker does not know of, or have reasonable grounds for suspecting, the existence of the drain, sewer or disposal main; or

(b) it is not reasonably practicable for the undertaker to discover the course of the drain, sewer or disposal main and it has not done so.

(8) Nothing in this section shall require a sewerage undertaker, at any time before 1st September 1999, to keep records of any particulars of any such drain, sewer or disposal main laid before 1st September 1989 as would not be excluded from its records by virtue of subsection (7) above unless—

(a) those particulars were shown on 31st August 1989 on a map kept by a local authority under section 32 of the Public Health Act 1936 (sewer maps); or

(b) it is a drain or sewer in relation to which a declaration of vesting, or an agreement to make such a declaration, has been made since 31st August 1989.

(9) The duties of a sewerage undertaker under this section shall be enforceable under section 18 above by the Secretary of State.

**200.**—(1) It shall be the duty of every sewerage undertaker so to provide local authorities, free of charge, with—

(a) copies of the contents of records kept under section 199 above; and

(b) copies of any modifications of those records,

as to ensure that every local authority to whose area any of those records relate are at all times informed of the contents for the time being of the records relating to their area.

(2) A local authority shall secure that so much of any information provided to them by virtue of this section as consists in the contents for the time being of records kept by a sewerage undertaker under section 199 above is available, at all reasonable times, for inspection by the public free of charge at an office of the authority.

(3) Any information which is required under this section to be provided to a local authority or to be made available by a local authority for inspection by the public shall be so provided or made available in the form of a map.

(4) The duties of a sewerage undertaker under this section shall be enforceable under section 18 above by the Secretary of State.

(5) In this section and, accordingly, in section 199(3) above "local authority", in relation to the Inner Temple and the Middle Temple, includes, respectively, the Sub-Treasurer of the Inner Temple and the Under-Treasurer of the Middle Temple.

### *Publication of certain information and advice*

**201.**—(1) The Secretary of State may arrange for the publication, in such form and in such manner as he considers appropriate, of such information relating to any matter which is connected with the carrying out by a company holding an appointment under Chapter I of Part II of this Act of the functions of a relevant undertaker as it may appear to him to be in the public interest to publish.

Publication of certain information and advice.

(2) The Director may arrange for the publication, in such form and in such manner as he considers appropriate, of such information and advice as it may appear to him to be expedient to give to any customer or potential customer of a company holding an appointment under Chapter I of Part II of this Act.

(3) In arranging for the publication of any such information or advice the Secretary of State or the Director shall have regard to the need for excluding, so far as that is practicable—

(a) any matter which relates to the affairs of an individual, where the publication of that matter would or might, in the opinion of the Secretary of State or (as the case may be) the Director, seriously and prejudicially affect the interests of that individual; and

(b) any matter which relates specifically to the affairs of a particular body of persons, whether corporate or unincorporate, where publication of that matter would or might, in the opinion of the Secretary of State or (as the case may be) the Director, seriously and prejudicially affect the interests of that body.

### *Powers to acquire and duties to provide information*

**202.**—(1) It shall be the duty of a company holding an appointment as a relevant undertaker to furnish the Secretary of State with all such information relating to any matter which—

Duties of undertakers to furnish the Secretary of State with information.

(a) is connected with, or with any proposals relating to, the carrying out by that company of the functions of a relevant undertaker; or

(b) is material to the carrying out by the Secretary of State of any of his functions under this Act, any of the other consolidation Acts or the Water Act 1989,

1989 c. 15.

as the Secretary of State may reasonably require.

(2) Information required under this section shall be furnished in such form and manner, and be accompanied or supplemented by such explanations, as the Secretary of State may reasonably require.

(3) The information which a company may be required to furnish to the Secretary of State under this section shall include information which, although it is not in the possession of that company or would not otherwise come into the possession of that company, is information which it is reasonable to require that company to obtain.

(4) A requirement for the purposes of this section shall be contained in a direction which—

    (a) may describe the information to be furnished in such manner as the Secretary of State considers appropriate;

    (b) may require the information to be furnished on a particular occasion, in particular circumstances or from time to time; and

    (c) may be given to a particular company, to companies of a particular description or to all the companies holding appointments under Chapter I of Part II of this Act.

(5) The obligations of a relevant undertaker under this section shall be enforceable under section 18 above by the Secretary of State.

(6) In this section "the other consolidation Acts" means the Water Resources Act 1991, the Statutory Water Companies Act 1991, so much of the Land Drainage Act 1991 as confers functions on the Secretary of State with respect to the NRA and the Water Consolidation (Consequential Provisions) Act 1991.

**203.**—(1) Where it appears to the Secretary of State or the Director that a company which holds an appointment as a relevant undertaker may be contravening, or may have contravened—

    (a) any condition of its appointment; or

    (b) any statutory or other requirement enforceable under section 18 above,

he may, for any purpose connected with such of his powers under Chapter II of Part II of this Act as are exercisable in relation to that matter, serve a notice under subsection (2) below on any person.

(2) A notice under this subsection is a notice signed by the Secretary of State or the Director and—

    (a) requiring the person on whom it is served to produce, at a time and place specified in the notice, to—

        (i) the Secretary of State or the Director; or

        (ii) any person appointed by the Secretary of State or the Director for the purpose,

    any documents which are specified or described in the notice and are in that person's custody or under his control; or

    (b) requiring that person, if he is carrying on a business, to furnish, at the time and place and in the form and manner specified in the notice, the Secretary of State or the Director with such information as may be specified or described in the notice.

(3) No person shall be required under this section to produce any documents which he could not be compelled to produce in civil proceedings in the High Court or, in complying with any requirement for the furnishing of information, to give any information which he could not be compelled to give in evidence in any such proceedings.

(4) A person who, without reasonable excuse, fails to do anything required of him by a notice under subsection (2) above shall be guilty of an offence and liable, on summary conviction, to a fine not exceeding level 5 on the standard scale.

(5) A person who intentionally alters, suppresses or destroys any document which he has been required by any notice under subsection (2) above to produce shall be guilty of an offence and liable—

    (a) on summary conviction, to a fine not exceeding the statutory maximum;

    (b) on conviction on indictment, to a fine.

(6) If a person makes default in complying with a notice under subsection (2) above, the High Court may, on the application of the Secretary of State or the Director, make such order as the Court thinks fit for requiring the default to be made good; and any such order may provide that all the costs or expenses of and incidental to the application shall be borne by the person in default or by any officers of a company or other association who are responsible for its default.

(7) Nothing in this section shall be construed as restricting any power of the Secretary of State or the Director under section 202 above or the conditions of an appointment under Chapter I of Part II of this Act to require a company holding such an appointment to produce any document to him or to furnish him with any information.

**204.**—(1) The owner or occupier of any land on or under which is situated any sewer, drain, pipe, channel or outlet used or intended to be used for discharging any trade effluent into a sewer of a sewerage undertaker shall, when requested to do so by the undertaker— *Provision of information to sewerage undertakers with respect to trade effluent discharges.*

    (a) produce to the undertaker all such plans of the sewer, drain, pipe, channel or outlet as the owner or, as the case may be, occupier possesses or is able without expense to obtain;

    (b) allow copies of the plans so produced by him to be made by, or under the directions of, the undertaker; and

    (c) furnish to the undertaker all such information as the owner or, as the case may be, occupier can reasonably be expected to supply with respect to the sewer, drain, pipe, channel or outlet.

(2) A request by a sewerage undertaker for the purposes of this section shall be made in writing.

(3) Every person who fails to comply with this section shall be guilty of an offence and liable, on summary conviction to a fine not exceeding level 3 on the standard scale.

(4) Expressions used in this section and in Chapter III of Part IV of this Act have the same meanings in this section as in that Chapter; and, accordingly, section 139 above shall have effect for the purposes of this section as it has effect for the purposes of that Chapter.

**205.**—(1) Where— *Exchange of metering information between undertakers.*

    (a) different services are provided in relation to the same premises by different relevant undertakers;

    (b) one of those undertakers has obtained a reading from a meter used in determining the amount of any charges fixed in relation to those premises;

    (c) the charges in relation to those premises of another of those undertakers are fixed by reference to any matter to which the reading is relevant; and

(d) that other undertaker has agreed to bear a reasonable proportion of the expenses of obtaining the reading together with the reasonable expenses of the disclosure of the reading to it,

it shall be the duty of the undertaker who obtained the reading to disclose the reading to the other undertaker.

(2) Any dispute between a relevant undertaker and any other person (including another such undertaker)—

(a) as to the terms to be contained in any agreement for the purposes of subsection (1)(d) above; or

(b) as to the amount of any expenses to be borne by any person under any such agreement,

shall be referred to the arbitration of a single arbitrator appointed by agreement between the undertaker and that person or, in default of agreement, by the Director.

(3) The duties of a relevant undertaker under this section shall be enforceable under section 18 above by the Secretary of State.

### *Restriction on disclosure of information*

**206.**—(1) Subject to the following provisions of this section, no information with respect to any particular business which—

(a) has been obtained by virtue of any of the provisions of this Act; and

(b) relates to the affairs of any individual or to any particular business,

shall, during the lifetime of that individual or so long as that business continues to be carried on, be disclosed without the consent of that individual or the person for the time being carrying on that business.

(2) No person shall disclose any information furnished to him under section 196 or 204 above or under Chapter III of Part IV of this Act except—

(a) with the consent of the person by whom the information was furnished;

(b) in connection with the execution of that Chapter;

(c) for the purposes of any proceedings arising under that Chapter (including any appeal, application to the Secretary of State or the Director or an arbitration);

(d) for the purposes of any criminal proceedings (whether or not so arising); or

(e) for the purposes of any report of any proceedings falling within paragraph (c) or (d) above.

(3) Subsection (1) above does not apply to any disclosure of information which is made—

(a) for the purpose of facilitating the carrying out by the Secretary of State, the Minister, the NRA, the Director, the Monopolies Commission or a county council or local authority of any of his, its or, as the case may be, their functions by virtue of this Act, any of the other consolidation Acts or the Water Act 1989;

(b) for the purpose of facilitating the performance by a relevant undertaker of any of the duties imposed on it by or under this Act, any of the other consolidation Acts or the Water Act 1989;

(c) in pursuance of any arrangements made by the Director under section 29(6) above or of any duty imposed by section 197(1)(a) or (2) or 203(1) or (2) of the Water Resources Act 1991 (information about water flow and pollution);

(d) for the purpose of facilitating the carrying out by any person mentioned in Part I of Schedule 15 to this Act of any of his functions under any of the enactments or instruments specified in Part II of that Schedule;

(e) for the purpose of enabling or assisting the Secretary of State to exercise any powers conferred on him by the Financial Services Act 1986 or by the enactments relating to companies, insurance companies or insolvency or for the purpose of enabling or assisting any inspector appointed by him under the enactments relating to companies to carry out his functions;

(f) for the purpose of enabling an official receiver to carry out his functions under the enactments relating to insolvency or for the purpose of enabling or assisting a recognised professional body for the purposes of section 391 of the Insolvency Act 1986 to carry out its functions as such;

(g) for the purpose of facilitating the carrying out by the Health and Safety Commission or the Health and Safety Executive of any of its functions under any enactment or of facilitating the carrying out by any enforcing authority, within the meaning of Part I of the Health and Safety at Work etc. Act 1974, of any functions under a relevant statutory provision, within the meaning of that Act;

(h) for the purpose of facilitating the carrying out by the Comptroller and Auditor General of any of his functions under any enactment;

(i) in connection with the investigation of any criminal offence or for the purposes of any criminal proceedings;

(j) for the purposes of any civil proceedings brought under or by virtue of this Act, any of the other consolidation Acts, the Water Act 1989 or any of the enactments or instruments specified in Part II of Schedule 15 to this Act, or of any arbitration under this Act, any of the other consolidation Acts or that Act of 1989; or

(k) in pursuance of a Community obligation.

(4) Nothing in subsection (1) above shall be construed—

(a) as limiting the matters which may be published under section 201 above or may be included in, or made public as part of, a report of the NRA, the Director, a customer service committee or the Monopolies Commission under any provision of this Act or of the Water Resources Act 1991; or

(b) as applying to any information which has been so published or has been made public as part of such a report or to any information exclusively of a statistical nature.

(5) Subject to subsection (6) below, nothing in subsection (1) above shall preclude the disclosure of information—

    (a) if the disclosure is of information relating to a matter connected with the carrying out of the functions of a relevant undertaker and is made by one Minister of the Crown or government department to another; or

    (b) if the disclosure is for the purpose of enabling or assisting any public or other authority for the time being designated for the purposes of this section by an order made by the Secretary of State to discharge any functions which are specified in the order.

(6) The power to make an order under subsection (5) above shall be exercisable by statutory instrument subject to annulment in pursuance of a resolution of either House of Parliament; and where such an order designates an authority for the purposes of paragraph (b) of that subsection, the order may—

    (a) impose conditions subject to which the disclosure of information is permitted by virtue of that paragraph; and

    (b) otherwise restrict the circumstances in which disclosure is so permitted.

(7) Any person who discloses any information in contravention of the preceding provisions of this section shall be guilty of an offence.

(8) A person who is guilty of an offence under this section by virtue of subsection (1) above shall be liable—

    (a) on summary conviction, to a fine not exceeding the statutory maximum;

    (b) on conviction on indictment, to imprisonment for a term not exceeding two years or to a fine or to both.

(9) A person who is guilty of an offence under this section by virtue of subsection (2) above shall be liable, on summary conviction, to imprisonment for a term not exceeding three months or to a fine not exceeding level 3 on the standard scale or to both.

1991 c. 57.
1991 c. 58.
1991 c. 59.
1991 c. 60.

(10) In this section "the other consolidation Acts" means the Water Resources Act 1991, the Statutory Water Companies Act 1991, the Land Drainage Act 1991 and the Water Consolidation (Consequential Provisions) Act 1991.

*Provision of false information*

Provision of false information.

**207.**—(1) If any person, in furnishing any information or making any application under or for the purposes of any provision of this Act, makes any statement which he knows to be false in a material particular, or recklessly makes any statement which is false in a material particular, he shall be guilty of an offence and liable—

    (a) on summary conviction, to a fine not exceeding the statutory maximum;

    (b) on conviction on indictment, to a fine.

(2) Proceedings for an offence under subsection (1) above shall not be instituted except by or with the consent of the Secretary of State, the Minister of Agriculture, Fisheries and Food or the Director of Public Prosecutions.

## PART VIII

### MISCELLANEOUS AND SUPPLEMENTAL

#### *Miscellaneous*

**208.**—(1) The Secretary of State may, after consultation with a relevant undertaker, give to that undertaker such directions of a general character as appear to the Secretary of State to be requisite or expedient in the interests of national security or for the purpose of mitigating the effects of any civil emergency which may occur.

Directions in the interests of national security.

(2) If it appears to the Secretary of State to be requisite or expedient to do so in the interests of national security or for the purpose of mitigating the effects of any civil emergency which has occurred or may occur, he may, after consultation with a relevant undertaker, give to that undertaker a direction requiring it to do, or not to do, a particular thing specified in the direction.

(3) It shall be the duty of a relevant undertaker, notwithstanding any other duty imposed on it (whether or not by or under this Act), to comply with any direction given to it by the Secretary of State under this section; and the duty of a relevant undertaker to comply with any such direction shall be enforceable under section 18 above by the Secretary of State.

(4) The Secretary of State shall lay before each House of Parliament a copy of every direction given under this section unless he is of the opinion that disclosure of the direction is against the interests of national security.

(5) A person shall not disclose, or be required by virtue of any enactment or otherwise to disclose, anything done by virtue of this section if the Secretary of State has notified him that the Secretary of State is of the opinion that disclosure of that thing is against the interests of national security.

(6) Any person who discloses any matter in contravention of subsection (5) above shall be guilty of an offence and liable, on conviction on indictment, to imprisonment for a term not exceeding two years or to a fine or to both.

(7) Any reference in this section to a civil emergency is a reference to any natural disaster or other emergency which, in the opinion of the Secretary of State, is or may be likely, in relation to any area—

(a) so to disrupt water supplies or sewerage services; or

(b) to involve such destruction of or damage to life or property in that area,

as seriously and adversely to affect all the inhabitants of that area, or a substantial number of them, whether by depriving them of any of the essentials of life or otherwise.

**209.**—(1) Where an escape of water, however caused, from a pipe vested in a water undertaker causes loss or damage, the undertaker shall be liable, except as otherwise provided in this section, for the loss or damage.

Civil liability of undertakers for escapes of water etc.

(2) A water undertaker shall not incur any liability under subsection (1) above if the escape was due wholly to the fault of the person who sustained the loss or damage or of any servant, agent or contractor of his.

(3) A water undertaker shall not incur any liability under subsection (1) above in respect of any loss or damage for which the undertaker would not be liable apart from that subsection and which is sustained—

    (a) by the NRA, a relevant undertaker or any statutory undertakers, within the meaning of section 336(1) of the Town and Country Planning Act 1990;

    (b) by any public gas supplier within the meaning of Part I of the Gas Act 1986 or the holder of a licence under section 6(1) of the ElectricityAct 1989;

    (c) by any highway authority; or

    (d) by any person on whom a right to compensation is conferred by section 82 of the New Roads and Street Works Act 1991.

(4) The Law Reform (Contributory Negligence) Act 1945, the Fatal Accidents Act 1976 and the Limitation Act 1980 shall apply in relation to any loss or damage for which a water undertaker is liable under this section, but which is not due to the undertaker's fault, as if it were due to its fault.

(5) Nothing in subsection (1) above affects any entitlement which a water undertaker may have to recover contribution under the Civil Liability (Contribution) Act 1978; and for the purposes of that Act, any loss for which a water undertaker is liable under that subsection shall be treated as if it were damage.

(6) Where a water undertaker is liable under any enactment or agreement passed or made before 1st April 1982 to make any payment in respect of any loss or damage the undertaker shall not incur liability under subsection (1) above in respect of the same loss or damage.

(7) In this section "fault" has the same meaning as in the Law Reform (Contributory Negligence) Act 1945.

(8) Until the coming into force of section 82 of the New Roads and Street Works Act 1991, subsection (3) above shall have effect as if for paragraph (d) there were substituted the following paragraphs—

    "(d) by any bridge authority, bridge managers, street authority or street managers within the meaning of the Public Utilities Street Works Act 1950; or

    (e) by any person on whom a right to compensation under section 26 of that Act of 1950 is conferred.";

but nothing in this section shall be taken to prejudice the power of the Secretary of State under that Act of 1991 to make an order bringing section 82 of that Act into force on different days for different purposes (including the purposes of this section).

### *Offences*

**210.**—(1) Where a body corporate is guilty of an offence under this Act and that offence is proved to have been committed with the consent or connivance of, or to be attributable to any neglect on the part of, any director, manager, secretary or other similar officer of the body corporate or any person who was purporting to act in any such capacity, then he, as well as the body corporate, shall be guilty of that offence and shall be liable to be proceeded against and punished accordingly.

(2) Where the affairs of a body corporate are managed by its members, subsection (1) above shall apply in relation to the acts and defaults of a member in connection with his functions of management as if he were a director of the body corporate.

**211.** Proceedings in respect of an offence created by or under any of the relevant sewerage provisions shall not, without the written consent of the Attorney-General, be taken by any person other than—

Limitation on right to prosecute in respect of sewerage offences.

    (a) a party aggrieved;

    (b) a sewerage undertaker; or

    (c) a body whose function it is to enforce the provisions in question.

### *Judicial disqualification*

**212.** No judge of any court or justice of the peace shall be disqualified from acting in relation to any proceedings to which a relevant undertaker is a party by reason only that he is or may become liable to pay a charge to that undertaker in respect of any service that is not the subject-matter of the proceedings.

Judicial disqualification.

### *Powers to make regulations*

**213.**—(1) The powers of the Secretary of State to make regulations under this Act shall be exercisable by statutory instrument subject (except in the case of regulations under section 8(1) or (2) above) to annulment in pursuance of a resolution of either House of Parliament.

Powers to make regulations.

(2) Subject to subsection (3) below, the provisions of any regulations made by the Secretary of State under this Act may include-

    (a) provision for any duty or other requirement imposed by the regulations on a water undertaker or sewerage undertaker to be enforceable under section 18 above by the Secretary of State, by the Director or by either of them;

    (b) provision, where such a duty or requirement is so enforceable by either of them, for enforcement by the Director to be subject to such consent or authorisation as may be prescribed;

    (c) provision which, in relation to the furnishing of any information or the making of any application under the regulations, makes provision corresponding to section 207 above;

    (d) provision for anything that may be prescribed by the regulations to be determined under the regulations and for anything falling to be so determined to be determined by such persons, in accordance with such procedure and by reference to such matters, and to the opinion of such persons, as may be prescribed;

    (e) different provision for different cases, including different provision in relation to different persons, circumstances or localities; and

    (f) such supplemental, consequential and transitional provision as the Secretary of State considers appropriate.

PART VIII

(3) Except to the extent that they would do so apart from this section, the power to make regulations under section 113, 125 or 126 above or under section 214 below or Schedule 8 to this Act—

    (a) shall not include the powers conferred by virtue of paragraphs (a) to (d) of subsection (2) above; and

    (b) in the case of the power to make regulations under section 214 below, shall also not include the powers conferred by virtue of paragraphs (e) and (f) of that subsection.

Power to prescribe forms.

**214.**—(1) The Secretary of State may by regulations prescribe the form of any notice or other document to be used for any of the purposes of the relevant sewerage provisions.

(2) If forms are prescribed under this section, those forms or forms to the like effect may be used in all cases to which those forms are applicable.

## *Local inquiries*

Local inquiries.

**215.**—(1) The Secretary of State may cause a local inquiry to be held in any case where he is authorised by any of the relevant sewerage provisions to determine any difference, to make any order, to give any consent or otherwise to act under any of those provisions.

1972 c. 70.

(2) Subject to subsection (3) below, subsections (2) to (5) of section 250 of the Local Government Act 1972 (which contain supplementary provisions with respect to local inquiries held in pursuance of that section) shall apply to local inquiries under subsection (1) above or any of the other provisions of this Act as they apply to inquiries under that section.

(3) Subsection (4) of the said section 250 shall apply in accordance with subsection (2) above in relation to such local inquiries under this Act as are held with respect to any matter affecting the carrying out of any function of the NRA as if the reference to a local authority in that subsection included a reference to the NRA.

## *Construction of Act*

Provisions relating to the service of documents.

**216.**—(1) Any document required or authorised by virtue of this Act to be served on any person may be served—

    (a) by delivering it to him or by leaving it at his proper address or by sending it by post to him at that address; or

    (b) if the person is a body corporate, by serving it in accordance with paragraph (a) above on the secretary or clerk of that body; or

    (c) if the person is a partnership, by serving it in accordance with paragraph (a) above on a partner or a person having the control of management of the partnership business.

1978 c. 30.

(2) For the purposes of this section and section 7 of the Interpretation Act 1978 (which relates to the service of documents by post) in its application to this section, the proper address of any person on whom a document is to be served shall be his last known address, except that—

    (a) in the case of service on a body corporate or its secretary or clerk, it shall be the address of the registered or principal office of the body;

(b) in the case of service on a partnership or a partner or a person having the control or management of a partnership business, it shall be the principal office of the partnership;

and for the purposes of this subsection the principal office of a company registered outside the United Kingdom or of a partnership carrying on business outside the United Kingdom is its principal office within the United Kingdom.

(3) If a person to be served by virtue of this Act with any document by another has specified to that other an address within the United Kingdom other than his proper address (as determined in pursuance of subsection (2) above) as the one at which he or someone on his behalf will accept documents of the same description as that document, that address shall also be treated as his proper address for the purposes of this section and for the purposes of the said section 7 in its application to this section.

(4) Where under any provision of this Act any document is required to be served on the owner, on a lessee or on the occupier of any premises then—

(a) if the name or address of the owner, of the lessee or, as the case may be, of the occupier of the premises cannot after reasonable inquiry be ascertained; or

(b) in the case of service on the occupier, if the premises appear to be or are unoccupied,

that document may be served either by leaving it in the hands of a person who is or appears to be resident or employed on the land or by leaving it conspicuously affixed to some building or object on the land.

(5) This section shall not apply to any document in relation to the service of which provision is made by rules of court.

**217.**—(1) The purposes to which this section applies shall be the construction of any enactment which, by reference to the functions of a relevant undertaker, confers any power on or in relation to that undertaker.

*Construction of provision conferring powers by reference to undertakers' functions.*

(2) For the purposes to which this section applies the functions of every relevant undertaker shall be taken to include joining with or acting on behalf of—

(a) the NRA;

(b) one or more other relevant undertakers; or

(c) the NRA and one or more other such undertakers,

for the purpose of carrying out any works or acquiring any land which at least one of the bodies with which it joins, or on whose behalf it acts, is authorised to carry out or acquire for the purposes of that body's functions under any enactment or of any function which is taken to be a function of that body for the purposes to which this section or section 3 of the Water Resources Act 1991 (functions of NRA for certain purposes) applies.

*1991 c. 57.*

(3) For the purposes to which this section applies the functions of every relevant undertaker shall be taken to include the protection against pollution—

(a) of any waters, whether on the surface or underground, which belong to the NRA or any water undertaker or from which the NRA or any water undertaker is authorised to take water;

(b) without prejudice to paragraph (a) above, of any reservoir which belongs to or is operated by the NRA or any water undertaker or which the NRA or any water undertaker is proposing to acquire or construct for the purpose of being so operated; and

1991 c. 57.

(c) of any underground strata from which the NRA or any water undertaker is for the time being authorised to abstract water in pursuance of a licence under Chapter II of Part II of the Water Resources Act 1991.

(4) For the purposes to which this section applies the functions of every relevant undertaker shall be taken to include the furtherance of research into matters in respect of which functions are conferred by or under this

1989 c. 15.

Act, the other consolidation Acts or the Water Act 1989 on the NRA, on water undertakers or on sewerage undertakers.

(5) For the purposes to which this section applies the functions of every relevant undertaker shall be taken to include the provision of houses and other buildings for the use of persons employed by that undertaker and the provision of recreation grounds for persons so employed.

(6) For the purposes to which this section applies the functions of every water undertaker shall be taken to include the provision of supplies of water in bulk, whether or not such supplies are provided for the purposes of, or in connection with, the carrying out of any other function of that undertaker.

(7) For the purposes to which this section applies the functions of every water undertaker shall be taken to include the doing of anything in pursuance of any arrangements under section 20 of the Water Resources Act 1991 between that undertaker and the NRA.

(8) In this section "the other consolidation Acts" has the same meaning as in section 206 above.

Meaning of "domestic purposes" in relation to water supply.

**218.**—(1) Subject to the following provisions of this section, in this Act references to domestic purposes, in relation to a supply of water to any premises or in relation to any cognate expression, are references to the drinking, washing, cooking, central heating and sanitary purposes for which water supplied to those premises may be used.

(2) Where the whole or any part of the premises are or are to be occupied as a house, those purposes shall be taken to include—

(a) the purposes of a profession carried on in that house or, where—

(i) that house and another part of the premises are occupied together; and

(ii) the house comprises the greater part of what is so occupied,

in that other part; and

(b) such purposes outside the house (including the washing of vehicles and the watering of gardens) as are connected with the occupation of the house and may be satisfied by a supply of water drawn from a tap inside the house and without the use of a hosepipe or similar apparatus.

(3) No such reference to domestic purposes shall be taken to include a reference—

    (a) to the use of a bath having a capacity, measured to the centre line of overflow or in such other manner as may be prescribed, of more than two hundred and thirty litres;

    (b) to the purposes of the business of a laundry; or

    (c) to any purpose of a business of preparing food or drink for consumption otherwise than on the premises.

**219.**—(1) In this Act, except in so far as the context otherwise requires—

    "accessories", in relation to a water main, sewer or other pipe, includes any manholes, ventilating shafts, inspection chambers, settling tanks, wash-out pipes, pumps, ferrules or stopcocks for the main, sewer or other pipe, or any machinery or other apparatus which is designed or adapted for use in connection with the use or maintenance of the main, sewer or other pipe or of another accessory for it, but does not include any telecommunication apparatus (within the meaning of Schedule 2 to the Telecommunications Act 1984) unless it—

        (a) is or is to be situated inside or in the close vicinity of the main, sewer or other pipe or inside or in the close vicinity of another accessory for it; and

        (b) is intended to be used only in connection with the use or maintenance of the main, sewer or other pipe or of another accessory for it;

    "analyse", in relation to any sample of land, water or effluent, includes subjecting the sample to a test of any description, and cognate expressions shall be construed accordingly;

    "conservancy authority" means any person who has a duty or power under any enactment to conserve, maintain or improve the navigation of a tidal water, and is not a harbour authority or navigation authority;

    "contravention" includes a failure to comply, and cognate expressions shall be construed accordingly;

    "customer or potential customer", in relation to a company holding an appointment under Chapter I of Part II of this Act, means—

        (a) any person for or to whom that company provides any services in the course of carrying out the functions of a water undertaker or sewerage undertaker; or

        (b) any person who might become such a person on making an application for the purpose to the company;

    "damage", in relation to individuals, includes death and any personal injury, including any disease or impairment of physical or mental condition;

    "the Director" means the Director General of Water Services;

    "disposal"—

        (a) in relation to land or any interest or right in or over land, includes the creation of such an interest or right and a disposal effected by means of the surrender or other termination of any such interest or right; and

(b) in relation to sewage, includes treatment;

and cognate expressions shall be construed accordingly;

"disposal main" means (subject to subsection (2) below) any outfall pipe or other pipe which—

(a) is a pipe for the conveyance of effluent to or from any sewage disposal works, whether of a sewerage undertaker or of any other person; and

(b) is not a public sewer;

"domestic purposes", except in relation to sewers, shall be construed in accordance with section 218 above;

"drain" means (subject to subsection (2) below) a drain used for the drainage of one building or of any buildings or yards appurtenant to buildings within the same curtilage;

"effluent" means any liquid, including particles of matter and other substances in suspension in the liquid;

"enactment" includes an enactment contained in this Act or in any Act passed after this Act;

"engineering or building operations", without prejudice to the generality of that expression, includes—

(a) the construction, alteration, improvement, maintenance or demolition of any building or structure or of any reservoir, watercourse, dam, weir, well, borehole or other works; and

(b) the installation, modification or removal of any machinery or apparatus;

"financial year" means the twelve months ending with 31st March;

"functions", in relation to a relevant undertaker, means the functions of the undertaker under or by virtue of any enactment and shall be construed subject to section 217 above;

"harbour authority" means a person who is a harbour authority within the meaning of the Prevention of Oil Pollution Act 1971 and is not a navigation authority;

1971 c. 60.

"highway" and "highway authority" have the same meanings as in the Highways Act 1980;

1980 c. 66.

"house" means any building or part of a building which is occupied as a dwelling-house, whether or not a private dwelling-house, or which, if unoccupied, is likely to be so occupied;

"information" includes anything contained in any records, accounts, estimates or returns;

"inland waters", has the same meaning as in the Water Resources Act 1991;

1991 c. 57.

"limited company" means a company within the meaning of the Companies Act 1985 which is limited by shares;

1985 c. 6.

"local authority" means the council of a district or of a London borough or the Common Council of the City of London;

"local statutory provision" means—

(a) a provision of a local Act (including an Act confirming a provisional order);

(b) a provision of so much of any public general Act as has effect with respect to a particular area, with respect to particular persons or works or with respect to particular provisions falling within any paragraph of this definition;

(c) a provision of an instrument made under any provision falling within paragraph (a) or (b) above; or

(d) a provision of any other instrument which is in the nature of a local enactment;

"meter" means any apparatus for measuring or showing the volume of water supplied to, or of effluent discharged from, any premises;

"micro-organism" includes any microscopic biological entity which is capable of replication;

"modifications" includes additions, alterations and omissions, and cognate expressions shall be construed accordingly;

"the Monopolies Commission" means the Monopolies and Mergers Commission;

"the NRA" means the National Rivers Authority;

"navigation authority" means any person who has a duty or power under any enactment to work, maintain, conserve, improve or control any canal or other inland navigation, navigable river, estuary, harbour or dock;

"notice" means notice in writing;

"owner", in relation to any premises, means the person who—

(a) is for the time being receiving the rack-rent of the premises, whether on his own account or as agent or trustee for another person; or

(b) would receive the rack-rent if the premises were let at a rack-rent,

and cognate expressions shall be construed accordingly;

"prescribed" means prescribed by regulations made by the Secretary of State;

"protected land", in relation to a company holding an appointment under Chapter I of Part II of this Act, means any land which, or any interest or right in or over which—

(a) was transferred to that company in accordance with a scheme under Schedule 2 to the Water Act 1989 or, where that company is a statutory water company, was held by that company at any time during the financial year ending with 31st March 1990;

1989 c. 15.

(b) is or has at any time on or after 1st September 1989 been held by that company for purposes connected with the carrying out of its functions as a water undertaker or sewerage undertaker (including any functions which for the purposes for which section 218 above has effect are taken to be such functions by virtue of subsection (6) or (7) of that section); or

G

(c) has been transferred to that company in accordance with a scheme under Schedule 2 to this Act from another company in relation to which that land was protected land when the other company held an appointment under that Chapter;

"public authority" means any Minister of the Crown or government department, the NRA, any local authority or county council or any person certified by the Secretary of State to be a public authority for the purposes of this Act;

"public sewer" means a sewer for the time being vested in a sewerage undertaker in its capacity as such, whether vested in that undertaker by virtue of a scheme under Schedule 2 to the Water Act 1989 or Schedule 2 to this Act or under section 179 above or otherwise, and "private sewer" shall be construed accordingly;

"railway undertakers" means the British Railways Board, London Regional Transport or any other person authorised by any enactment, or by any order, rule or regulation made under any enactment, to construct, work or carry on any railway;

"records" includes computer records and any other records kept otherwise than in a document;

"the relevant sewerage provisions" means the following provisions of this Act, that is to say—

(a) Chapters II and III of Part IV (except sections 98 to 101 and 110 and so much of Chapter III of that Part as provides for regulations under section 138 or has effect by virtue of any such regulations);

(b) sections 160, 171, 172(4), 178, 184, 189, 196 and 204 and paragraph 4 of Schedule 12; and

(c) the other provisions of this Act so far as they have effect for the purposes of any provision falling within paragraph (a) or (b) of this definition;

"relevant undertaker" means a water undertaker or sewerage undertaker;

"resource main" means (subject to subsection (2) below) any pipe, not being a trunk main, which is or is to be used for the purpose of—

(a) conveying water from one source of supply to another, from a source of supply to a regulating reservoir or from a regulating reservoir to a source of supply; or

(b) giving or taking a supply of water in bulk;

"service pipe" means (subject to subsection (2) below) so much of a pipe which is, or is to be, connected with a water main for supplying water from that main to any premises as—

(a) is or is to be subject to water pressure from that main; or

(b) would be so subject but for the closing of some valve,

and includes part of any service pipe;

"services" includes facilities;

"sewer" includes (without prejudice to subsection (2) below) all sewers and drains (not being drains within the meaning given by this subsection) which are used for the drainage of buildings and yards appurtenant to buildings;

"sewerage services" includes the disposal of sewage and any other services which are required to be provided by a sewerage undertaker for the purpose of carrying out its functions;

"special administration order" has the meaning given by section 23 above;

"statutory water company" means any company which was a statutory water company for the purposes of the Water Act 1973 immediately before 1st September 1989; 1973 c. 37.

"stopcock" includes any box or pit in which a stopcock is enclosed and the cover to any such box or pit;

"street" has, subject to subsection (5) below, the same meaning as in Part III of the New Roads and Street Works 1991; 1991 c. 22.

"subordinate legislation" has the same meaning as in the Interpretation Act 1978; 1978 c. 30.

"substance" includes micro-organisms and any natural or artificial substance or other matter, whether it is in solid or liquid form or in the form of a gas or vapour;

"supply of water in bulk" means a supply of water for distribution by a water undertaker taking the supply;

"surface water" includes water from roofs;

"trunk main" means a water main which is or is to be used by a water undertaker for the purpose of—

(a) conveying water from a source of supply to a filter or reservoir or from one filter or reservoir to another filter or reservoir; or

(b) conveying water in bulk, whether in the course of taking a supply of water in bulk or otherwise, between different places outside the area of the undertaker, from such a place to any part of that area or from one part of that area to another part of that area;

"underground strata" means strata subjacent to the surface of any land;

"vessel" includes a hovercraft within the meaning of the Hovercraft Act 1968; 1968 c. 59.

"water main" means (subject to subsection (2) below) any pipe, not being a pipe for the time being vested in a person other than the undertaker, which is used or to be used by a water undertaker for the purpose of making a general supply of water available to customers or potential customers of the undertaker, as distinct from for the purpose of providing a supply to particular customers;

"watercourse" includes all rivers, streams, ditches, drains, cuts, culverts, dykes, sluices, sewers and passages through which water flows except mains and other pipes which belong to the NRA or a water undertaker or are used by a water undertaker or any other person for the purpose only of providing a supply of water to any premises.

(2) In this Act—

> (a) references to a pipe, including references to a main, a drain or a sewer, shall include references to a tunnel or conduit which serves or is to serve as the pipe in question and to any accessories for the pipe; and

> (b) references to any sewage disposal works shall include references to the machinery and equipment of those works and any necessary pumping stations and outfall pipes;

and, accordingly, references to the laying of a pipe shall include references to the construction of such a tunnel or conduit, to the construction or installation of any such accessories and to the making of a connection between one pipe and another.

(3) Nothing in Part III or IV of this Act by virtue of which a relevant undertaker owes a duty to any particular person to lay any water main, resource main or service pipe or any sewer, disposal main or discharge pipe shall be construed—

> (a) as conferring any power in addition to the powers conferred apart from those Parts; or

> (b) as requiring the undertaker to carry out any works which it has no power to carry out.

(4) References in this Act to the fixing of charges in relation to any premises by reference to volume are references to the fixing of those charges by reference to the volume of water supplied to those premises, to the volume of effluent discharged from those premises, to both of those factors or to one or both of those factors taken together with other factors.

1991 c. 22.

1950 c. 39.

(5) Until the coming into force of Part III of the New Roads and Street Works Act 1991, the definition of "street" in subsection (1) above shall have effect as if the reference to that Part were a reference to the Public Utilities Street Works Act 1950; but nothing in this section shall be taken—

> (a) to prejudice the power of the Secretary of State under that Act of 1991 to make an order bringing Part III of that Act into force on different days for different purposes (including the purposes of this section); or

> (b) in the period before the coming into force of that Part, to prevent references in this Act to a street, where the street is a highway which passes over a bridge or through a tunnel, from including that bridge or tunnel.

(6) For the purposes of any provision of this Act by or under which power is or may be conferred on any person to recover the expenses incurred by that person in doing anything, those expenses shall be assumed to include such sum as may be reasonable in respect of establishment charges or overheads.

(7) References in this Act to the later or latest of two or more different times or days are, in a case where those times or days coincide, references to the time at which or, as the case may be, the day on which they coincide.

(8) Where by virtue of any provision of this Act any function of a Minister of the Crown is exercisable concurrently by different Ministers, that function shall also be exercisable jointly by any two or more of those Ministers.

(9) Sub-paragraph (1) of paragraph 1 of Schedule 2 to the Water Consolidation (Consequential Provisions) Act 1991 has effect (by virtue of sub-paragraph (2)(b) of that paragraph) so that references in this Act to things done under or for the purposes of provisions of this Act or the Water Resources Act 1991 include references to things done, or treated as done, under or for the purposes of the corresponding provisions of the law in force before the commencement of this Act.

PART VIII
1991 c. 60.

1991 c. 57.

**220.** Subject to any provision to the contrary which is contained in Schedule 26 to the Water Act 1989 or in the Water Consolidation (Consequential Provisions) Act 1991, nothing in any local statutory provision passed or made before 1st September 1989 shall be construed as relieving any relevant undertaker from any liability arising by virtue of this Act in respect of any act or omission occurring on or after that date.

Effect of local Acts.

### *Other supplemental provisions*

**221.**—(1) Subject to the following provisions of this section, the provisions of this Act shall have effect in relation to land in which there is a Crown or Duchy interest as they have effect in relation to land in which there is no such interest.

Crown application.

(2) Subject to subsection (3) below, a power which is conferred by or under this Act in relation to land shall be exercisable in relation to any land in which there is a Crown or Duchy interest only with the consent of the appropriate authority.

(3) Subsection (2) above shall not require any consent to be given—

(a) for the exercise of any power in relation to any land in which there is a Crown or Duchy interest to the extent that that power would be so exercisable apart from subsection (1) above;

(b) for the imposition in relation to any premises in which there is a Crown or Duchy interest of any charges for a service provided by a relevant undertaker in the course of carrying out its functions; or

(c) for the purposes of any provision having effect by virtue of so much of section 167 above and Schedule 11 to this Act as relates to the granting of authority for discharges of water.

(4) A consent given for the purposes of subsection (2) above may be given on such financial and other conditions as the appropriate authority giving the consent may consider appropriate.

(5) In this section—

"the appropriate authority" has the same meaning as in section 293 of the Town and Country Planning Act 1990; and

1990 c. 8.

"Crown or Duchy interest" means an interest belonging to Her Majesty in right of the Crown or of the Duchy of Lancaster, or to the Duchy of Cornwall, or belonging to a government department or held in trust for Her Majesty for the purposes of a government department;

and the provisions of subsection (3) of that section 293 as to the determination of questions shall apply for the purposes of this section.

**222.**—(1) Subject to the provisions of any order under this section, nothing in this Act shall require or authorise any function, duty or power to be carried out, performed or exercised in relation to the Isles of Scilly by the NRA or any relevant undertaker; and references in the preceding provisions of this Act to England and Wales shall not include references to those Isles.

(2) The Secretary of State may, on the application of the Council of the Isles of Scilly, by order make provision with respect to the carrying out in those Isles of functions falling under this Act to be carried out in relation to other parts of England and Wales by the NRA or by a relevant undertaker.

(3) Without prejudice to the generality of the power conferred by subsection (2) above, an order under this section may apply any provision of this Act, of the Water Consolidation (Consequential Provisions) Act 1991 or of the Water Act 1989 in relation to the Isles of Scilly with or without modifications.

(4) The power of the Secretary of State to make an order under this section shall be exercisable by statutory instrument subject to annulment in pursuance of a resolution of either House of Parliament.

(5) An order under this section may—

(a) make different provision for different cases, including different provision in relation to different persons, circumstances or localities; and

(b) contain such supplemental, consequential and transitional provision as the Secretary of State considers appropriate, including provision saving provision repealed by or under any enactment.

(6) Chapter IV of Part III of this Act, except section 90, shall apply to the Isles of Scilly as if the Council of the Isles of Scilly were a water undertaker and the Isles were the area of the undertaker.

(7) The exception of section 90 above from the provisions of subsection (6) above shall be without prejudice to the power to make provision by an order under this section in relation to that section.

**223.**—(1) This Act may be cited as the Water Industry Act 1991.

(2) This Act shall come into force on 1st December 1991.

(3) Except for the purpose of giving effect to any scheme under Schedule 2 to this Act, this Act extends to England and Wales only.

# SCHEDULES

### THE DIRECTOR GENERAL OF WATER SERVICES

*Remuneration, pensions etc.*

1.—(1) There shall be paid to the Director such remuneration, and such travelling and other allowances, as the Secretary of State may determine.

(2) In the case of any such holder of the office of the Director as may be determined by the Secretary of State, there shall be paid such pension, allowances or gratuities to or in respect of him, or such payments towards provision for the payment of a pension, allowances or gratuities to or in respect of him, as may be so determined.

(3) If, when any person ceases to hold office as the Director, the Secretary of State determines that there are special circumstances which make it right that he should receive compensation, there may be paid to him a sum by way of compensation of such amount as may be determined by the Secretary of State.

(4) The approval of the Treasury shall be required for the making of a determination under this paragraph.

*Staff*

2.—(1) The Director may, with the approval of the Treasury as to numbers and terms and conditions of service, appoint such staff as he may determine.

(2) Anything authorised or required by or under any enactment to be done by the Director may be done by any member of the staff of the Director who has been authorised for the purpose, whether generally or specially, by the Director.

*Expenses of the Director and his staff*

3. There shall be paid out of money provided by Parliament—

    (a) the remuneration of, and any travelling or other allowances payable under this Act to, the Director and any staff of the Director; and

    (b) any expenses duly incurred by the Director or by any of his staff in consequence of the provisions of this Act.

*Official seal*

4. The Director shall have an official seal for the authentication of documents required for the purposes of his functions.

*Documentary evidence*

5. The Documentary Evidence Act 1868 shall have effect as if the Director were included in the first column of the Schedule to that Act, as if the Director and any person authorised to act on behalf of the Director were mentioned in the second column of that Schedule, and as if the regulations referred to in that Act included any document issued by the Director or by any such person.     1868 c. 37.

## SCHEDULE 2

TRANSITIONAL PROVISION ON TERMINATION OF APPOINTMENTS

*Cases where Schedule applies*

1.—(1) This Schedule shall apply in each of the cases specified in sub-paragraphs (2) and (3) below.

(2) The first case in which this Schedule applies is where—

(a) the Secretary of State or the Director is proposing to make an appointment or variation replacing a company as a relevant undertaker; and

(b) by virtue of that appointment a company ("the new appointee") will hold an appointment as the water undertaker or sewerage undertaker for an area which is or includes the whole or any part of the area for which, until the relevant date, another company ("the existing appointee") holds an appointment as the water undertaker or, as the case may be, sewerage undertaker.

(3) The second case in which this Schedule applies is where—

(a) the High Court has made a special administration order in relation to any company ("the existing appointee"); and

(b) it is proposed that on and after the relevant date another company ("the new appointee") should, without any such appointment or variation as is mentioned in sub-paragraph (2) above having been made, hold an appointment as water undertaker or sewerage undertaker for an area which is or includes the whole or any part of the area for which until that date the existing appointee holds an appointment as water undertaker or, as the case may be, sewerage undertaker.

(4) In this Schedule—

"existing appointee" and "new appointee" shall be construed in accordance with sub-paragraph (2) or (3) above according to whether this Schedule is applying in the case mentioned in the first or second of those sub-paragraphs;

"other appointees" means any companies, other than the existing appointee and the new appointee, which are likely on or at a time after the relevant date to be holding appointments as water undertakers or sewerage undertakers for any area which is or includes any part of the area for which the existing appointee has at any time held an appointment as water undertaker or sewerage undertaker;

"the relevant date" means—

(a) where this Schedule applies by virtue of sub-paragraph (2) above, the coming into force of the appointment or variation mentioned in paragraph (a) of that sub-paragraph; and

(b) where this Schedule applies by virtue of sub-paragraph (3) above, such day, being a day before the discharge of the special administration order takes effect, as the High Court may appoint for the purposes of this Schedule; and

"special administrator", in relation to a company in relation to which a special administration order has been made, means the person for the time being holding office for the purposes of section 23(1) of this Act.

*Making and modification of transfer schemes*

2.—(1) The existing appointee, acting with the consent of the new appointee and, in relation to the matters affecting them, of any other appointees, may make a scheme under this Schedule for the transfer of property, rights and liabilities from the existing appointee to the new appointee.

(2) A scheme under this Schedule shall not take effect unless it is approved by the Secretary of State or the Director.

(3) Where a scheme under this Schedule is submitted to the Secretary of State or the Director for his approval, he may, with the consent of the new appointee, of the existing appointee and, in relation to the matters affecting them, of any other appointees, modify the scheme before approving it.

(4) If at any time after a scheme under this Schedule has come into force in relation to the property, rights and liabilities of any company the Secretary of State considers it appropriate to do so and the existing appointee, the new appointee and, in relation to the provisions of the order which affect them, any other appointees consent to the making of the order, the Secretary of State may by order provide that that scheme shall for all purposes be deemed to have come into force with such modifications as may be specified in the order.

(5) An order under sub-paragraph (4) above may make, with effect from the coming into force of the scheme to which it relates, any such provision as could have been made by the scheme and, in connection with giving effect to that provision from that time, may contain such supplemental, consequential and transitional provision as the Secretary of State considers appropriate.

(6) In determining, in accordance with his duties under Part I of this Act, whether and in what manner to exercise any power conferred on him by this paragraph the Secretary of State or the Director shall have regard to the need to ensure that any provision for the transfer of property, rights and liabilities in accordance with a scheme under this Schedule allocates property, rights and liabilities to the different companies affected by the scheme in such proportions as appear to him to be appropriate in the context of the different functions which will, by virtue of this Act, be carried out at different times on and after the relevant date by the new appointee, by the existing appointee and by any other appointees.

(7) It shall be the duty of the new appointee, of the existing appointee and of any other appointees to provide the Secretary of State or the Director with all such information and other assistance as he may reasonably require for the purposes of, or in connection with, the exercise of any power conferred on him by this paragraph.

(8) A company which without reasonable excuse fails to do anything required of it by virtue of sub-paragraph (7) above shall be guilty of an offence and liable, on summary conviction, to a fine not exceeding level 5 on the standard scale.

(9) Without prejudice to the other provisions of this Act relating to the special administrator of a company, anything which is required by this paragraph to be done by a company shall, where that company is a company in relation to which a special administration order is in force, be effective only if it is done on the company's behalf by its special administrator.

*Transfers by scheme*

3.—(1) A scheme under this Schedule for the transfer of the existing appointee's property, rights and liabilities shall come into force on the relevant date and, on coming into force, shall have effect, in accordance with its provisions and without further assurance, so as to transfer the property, rights and liabilities to which the scheme relates to the new appointee.

(2) For the purpose of making any division of property, rights or liabilities which it is considered appropriate to make in connection with the transfer of property, rights and liabilities in accordance with a scheme under this Schedule, the provisions of that scheme may—

(a) create for the existing appointee, the new appointee or any other appointees an interest in or right over any property to which the scheme relates;

(b) create new rights and liabilities as between any two or more of those companies; and

(c) in connection with any provision made by virtue of paragraph (a) or (b) above, make incidental provision as to the interests, rights and liabilities of other persons with respect to the subject-matter of the scheme.

(3) A scheme under this Schedule may contain provision for the consideration to be provided by the new appointee and by any other appointees in respect of the transfer or creation of property, rights and liabilities by means of the scheme; and any such provision shall be enforceable in the same way as if the property, rights and liabilities had been created or transferred, and (if the case so requires) had been capable of being created or transferred, by agreement between the parties.

(4) The property, rights and liabilities of the existing appointee that shall be capable of being transferred in accordance with a scheme under this Schedule shall include—

(a) property, rights and liabilities that would not otherwise be capable of being transferred or assigned by the existing appointee;

(b) such property, rights and liabilities to which the existing appointee may become entitled or subject after the making of the scheme and before the relevant date as may be described in the scheme;

(c) property situated anywhere in the United Kingdom or elsewhere;

(d) rights and liabilities under enactments;

(e) rights and liabilities under the law of any part of the United Kingdom or of any country or territory outside the United Kingdom.

(5) The provision that may be made by virtue of sub-paragraph (2)(b) above includes—

(a) provision for treating any person who is entitled by virtue of a scheme under this Schedule to possession of a document as having given another person an acknowledgement in writing of the right of that other person to the production of the document and to delivery of copies thereof; and

1925 c. 20.     (b) provision applying section 64 of the Law of Property Act 1925 (production and safe custody of documents) in relation to any case in relation to which provision falling within paragraph (a) above has effect.

(6) For the avoidance of doubt, it is hereby declared that the transfers authorised by paragraph (a) of sub-paragraph (4) above include transfers which, by virtue of that paragraph, are to take effect as if there were no such contravention, liability or interference with any interest or right as there would be, in the case of a transfer or assignment otherwise than in accordance with a scheme under this Schedule, by reason of any provision having effect (whether under any enactment or agreement or otherwise) in relation to the terms on which the existing appointee is entitled or subject to the property, right or liability in question.

*Transfer of appointment*

4.—(1) Where a scheme under this Schedule is made in the case specified in paragraph 1(3) above, the scheme may provide for the transfer to the new appointee, with such modifications as may be specified in the scheme, of the appointment under Chapter I of Part II of this Act which is held by the existing appointee.

(2) In such a case different schemes under this Schedule may provide for the transfer of such an appointment to different companies as respects different parts of the area to which the appointment relates.

*Supplemental provisions of schemes*

5.—(1) A scheme under this Schedule may contain supplemental, consequential and transitional provision for the purposes of, or in connection with, the provision for the transfers or any other provision made by the scheme.

(2) Without prejudice to the generality of sub-paragraph (1) above, a scheme under this Schedule may provide—

    (a) that for purposes connected with any transfers made in accordance with the scheme (including the transfer of rights and liabilities under an enactment) the new appointee is to be treated as the same person in law as the existing appointee;

    (b) that, so far as may be necessary for the purposes of or in connection with any such transfers, agreements made, transactions effected and other things done by or in relation to the existing appointee are to be treated as made, effected or done by or in relation to the new appointee;

    (c) that, so far as may be necessary for the purposes of or in connection with any such transfers, references in any agreement (whether or not in writing) or in any deed, bond, instrument or other document to, or to any officer of, the existing appointee are to have effect with such modifications as are specified in the scheme;

    (d) that proceedings commenced by or against the existing appointee are to be continued by or against the new appointee;

    (e) that the effect of any transfer under the scheme in relation to contracts of employment with the existing appointee is not to be to terminate any of those contracts but is to be that periods of employment with the existing appointee are to count for all purposes as periods of employment with the new appointee;

    (f) that disputes as to the effect of the scheme between the existing appointee and the new appointee, between either of them and any other appointee or between different companies which are other appointees are to be referred to such arbitration as may be specified in or determined under the scheme;

    (g) that determinations on such arbitrations and certificates given jointly by two or more such appointees as are mentioned in paragraph (f) above as to the effect of the scheme as between the companies giving the certificates are to be conclusive for all purposes.

*Duties of existing appointee after the scheme comes into force*

6.—(1) A scheme under this Schedule may provide for the imposition of duties on the existing appointee and on the new appointee to take all such steps as may be requisite to secure that the vesting in the new appointee, by virtue of the scheme, of any foreign property, right or liability is effective under the relevant foreign law.

(2) The provisions of a scheme under this Schedule may require the existing appointee to comply with any directions of the new appointee in performing any duty imposed on the existing appointee by virtue of a provision included in the scheme under sub-paragraph (1) above.

(3) A scheme under this Schedule may provide that, until the vesting of any foreign property, right or liability of the existing appointee in the new appointee is effective under the relevant foreign law, it shall be the duty of the existing appointee to hold that property or right for the benefit of, or to discharge that liability on behalf of, the new appointee.

(4) Nothing in any provision included by virtue of this paragraph in a scheme under this Schedule shall be taken as prejudicing the effect under the law of any part of the United Kingdom of the vesting by virtue of the scheme in the new appointee of any foreign property, right or liability.

SCH. 2    (5) A scheme under this Schedule may provide that, in specified cases, foreign property, rights or liabilities that are acquired or incurred by an existing appointee after the scheme comes into force are immediately to become property, rights or liabilities of the new appointee; and such a scheme may make the same provision in relation to any such property, rights or liabilities as can be made, by virtue of the preceding provisions of this paragraph, in relation to foreign property, rights and liabilities vested in the existing appointee when the scheme comes into force.

(6) References in this paragraph to any foreign property, right or liability are references to any property, right or liability as respects which any issue arising in any proceedings would have to be determined (in accordance with the rules of private international law) by reference to the law of a country or territory outside the United Kingdom.

(7) Any expenses incurred by an existing appointee in consequence of any provision included by virtue of this paragraph in a scheme under this Schedule shall be met by the new appointee.

(8) Duties imposed on a company by virtue of this paragraph shall be enforceable in the same way as if they were imposed by a contract between the existing appointee and the new appointee.

*Further transitional provision and local statutory provisions*

7.—(1) The Secretary of State may, if he thinks it appropriate to do so for the purposes of, or in connection with, any appointment or variation replacing a company as a relevant undertaker or any scheme under this Schedule, by order made by statutory instrument—

1989 c. 15.

(a) make any provision which corresponds, in relation to any enactment referred to at the passing of the Water Act 1989 in Schedule 26 to that Act, to any provision originally made by that Schedule or makes similar provision in relation to any other enactment; or

(b) amend or repeal any local statutory provision.

(2) An order under this paragraph may—

(a) make provision applying generally in relation to local statutory provisions of a description specified in the order;

(b) make different provision for different cases, including different provision in relation to different persons, circumstances or localities; and

(c) contain such supplemental, consequential and transitional provision as the Secretary of State considers appropriate.

Section 23.

SCHEDULE 3

SPECIAL ADMINISTRATION ORDERS

PART I

MODIFICATIONS OF THE 1986 ACT

*General application of provisions of 1986 Act*

1. Where a special administration order has been made, sections 11 to 15, 17 to 23 and 27 of the 1986 Act (which relate to administration orders under Part II of that Act) shall apply, with the modifications specified in the following provisions of this Part of this Schedule—

(a) as if references in those sections to an administration order were references to a special administration order and references to an administrator were references to a special administrator; and

(b) where the company in relation to which the order has been made is a statutory water company that is not a limited company, as if references to a company included references to such a company.

### *Effect of order*

2. In section 11 of the 1986 Act (effect of order), as applied by this Part of this Schedule—

   (a) the requirement in subsection (1)(a) that any petition for the winding up of the company shall be dismissed shall be without prejudice to the special administration order in a case where the order is made by virtue of section 25 of this Act;

   (b) the references in subsections (1)(b), (3)(b) and (4) to an administrative receiver, in relation to a statutory water company that is not a limited company, shall include references to any receiver whose functions in relation to that company correspond to those of an administrative receiver in relation to a limited company; and

   (c) the reference in subsection (3)(d) to proceedings shall include a reference to any proceedings under or for the purposes of section 18 of this Act.

### *Appointment of special administrator*

3. In section 13 of the 1986 Act (appointment of administrator), as applied by this Part of this Schedule, for subsection (3) there shall be substituted the following subsection—

   "(3) An application for an order under subsection (2) may be made—

   (a) by the Secretary of State;

   (b) with the consent of the Secretary of State, by the Director General of Water Services;

   (c) by any continuing special administrator of the company or, where there is no such special administrator, by the company, the directors or any creditor or creditors of the company."

### *General powers of special administrator*

4. In section 14 of the 1986 Act (general powers of administrator), as applied by this Part of this Schedule—

   (a) in subsection (1)(b), the reference to the powers specified in Schedule 1 to that Act shall be deemed to include a reference to a power to act on behalf of the company for the purposes of this Act, any local statutory provision or the exercise or performance of any power or duty which is conferred or imposed on the company by virtue of its holding an appointment under Chapter I of Part II of this Act; and

   (b) in subsection (4), the reference to a power conferred by the company's memorandum or articles of association shall be deemed to include a reference to a power conferred by a local statutory provision or by virtue of the company's holding such an appointment.

### *Power to deal with charged property*

5.—(1) Section 15 of the 1986 Act (power to deal with charged property), as applied by this Part of this Schedule, shall have effect as follows.

(2) In subsection (5)(b) (amount to be paid to chargeholder not to be less than open market value), for the words "in the open market by a willing vendor" there shall be substituted the words "for the best price which is reasonably available on a sale which is consistent with the purposes of the special administration order".

(3) Subsections (7) and (8) (notice to registrar) shall not apply where the company in relation to which the special administration order is made is a statutory water company that is not a limited company.

#### Duties of special administrator

6.—(1) Section 17 of the 1986 Act (duties of administrator), as applied by this Part of this Schedule, shall have effect as follows.

(2) For subsection (2) there shall be substituted the following subsection—

"(2) Subject to any directions of the court, it shall be the duty of the special administrator to manage the affairs, business and property of the company in accordance with proposals, as for the time being revised under section 23, which have been prepared for the purposes of that section by him or any predecessor of his."

(3) In subsection (3), paragraph (a) (right of creditors to require the holding of a creditors' meeting) shall be omitted.

#### Discharge of order

7.—(1) Section 18 of the 1986 Act (discharge and variation of administration order), as applied by this Part of this Schedule, shall have effect as follows.

(2) For subsections (1) and (2) there shall be substituted the following subsection—

"(1) An application for a special administration order to be discharged may be made—

(a) by the special administrator, on the ground that the purposes of the order have been achieved; or

(b) by the Secretary of State or, with the consent of the Secretary of State, the Director General of Water Services, on the ground that it is no longer necessary that those purposes are achieved."

(3) In subsection (3), the words "or vary" shall be omitted.

(4) In subsection (4), the words "or varied" and "or variation" shall be omitted and for the words "to the registrar of companies" there shall be substituted—

(a) where the company in relation to which the special administration order is made is a statutory water company that is not a limited company, the words "to the Director General of Water Services"; and

(b) in any other case, the words "to the registrar of companies and to the Director General of Water Services".

#### Notice of making of order

8. In section 21(2) of the 1986 Act (notice of order to be given by administrator), as applied by this Part of this Schedule, for the words "to the registrar of companies" there shall be substituted—

(a) where the company in relation to which the special administration order is made is a statutory water company that is not a limited company, the words "to the Director General of Water Services"; and

(b) in any other case, the words "to the registrar of companies, to the Director General of Water Services".

*Statement of proposals*

9. In section 23 of the 1986 Act (statement of proposals), as applied by this Part of this Schedule, for subsections (1) and (2) there shall be substituted the following subsections—

"(1) Where a special administration order has been made, the special administrator shall, within 3 months (or such longer period as the court may allow) after the making of the order, send a statement of his proposals for achieving the purposes of the order—

(a) to the Secretary of State and to the Director General of Water Services;

(b) so far as he is aware of their addresses, to all creditors of the company; and

(c) except where the company in relation to which the special administration order is made is a statutory water company that is not a limited company, to the registrar of companies;

and may from time to time revise those proposals.

(2) If at any time—

(a) the special administrator proposes to make revisions of the proposals for achieving the purposes of the special administration order; and

(b) those revisions appear to him to be substantial,

the special administrator shall, before making those revisions, send a statement of the proposed revisions to the Secretary of State, to the Director General of Water Services, (so far as he is aware of their addresses) to all creditors of the company and, except where the company in relation to which the special administration order is made is a statutory water company that is not a limited company, to the registrar of companies.

(2A) Where the special administrator is required by subsection (1) or (2) to send any person a statement before the end of any period or before making any revision of any proposals, he shall also, before the end of that period or, as the case may be, before making those revisions either—

(a) send a copy of the statement (so far as he is aware of their addresses) to all members of the company; or

(b) publish in the prescribed manner a notice stating an address to which members should write for copies of the statement to be sent to them free of charge."

*Applications to court*

10.—(1) Section 27 of the 1986 Act (protection of interests of creditors and members), as applied by this Part of this Schedule, shall have effect as follows.

(2) After subsection (1) there shall be inserted the following subsection—

"(1A) At any time when a special administration order is in force the Secretary of State or, with the consent of the Secretary of State, the Director General of Water Services may apply to the High Court by petition for an order under this section on the ground that the special administrator has exercised or is exercising, or proposing to exercise, his powers in relation to the company in a manner which—

(a) will not best ensure the achievement of the purposes of the order; or

SCH. 3

(b) without prejudice to paragraph (a) above, involves either a contravention of the conditions of the company's appointment under Chapter I of Part II of the Water Industry Act 1991 or of any statutory or other requirement imposed on the company in consequence of that appointment."

(3) In subsection (3) (order not to prejudice or prevent voluntary arrangements or administrator's proposals), for paragraphs (a) and (b) there shall be substituted the words "the achievement of the purposes of the order".

(4) Subsections (4)(d) and (6) (power of court to order discharge) shall be omitted.

## PART II

### SUPPLEMENTAL

#### *General adaptations and saving*

11.—(1) Subject to the preceding provisions of this Schedule, references in the 1986 Act (except in sections 8 to 10 and 24 to 26), or in any other enactment passed before 6th July 1989, to an administration order under Part II of that Act, to an application for such an order and to an administrator shall include references, respectively, to a special administration order, to an application for a special administration order and to a special administrator.

(2) Subject as aforesaid and to sub-paragraph (3) below, references in the 1986 Act, or in any other enactment passed before 6th July 1989, to an enactment contained in Part II of that Act shall include references to that enactment as applied by section 24 of this Act or Part I of this Schedule.

(3) Sub-paragraphs (1) and (2) above shall apply in relation to a reference in an enactment contained in Part II of the 1986 Act only so far as necessary for the purposes of the operation of the provisions of that Part as so applied.

(4) The provisions of this Schedule shall be without prejudice to the power conferred by section 411 of the 1986 Act (company insolvency rules), as modified by sub-paragraphs (1) and (2) above.

#### *Interpretation*

1986 c. 45.

12.—(1) In this Schedule "the 1986 Act" means the Insolvency Act 1986.

(2) In this Schedule, and in any modification of the 1986 Act made by this Schedule, "special administrator", in relation to a special administration order, means any person appointed in relation to that order for the purposes of section 23(1) of this Act; and in any such modification "special administration order" has the same meaning as in this Act.

Section 28.

## SCHEDULE 4

### CUSTOMER SERVICE COMMITTEES

#### *Sub-committees*

1. A customer service committee may, with the approval of the Director —

(a) establish local and other sub-committees through which the customer service committee may carry out such of its functions as it may determine;

(b) appoint such persons as it may determine (including persons who are not members of the committee) to be members of any such sub-committee; and

(c) regulate the procedure of any such sub-committee and, subject to paragraph 3 below, the terms and conditions of service of any person appointed to be a member of any such sub-committee.

*Remuneration, pensions etc. of the chairman of a customer service committee*

2.—(1) There shall be paid to the chairman of a customer service committee such remuneration, and such travelling and other allowances, as the Director may determine.

(2) There shall be paid—

(a) such pension, allowances or gratuities to or in respect of a person who has held or holds office as the chairman of a customer service committee; or

(b) such payments towards provision for the payment of a pension, allowances or gratuities to or in respect of such a person,

as may be determined by the Director.

(3) If, when any person ceases to hold office as such a chairman, the Director determines that there are special circumstances which make it right that that person should receive compensation, there may be paid to him a sum by way of compensation of such amount as may be determined by the Director.

(4) The approval of the Treasury shall be required for the making of a determination under this paragraph.

*Expenses of other members of a customer service committee etc.*

3. Subject to paragraph 2 above, neither the members of a customer service committee nor the members of any sub-committee of any such committee shall be paid any sums by the Director for or in respect of their services except—

(a) in the case of services as a member of a customer service committee, sums reimbursing the member for loss of remuneration, for travelling expenses or for any other out-of-pocket expenses; and

(b) in the case of services as a member of a sub-committee of a customer service committee, sums reimbursing the member for travelling expenses or for any other out-of-pocket expenses which do not relate to loss of remuneration.

*Staff*

4.—(1) The Director may, with the approval of the Treasury as to numbers and terms and conditions of service, appoint such officers and employees of a customer service committee or of any sub-committee of a customer service committee as he may determine.

(2) Anything authorised or required by or under this Act to be done by a customer service committee may be done by any of the officers or employees of the committee, or of any of its sub-committees, who has been authorised for the purpose, whether generally or specially, by the committee or, in accordance with the terms of its appointment, by a sub-committee of the committee.

*Financial provisions*

5.—(1) The following shall be paid by the Director out of money provided by Parliament, that is to say—

(a) any sums required to be paid to or in respect of any person under paragraph 2 or 3 above; and

(b) any expenses incurred by a customer service committee in accordance with any statement approved under sub-paragraph (3) below.

SCH. 4    (2) A customer service committee shall prepare in respect of each financial year a statement of the expenses which it expects to incur in respect of that year—

(a) in relation to officers and employees of the committee and its sub-committees; or

(b) otherwise for the purposes of, or in connection with, the carrying out of its functions;

and that statement shall be sent to the Director, in the case of the statement in respect of the financial year current at the establishment of the committee, as soon as practicable after the establishment of the committee and, in any other case, before the beginning of the financial year to which the statement relates.

(3) The Director shall consider any statement sent to him under sub-paragraph (2) above and shall either approve the statement or approve it with such modifications as he considers appropriate.

Section 65.

## SCHEDULE 5

PROCEDURE FOR ORDERS RELATING TO PRESSURE AND CONSTANCY OF SUPPLY

*Applications for orders*

1.—(1) Where the Director or a water undertaker applies to the Secretary of State for an order under section 65(5) of this Act, the applicant shall—

(a) submit to the Secretary of State a draft of the order applied for;

(b) publish a notice with respect to the application, at least once in each of two successive weeks, in one or more newspapers circulating in the locality which would be affected by the provision proposed to be made by the order;

(c) not later than the date on which that notice is first published serve a copy of the notice on every affected local authority and every affected water undertaker; and

(d) publish a notice in the London Gazette which-

(i) states that the draft order has been submitted to the Secretary of State;

(ii) names every local authority on whom a notice is required to be served under this paragraph;

(iii) specifies a place where a copy of the draft order and of any relevant map or plan may be inspected; and

(iv) gives the name of every newspaper in which the notice required by virtue of paragraph (b) above was published and the date of an issue containing the notice.

(2) The notice required by virtue of sub-paragraph (1)(b) above to be published with respect to an application for an order shall—

(a) state the general effect of the order applied for;

(b) specify a place where a copy of the draft order and of any relevant map or plan may be inspected by any person free of charge at all reasonable times during the period of twenty-eight days beginning with the date of the first publication of the notice; and

(c) state that any person may, within that period, by notice to the Secretary of State object to the making of the order.

(3) For the purposes of subsection (1)(c) above a local authority or a water undertaker which is not the applicant shall be affected by an application for an order if its area includes the whole or any part of the locality which would be affected by the provision proposed to be made by the order.

*Supply of copies of draft orders*

2. The applicant for an order under section 65(5) of this Act shall, at the request of any person and on payment by that person of such charge (if any) as the applicant may reasonably require, furnish that person with a copy of the draft order submitted to the Secretary of State under paragraph 1 above.

*Modifications of proposals*

3.—(1) On an application for an order under section 65(5) of this Act, the Secretary of State may make the order either in the terms of the draft order submitted to him or, subject to sub-paragraph (2) below, in those terms as modified in such manner as he thinks fit, or may refuse to make an order.

(2) The Secretary of State shall not make such a modification of a draft order submitted to him as he considers is likely adversely to affect any persons unless he is satisfied that the applicant for the order has given and published such additional notices, in such manner, as the Secretary of State may have required.

*Consideration of objections etc.*

4. Where an application for an order to which this Schedule applies has been made, the Secretary of State may, if he considers it appropriate to do so, hold a local inquiry before making any order on the application.

SCHEDULE 6

SUPPLEMENTAL PROVISIONS RELATING TO RIGHTS OF ENTRY

Sections 71 to 84 & 162 to 172.

PART I

RIGHTS REQUIRING NOTICE FOR ENTRY TO NON-BUSINESS PREMISES

*Notice of entry*

1.—(1) Where this Part of this Schedule applies to any right of entry conferred by a provision of this Act, admission to any premises which are not business premises shall not be demanded as of right by virtue of that provision, unless twenty-four hours notice of the intended entry has been given to the occupier of the premises.

(2) In this paragraph "business premises" means—

(a) any factory; or

(b) any place in which persons are employed otherwise than in domestic service;

and in this sub-paragraph "factory" has the same meaning as in the Factories Act 1961.

1961 c. 34.

*Warrants to exercise right*

2.—(1) Subject to sub-paragraph (3) below, if it is shown to the satisfaction of a justice of the peace, on sworn information in writing—

(a) that any one or more of the conditions specified in sub-paragraph (2) below is fulfilled in relation to any premises which a person is entitled to enter by virtue of a right of entry to which this Part of this Schedule applies; and

(b) that there is reasonable ground for entry to the premises for any purpose for which the right is exercisable,

the justice may by a warrant under his hand authorise that person to enter the premises, if need be by force.

(2) The conditions mentioned in sub-paragraph (1) above are—

(a) that admission to the premises has been refused to the person having the right to enter them;

(b) that such refusal is apprehended;

(c) that the premises are unoccupied or the occupier is temporarily absent;

(d) that the case is one of urgency;

(e) that an application for admission would defeat the object of the entry.

(3) A warrant under this Part of this Schedule shall not be issued by a justice of the peace in a case in which he is satisfied that the condition mentioned in paragraph (a) or (b) of sub-paragraph (2) above is fulfilled unless he is also satisfied—

(a) that notice of the intention to apply for a warrant has been given to the occupier;

(b) that a condition mentioned in either of paragraphs (c) and (d) of that sub-paragraph is also fulfilled in relation to the premises; or

(c) that the giving of such notice as is mentioned in paragraph (a) above would defeat the object of the entry.

(4) Every warrant under this Part of this Schedule shall continue in force until the purpose for which the entry is necessary has been fulfilled.

(5) A person leaving any unoccupied premises which he has entered by virtue of a warrant under this Part of this Schedule shall leave them as effectually secured against trespassers as he found them.

### Supplementary power of person making entry

3. Any person entitled to enter any premises by virtue of a right to which this Part of this Schedule applies, or of a warrant under this Part of this Schedule, may take with him such other persons as may be necessary.

### Obstruction of person exercising right

4. Any person who wilfully obstructs any person upon whom a right of entry has been conferred by virtue of—

(a) any provision of this Act relating to a right of entry to which this Part of this Schedule applies; or

(b) a warrant under this Part of this Schedule,

shall be guilty of an offence and liable, on summary conviction, to a fine not exceeding level 1 on the standard scale.

### Duty of persons exercising rights to maintain confidentiality

5.—(1) Without prejudice to section 206 of this Act and subject to sub-paragraphs (2) and (3) below, any person who is admitted to any premises in compliance—

(a) with any provision of this Act relating to a right of entry to which this Part of this Schedule applies; or

(b) with a warrant under this Part of this Schedule,

shall be guilty of an offence under this paragraph if he discloses to any person any information obtained by him there with regard to any manufacturing process or trade secret.

(2) A person shall not be guilty of an offence under this paragraph in respect of any disclosure made in the performance of his duty.

(3) For the purposes of the application of this Part of this Schedule to the right ScH. 6 conferred by section 171 of this Act, the reference to premises in subsection (1) above shall have effect as a reference only to business premises, within the meaning of paragraph 1 above.

(4) A person who is guilty of an offence under this paragraph, other than such a person as is mentioned in sub-paragraph (5) below, shall be liable—

    (a) on summary conviction, to imprisonment for a term not exceeding three months or to a fine not exceeding the statutory maximum or to both;

    (b) on conviction on indictment, to imprisonment for a term not exceeding three months or to a fine or to both.

(5) A person who is guilty of an offence under this paragraph by virtue of the application of this Part of this Schedule to the rights conferred by section 171 of this Act shall be liable, on summary conviction, to imprisonment for a term not exceeding three months or to a fine not exceeding level 3 on the standard scale or to both.

## PART II

### OTHER RIGHTS OF ENTRY AND RELATED POWERS

#### *Notice of entry*

6.—(1) Without prejudice to any power exercisable by virtue of a warrant under this Part of this Schedule, no person shall make an entry into any premises by virtue of any right or power to which this Part of this Schedule applies except—

    (a) in an emergency; or

    (b) at a reasonable time and after the required notice of the intended entry has been given to the occupier of the premises.

(2) For the purposes of this paragraph the required notice is—

    (a) in the case of the rights and powers conferred by virtue of any of sections 74(4), 84(2) and (3), 86(4) and 170(1)(c) and (3) of this Act, twenty-four hours' notice; and

    (b) in any other case, seven days' notice.

(3) For the purposes of the application of this Part of this Schedule to any right or power conferred by section 168 of this Act the reference in sub-paragraph (1) above to an emergency—

    (a) in relation to any entry to premises for the purposes of, or for purposes connected with, the exercise or proposed exercise of any power in relation to a street, includes a reference to any circumstances requiring the carrying out of emergency works within the meaning of Part III of 1991 c. 22. the New Roads and Street Works Act 1991; and

    (b) in relation to any other entry to premises, includes a reference to any danger to property and to any interruption of a supply of water provided to any premises by any person and to any interruption of the provision of sewerage services to any premises.

(4) Until the coming into force of section 52 of the New Roads and Street Works Act 1991, sub-paragraph (3)(a) above shall have effect as if the reference to Part III of that Act were a reference to the Public Utilities Street Works Act 1950 c. 39. 1950; but nothing in this sub-paragraph shall be taken to prejudice the power of the Secretary of State under that Act of 1991 to make an order bringing that section 52 into force on different days for different purposes (including the purposes of this paragraph).

(5) For the purposes of the application of this Part of this Schedule to the rights and other powers conferred by section 172 of this Act sub-paragraph (1) above shall have effect as if the power in an emergency to make an entry to any premises otherwise than at a reasonable time and after the required notice were omitted.

### *Warrant to exercise right or power*

7.—(1) If it is shown to the satisfaction of a justice of the peace on sworn information in writing—

(a) that there are reasonable grounds for the exercise in relation to any premises of a right or power to which this Part of this Schedule applies; and

(b) that one or more of the conditions specified in sub-paragraph (2) below is fulfilled in relation to those premises,

the justice may by warrant authorise the relevant authority to designate a person who shall be authorised to exercise the right or power in relation to those premises in accordance with the warrant and, if need be, by force.

(2) The conditions mentioned in sub-paragraph (1)(b) above are—

(a) that the exercise of the right or power in relation to the premises has been refused;

(b) that such a refusal is reasonably apprehended;

(c) that the premises are unoccupied;

(d) that the occupier is temporarily absent from the premises;

(e) that the case is one of urgency; or

(f) that an application for admission to the premises would defeat the object of the proposed entry.

(3) A justice of the peace shall not issue a warrant under this Part of this Schedule by virtue only of being satisfied that the exercise of a right or power in relation to any premises has been refused, or that a refusal is reasonably apprehended, unless he is also satisfied—

(a) that notice of the intention to apply for the warrant has been given to the occupier of the premises; or

(b) that the giving of such a notice would defeat the object of the proposed entry.

(4) For the purposes of the application of this Part of this Schedule to the rights and powers conferred by section 169 of this Act in a case to which subsection (4) of that section applies, a justice of the peace shall not issue a warrant under this Part of this Schedule unless he is satisfied that the Secretary of State has given his authorisation for the purposes of that subsection in relation to that case.

(5) Every warrant under this Part of this Schedule shall continue in force until the purposes for which the warrant was issued have been fulfilled.

### *Manner of exercise of right or power*

8. A person designated as the person who may exercise any right or power to which this Part of this Schedule applies shall produce evidence of his designation and other authority before he exercises the right or power.

*Supplementary powers of person making entry etc.*

9. A person authorised to enter any premises by virtue of any right or power to which this Part of this Schedule applies shall be entitled, subject in the case of a right or power exercisable under a warrant to the terms of the warrant, to take with him on to the premises such other persons and such equipment as may be necessary.

*Duty to secure premises*

10. A person who enters any premises in the exercise of any right or power to which this Part of this Schedule applies shall leave the premises as effectually secured against trespassers as he found them.

*Compensation*

11.—(1) Where any person exercises any right or power to which this Part of this Schedule applies, it shall be the duty of the relevant authority to make full compensation to any person who has sustained loss or damage by reason of—

(a) the exercise by the designated person of that right or power or of any power to take any person or equipment with him when entering the premises in relation to which the right or power is exercised; or

(b) the performance of, or failure of the designated person to perform, the duty imposed by paragraph 10 above.

(2) Compensation shall not be payable by virtue of sub-paragraph (1) above in respect of any loss or damage if the loss or damage—

(a) is attributable to the default of the person who sustained it; or

(b) is loss or damage in respect of which compensation is payable by virtue of any other provision of this Act.

(3) Any dispute as to a person's entitlement to compensation under this paragraph or as to the amount of any such compensation, shall be referred to the arbitration of a single arbitrator appointed by agreement between the relevant authority and the person who claims to have sustained the loss or damage or, in default of agreement—

(a) by the President of the Lands Tribunal where the relevant authority is the Secretary of State; and

(b) by the Secretary of State, in any other case.

*Obstruction of person exercising right or power*

12. A person who intentionally obstructs another person acting in the exercise of any right or power to which this Part of this Schedule applies shall be guilty of an offence and liable, on summary conviction, to a fine not exceeding level 3 on the standard scale.

*Interpretation of Part II*

13.—(1) In this Part of this Schedule "relevant authority", in relation to a right or power to which this Part of this Schedule applies, means the person who, by virtue of—

(a) the provision by which the right or power is conferred; or

(b) (except in paragraph 7 above) the warrant,

is entitled to designate the person by whom the right or power may be exercised.

(2) References in this Part of this Schedule, except in paragraph 7 above, to a right or power to which this Part of this Schedule applies include references to a right or power exercisable by virtue of a warrant under this Part of this Schedule.

(3) For the purposes of paragraphs 10 and 11 above a person enters any premises by virtue of a right or power to which this Part of this Schedule applies notwithstanding that he has failed (whether by virtue of the waiver of the requirement by the occupier of the premises or otherwise) to comply with-

(a) any requirement to enter those premises at a reasonable time or after giving notice of his intended entry; or

(b) the requirement imposed by paragraph 8 above.

Section 91.

# SCHEDULE 7

### PRE-1985 FLUORIDATION SCHEMES

*Operation of pre-1985 schemes*

1.—(1) Where in pursuance of any such arrangements entered into by a water authority or statutory water company before 20th December 1984 as have effect immediately before the coming into force of this Act as arrangements entered into by a water undertaker—

(a) a scheme for increasing the fluoride content of water supplied by the authority or company in any part of England and Wales was in operation immediately before that date; or

(b) work had been begun by the authority or company before that date for enabling such a scheme to be brought into operation,

that water undertaker may, while the conditions mentioned in sub-paragraph (2) below are satisfied, operate the scheme.

(2) The conditions referred to in sub-paragraph (1) above are that the arrangements require—

(a) fluoridation to be effected only by the addition of one or more of the compounds of fluorine mentioned in subsection (4) of section 87 of this Act; and

(b) the concentrations of fluoride in the water supplied to consumers to be maintained, so far as reasonably practicable, at one milligram per litre.

*Supplies by other undertakers and revocation or variation of scheme*

2.—(1) Where a water undertaker is operating a fluoridation scheme by virtue of this Schedule—

(a) subsections (6) and (7) of section 87 of this Act shall apply in relation to the scheme as they apply in relation to any scheme operated in exercise of the power conferred by that section or section 1 of the Water (Fluoridation) Act 1985;

(b) the scheme shall cease to have effect upon the appropriate authority giving to the undertaker reasonable notice of the authority's desire to terminate it; and

(c) the arrangements under which the scheme is operated may be varied to take account of any amendment of section 87(2) of this Act which is made under section 88 of this Act.

1985 c. 63.

(2) In this paragraph "appropriate authority", in relation to a fluoridation scheme which is operated under this Schedule, means the Regional or District Health Authority to which the water undertaker concerned is answerable in accordance with the arrangements under which the scheme is operated.

*Publicity and consultation*

3.—(1) Section 89 of this Act (including the power of the Secretary of State under subsection (6) of that section to dispense with the other requirements of that section) shall apply where a District Health Authority propose to terminate a scheme which may be operated by virtue of this Schedule as it applies where such an authority propose to withdraw an application under section 87 of this Act.

(2) Accordingly, in subsection (7) of section 89 of this Act, the reference to the question whether an application under section 87 of this Act should be withdrawn shall be treated by virtue of sub-paragraph (1) above as a reference to whether a scheme should be terminated under this Schedule.

SCHEDULE 8

Section 140.

PRE-1989 ACT TRANSITIONAL AUTHORITY FOR TRADE EFFLUENT DISCHARGES ETC.

*Trade effluent agreements*

1. Nothing in Chapter III of Part IV of this Act (except so far as it relates to special category effluent) or in the repeals made by the Water Consolidation (Consequential Provisions) Act 1991 shall affect—

1991 c. 60.

   (a) any agreement with respect to any trade effluent to which a sewerage undertaker is a party by virtue of its having been duly made before 1st July 1937 between a predecessor of the undertaker and the owner or occupier of any trade premises; or

   (b) any agreement saved by section 63(8) of the Public Health Act 1961 (pre-1961 Act agreements with respect to discharges from premises used for farming or for scientific research or experiment).

1961 c. 64.

*Authorisations having effect as deemed consents under the Control of Pollution Act 1974*

2.—(1) Where, by virtue of section 43(2) of the Control of Pollution Act 1974 there is, immediately before the commencement of this Act, a deemed consent for the purposes of the Public Health (Drainage of Trade Premises) Act 1937 which has effect under the Water Act 1989 in relation to any sewerage undertaker, that deemed consent shall have effect as a deemed consent for the purposes of Chapter III of Part IV of this Act subject to the following provisions of this paragraph.

1974 c. 40.

1937 c. 40.
1989 c. 15.

(2) The sewerage undertaker—

   (a) may at any time; and

   (b) shall if requested to do so by any person entitled to make a discharge in pursuance of the deemed consent,

by notice served on the owner and any occupier of the premises in question cancel the deemed consent and, subject to sub-paragraph (3) below, give its actual consent for such discharges as were authorised by the deemed consent.

(3) An actual consent given under sub-paragraph (2) above shall be so given either conditionally or subject to any conditions which may be attached to consents by virtue of section 121 of this Act.

(4) It is hereby declared that the provisions of Chapter III of Part IV of this Act with respect to the variation of conditions of a consent apply in relation to an actual consent under sub-paragraph (2) above as they apply in relation to any other actual consent under Chapter III of Part IV of this Act.

(5) A notice signifying an actual consent under sub-paragraph (2) above shall indicate that a right of appeal is conferred under the following paragraph in respect of the notice.

### Appeals in respect of consents under paragraph 2

3.—(1) A person on whom notice is served in pursuance of paragraph 2(2) above may, in accordance with regulations made by the Secretary of State, appeal to the Director.

(2) Section 137 of this Act shall apply, with the necessary modifications, in relation to appeals under this paragraph as it applies in relation to appeals under section 122 of this Act.

(3) On an appeal under this paragraph the Director may give the sewerage undertaker in question any such direction as he thinks fit with respect to the notice and it shall be the duty of the undertaker to comply with the direction.

### Determinations of disputes as to transitional matters

4.—(1) Any dispute in so far as it—

(a) arises after the commencement of this Act and relates to a deemed consent in respect of discharges previously authorised under section 4 of the Public Health (Drainage of Trade Premises) Act 1937; and

(b) is a dispute as to the nature or composition of any trade effluent discharged from any trade premises into a sewer during any period, as to the quantity of trade effluent so discharged on any one day during any period or as to the rate of trade effluent so discharged during any period,

shall, unless the parties otherwise agree, be referred to the Director for determination.

1937 c. 40.

(2) On a reference under this paragraph the Director may make such order in the matter as he thinks just.

(3) An order on a reference under this paragraph shall be final; but section 137 of this Act shall apply, with the necessary modifications, in relation to references under this paragraph as it applies in relation to appeals under section 122 of this Act.

### Regulations as to residue of agreements

1974 c. 40.

5. The Secretary of State may by regulations make provisions in relation to the provisions of any agreement to which subsection (1) of section 43 of the Control of Pollution Act 1974 applied and which apart from that section would be in force after the commencement of this Act—

(a) for determining, by arbitration or otherwise, whether any such agreement continues to have effect as relating to a matter other than the discharge of trade effluent into a sewerage undertaker's sewer;

(b) for determining, by arbitration or otherwise, what modifications (if any) are appropriate in consequence of any prescribed provision of section 43 of that Act or any provision of this Schedule re-enacting any such provision; and

(c) in a case in which the conditions on which any discharges authorised by such an agreement included, immediately before the coming into force of section 43 of that Act, a condition as to charges in respect of the discharges and other matters—

(i) for determining, by arbitration or otherwise, the proportion of the charges attributable to the discharges; and

(ii) for limiting accordingly the conditions which are to be treated by virtue of section 43 of that Act as included in the deemed consent which has effect by virtue of this Schedule.

## SCHEDULE 9

### Mᴏᴅɪғɪᴄᴀᴛɪᴏɴ ᴏғ Cᴏᴍᴘᴇɴsᴀᴛɪᴏɴ Pʀᴏᴠɪsɪᴏɴs ᴇᴛᴄ. ɪɴ ʀᴇʟᴀᴛɪᴏɴ ᴛᴏ ᴛʜᴇ Cʀᴇᴀᴛɪᴏɴ ᴏғ Nᴇᴡ Rɪɢʜᴛs

*Compensation enactments*

1. Subject to the following provisions of this Schedule, the enactments for the time being in force with respect to compensation for the compulsory purchase of land shall apply with the necessary modifications as respects compensation in the case of a compulsory acquisition under section 155 of this Act of a right by the creation of a new right as they apply as respects compensation on the compulsory purchase of land and interests in land.

*Adaptation of the Compulsory Purchase Act 1965*

2.—(1) The Compulsory Purchase Act 1965 (in the following provisions of this Schedule referred to as "the 1965 Act") shall have effect with the modifications necessary to make it apply to the compulsory acquisition under section 155 of this Act of a right by the creation of a new right as it applies to the compulsory acquisition under that section of land, so that, in appropriate contexts, references in that Act to land are to be read (according to the requirements of the particular context) as referring to, or as including references to—

(a) the right acquired or to be acquired; or

(b) the land over which the right is or is to be exercisable.

(2) Without prejudice to the generality of sub-paragraph (1) above, Part I of the 1965 Act shall apply in relation to the compulsory acquisition under section 155 of this Act of a right by the creation of a new right with the modifications specified in the following provisions of this Schedule.

*Section 7 of the 1965 Act*

3. For section 7 of the 1965 Act (measure of compensation) there shall be substituted the following section—

"7. In assessing the compensation to be paid by the acquiring authority under this Act regard shall be had not only to the extent (if any) to which the value of the land over which the right is to be acquired is depreciated by the acquisition of the right but also to the damage (if any) to be sustained by the owner of the land by reason of its severance from other land of his, or injuriously affecting that other land by the exercise of the powers conferred by this or the special Act."

*Section 8 of the 1965 Act*

4. For subsection (1) of section 8 of the 1965 Act (protection for vendor against severance of house, garden, etc.) there shall be substituted the following subsections—

"(1) No person shall be required to grant any right over part only—

(a) of any house, building or manufactory; or

(b) of a park or garden belonging to a house,

if he is willing to sell the whole of the house, building, manufactory, park or garden, unless the Lands Tribunal determine that—

    (i) in the case of a house, building or manufactory, the part over which the right is proposed to be acquired can be made subject to that right without material detriment to the house, building or manufactory; or

    (ii) in the case of a park or garden, the part over which the right is proposed to be acquired can be made subject to that right without seriously affecting the amenity or convenience of the house;

and, if the Lands Tribunal so determine, the Tribunal shall award compensation in respect of any loss due to the acquisition of the right, in addition to its value; and thereupon the party interested shall be required to grant to the acquiring authority that right over the part of the house, building, manufactory, park or garden.

(1A) In considering the extent of any material detriment to a house, building or manufactory, or any extent to which the amenity or convenience of a house is affected, the Lands Tribunal shall have regard not only to the right which is to be acquired over the land, but also to any adjoining or adjacent land belonging to the same owner and subject to compulsory purchase."

### *Effect of deed poll*

5. The following provisions of the 1965 Act (being provisions stating the effect of a deed poll executed in various circumstances where there is no conveyance by persons with interests in the land), that is to say—

    (a) section 9(4) (refusal by owners to convey);

    (b) paragraph 10(3) of Schedule 1 (owners under incapacity);

    (c) paragraph 2(3) of Schedule 2 (absent and untraced owners); and

    (d) paragraphs 2(3) and 7(2) of Schedule 4 (common land),

shall be so modified as to secure that, as against persons with interests in the land which are expressed to be overridden by the deed, the right which is to be compulsorily acquired is vested absolutely in the acquiring authority.

### *Section 11 of the 1965 Act*

6. Section 11 of the 1965 Act (powers of entry) shall be so modified as to secure that, as from the date on which the acquiring authority have served notice to treat in respect of any right, they have power, exercisable in the like circumstances and subject to the like conditions, to enter for the purpose of exercising that right (which shall be deemed for this purpose to have been created on the date of service of the notice); and sections 12 (penalty for unauthorised entry) and 13 (entry on warrant in the event of obstruction) shall be modified correspondingly.

### *Section 20 of the 1965 Act*

7. Section 20 of the 1965 Act (protection for interests of tenants at will etc.) shall apply with the modifications necessary to secure that persons with such interests as are mentioned in that section are compensated in a manner corresponding to that in which they would be compensated on a compulsory acquisition under section 155 of this Act of that land, but taking into account only the extent (if any) of such interference with such an interest as is actually caused, or likely to be caused, by the exercise of the right in question.

*Section 22 of the 1965 Act*

8. Section 22 of the 1965 Act (protection of acquiring authority's possession where by inadvertence an estate, right or interest has not been got in) shall be so modified as to enable the acquiring authority, in circumstances corresponding to those referred to in that section, to continue entitled to exercise the right acquired, subject to compliance with that section as respects compensation.

## SCHEDULE 10

### PROCEDURE RELATING TO BYELAWS UNDER SECTION 157

*Confirmation of byelaws*

1.—(1) No byelaw made by a relevant undertaker under section 157 of this Act shall have effect until confirmed by the Secretary of State under this Schedule.

(2) At least one month before it applies for the confirmation of any such byelaw, a relevant undertaker shall—

    (a) cause a notice of its intention to make the application to be published in the London Gazette and in such other manner as it considers appropriate for the purpose of bringing the proposed byelaw to the attention of persons likely to be affected by it; and

    (b) cause copies of the notice to be served on any persons carrying out functions under any enactment who appear to it to be concerned.

(3) For at least one month before an application is made by a relevant undertaker for the confirmation of any such byelaw, a copy of it shall be deposited at one or more of the offices of the relevant undertaker, including (if there is one) at an office in the area to which the byelaw would apply.

(4) A relevant undertaker shall provide reasonable facilities for the inspection free of charge of a byelaw deposited under sub-paragraph (3) above.

(5) Every person shall be entitled, on application to a relevant undertaker, to be furnished free of charge with a printed copy of a byelaw so deposited.

*Confirmation with or without modifications*

2.—(1) The Secretary of State, with or without a local inquiry, may refuse to confirm any byelaw submitted to him by a relevant undertaker for confirmation under this Schedule, or may confirm the byelaw either without or, if the relevant undertaker consents, with modifications.

(2) The relevant undertaker which has so submitted a byelaw shall, if so directed by the Secretary of State, cause notice of any proposed modifications to be given in accordance with his directions.

*Commencement of byelaw*

3.—(1) The Secretary of State may fix the date on which any byelaw confirmed under this Schedule is to come into force.

(2) If no date is so fixed, the byelaw shall come into force at the end of the period of one month beginning with the date of confirmation.

*Availability of confirmed byelaws*

4.—(1) Every byelaw made by a relevant undertaker and confirmed under this Schedule shall be printed and deposited at one or more of the offices of the relevant undertaker, including (if there is one) at an office in the area to which the byelaw applies; and copies of the byelaw shall be available at those offices, at all reasonable times, for inspection by the public free of charge.

(2) Every person shall be entitled, on application to a relevant undertaker and on payment of such reasonable sum as the relevant undertaker may determine, to be furnished with a copy of any byelaw so deposited by that undertaker.

### Revocation of byelaws

1991 c. 60.

5. Without prejudice to subsection (5) of section 157 of this Act and subject to paragraph 4(4) of Schedule 2 to the Water Consolidation (Consequential Provisions) Act 1991, if it appears to the Secretary of State that the revocation of a byelaw under that section is necessary or expedient, he may, after—

(a) giving notice to the relevant undertaker which made the byelaw;

(b) considering any representations or objections made by that undertaker; and

(c) if required by that undertaker, holding a local inquiry,

revoke that byelaw.

### Proof of byelaws etc.

6. The production of a printed copy of a byelaw purporting to be made by a relevant undertaker upon which is indorsed a certificate, purporting to be signed on its behalf, stating—

(a) that the byelaw was made by that undertaker;

(b) that the copy is a true copy of the byelaw;

(c) that on a specified date the byelaw was confirmed under this Schedule; and

(d) the date, if any, fixed under paragraph 3 above for the coming into operation of the byelaw,

shall be prima facie evidence of the facts stated in the certificate, and without proof of the handwriting or official position of any person purporting to sign the certificate.

Section 167.

## SCHEDULE 11

### ORDERS CONFERRING COMPULSORY WORKS POWERS

#### Applications for orders

1.—(1) Where a water undertaker applies to the Secretary of State for a compulsory works order, it shall—

(a) submit to the Secretary of State a draft of the order applied for;

(b) publish a notice with respect to the application, at least once in each of two successive weeks, in one or more newspapers circulating in each relevant locality;

(c) not later than the date on which that notice is first published—

(i) serve a copy of the notice on each of the persons specified in relation to the application in sub-paragraph (3) below; and

(ii) in the case of a draft order which would authorise the stopping-up or diversion of a footpath or bridleway, cause such a copy, together with a plan showing the general effect of the draft order so far as it relates to the footpath or bridleway, to be displayed in a prominent position at the ends of the part of the path or way to be stopped up or diverted;

and

(d) publish a notice in the London Gazette which—

(i) states that the draft order has been submitted to the Secretary of State;

(ii) names every local authority on whom a notice is required to be served under this paragraph;

(iii) specifies a place where a copy of the draft order and of any relevant map or plan may be inspected; and

(iv) gives the name of every newspaper in which the notice required by virtue of paragraph (b) above was published and the date of an issue containing the notice.

(2) The notice required by virtue of sub-paragraph (1)(b) above to be published with respect to an application for an order by a water undertaker shall—

(a) state the general effect of the order applied for;

(b) in the case of an application made wholly or partly for the purpose of enabling any discharges of water to be made—

(i) contain particulars of the proposed discharges, stating the purposes of the discharges and specifying each place of discharge;

(ii) specify the places at which the water to be comprised in the proposed discharges is to be taken and the treatment (if any) which the draft order proposes to require the water, or any of it, to receive before being discharged under the order; and

(iii) state the effect which, in the opinion of the undertaker, the proposed discharges would have on the flow, level and quality of water in any inland waters or underground strata;

(c) specify a place where a copy of the draft order and of any relevant map or plan may be inspected by any person free of charge at all reasonable times during the period of twenty-eight days beginning with the date of the first publication of the notice; and

(d) state that any person may, within that period, by notice to the Secretary of State object to the making of the order.

(3) The persons mentioned in sub-paragraph (1)(c) above in relation to an application for a compulsory works order a draft of which has been submitted to the Secretary of State are—

(a) the NRA;

(b) every local authority whose area is or includes the whole or any part of a relevant locality;

(c) every water undertaker, not being the applicant, whose area is or includes the whole or any part of such a locality;

(d) every navigation authority, harbour authority and conservancy authority which would be affected by, or has functions in relation to any inland waters which would be affected by, any provision proposed to be made by the order;

(e) every owner, lessee or occupier (except tenants for a month or for any period of less than a month) of any land in relation to which compulsory powers would become exercisable if the order were made in the terms of the draft order;

(f) every person who has given notice to the water undertaker requiring it to notify him of applications for compulsory works orders and has paid such reasonable charge as the undertaker may have required him to pay for being notified by virtue of this paragraph;

(g) such other persons as may be prescribed.

(4) In this paragraph "relevant locality", in relation to an application for an order a draft of which is submitted to the Secretary of State by a water undertaker, means—

(a) any locality which would be affected by any provision proposed to be made by the order for the purpose of enabling any engineering or building operations to be carried out; and

(b) where provision is proposed to be made by the order for the purpose of enabling discharges of water to be made, each locality in which the place of any of the proposed discharges is situated or in which there appears to that undertaker to be any inland waters or underground strata the flow, level or quality of water in which may be affected by any of the proposed discharges.

### *Supply of copies of draft orders*

2. A water undertaker applying for a compulsory works order shall, at the request of any person and on payment by that person of such charge (if any) as the undertaker may reasonably require, furnish that person with a copy of the draft order submitted to the Secretary of State under paragraph 1 above and of any relevant map or plan.

### *Powers on an application*

3.—(1) On an application for a compulsory works order, the Secretary of State may make the order either in the terms of the draft order submitted to him or, subject to sub-paragraphs (2) and (3) below, in those terms as modified in such manner as he thinks fit, or may refuse to make an order.

(2) The Secretary of State shall not make such a modification of a draft order submitted to him by any water undertaker as he considers is likely adversely to affect any persons unless he is satisfied that the undertaker has given and published such additional notices, in such manner, as the Secretary of State may have required.

(3) The Secretary of State shall not, unless all interested parties consent, make a compulsory works order so as to confer in relation to any land any powers of compulsory acquisition which would not have been conferred in relation to that land if the order were made in the terms of the draft order submitted to him under paragraph 1 above.

(4) Where, on an application by a water undertaker for a compulsory works order, the Secretary of State refuses to make an order, the undertaker shall, as soon as practicable after the refusal, notify the refusal to every person on whom it was, by virtue of paragraph 1(1)(c)(i) above, required to serve a copy of the notice with respect to the application.

(5) The duty of a water undertaker under sub-paragraph (4) above shall be enforceable under section 18 of this Act by the Secretary of State.

### *Consideration of objections etc.*

4.—(1) If, where an application for a compulsory works order has been made by a water undertaker, any notice of an objection to it is received, before the end of the relevant period, by the Secretary of State from—

(a) any person on whom a notice under paragraph 1 or 3 above is required to be served; or

(b) from any other person appearing to the Secretary of State to be affected by the order as submitted to him or as proposed to be modified under paragraph 3 above,

then, unless the objection is withdrawn, the Secretary of State shall, before making the order, either cause a local inquiry to be held or afford to the objector and to the undertaker an opportunity of appearing before, and being heard by, a person appointed by the Secretary of State for the purpose.

(2) Where any objection received by the Secretary of State as mentioned in sub-paragraph (1) above relates to any powers of compulsory acquisition, the Secretary of State may require the objector to state in writing the grounds of his objection; and if the Secretary of State is satisfied that the objection relates exclusively to matters that can be dealt with in the assessment of compensation, he may disregard the objection for the purposes of that sub-paragraph.

(3) In this paragraph "the relevant period", in relation to an application for any order, means the period ending with whichever is the later of—

    (a) the end of the period of twenty-eight days beginning with the date of the first publication of the notice published with respect to the application for the purposes of paragraph 1(1)(b) above; and

    (b) the end of the period of twenty-five days beginning with the date of the publication in the London Gazette of the notice published for the purposes of the application by virtue of paragraph 1(1)(d) above,

together, in the case of an application for an order modifications to which have been proposed by the Secretary of State, with any further periods specified with respect to the modifications in notices under paragraph 3(2) above.

### *Notice after making of order*

5.—(1) As soon as practicable after a compulsory works order has been made, the undertaker on whose application it is made shall—

    (a) publish a notice of the making of the order, at least once in each of two successive weeks, in one or more newspapers circulating in each relevant locality; and

    (b) not later than the date on which that notice is first published—

        (i) serve a copy of the notice on every person on whom that undertaker was, by virtue of paragraph 1(1)(c)(i) above, required to serve a copy of the notice with respect to the application for the order; and

        (ii) in the case of an order authorising the stopping-up or diversion of a footpath or bridleway, cause such a copy, together with a plan showing the general effect of the order so far as it relates to the footpath or bridleway, to be displayed in a prominent position at the ends of the appropriate part of the path or way.

(2) The notice required by virtue of sub-paragraph (1)(a) above to be published with respect to a compulsory works order shall—

    (a) state the general effect of the order;

    (b) in the case of an order made wholly or partly for the purpose of enabling any discharges of water to be made—

        (i) contain particulars of the discharges, stating the purposes of the discharges and specifying each place of discharge;

        (ii) specify the places at which the water to be comprised in the discharges is to be taken and the treatment (if any) which the order requires the water, or any of it, to receive before being discharged under the order; and

        (iii) state the effect which, in the opinion of the applicant undertaker, the discharges would have on the flow, level and quality of water in any inland waters or underground strata;

    and

    (c) specify a place where a copy of the order and of any relevant map or plan may be inspected by any person free of charge at all reasonable times.

(3) Where a compulsory works order has been made, the undertaker on whose application it was made shall, at the request of any person and on payment by that person of such charge (if any) as that undertaker may reasonably require, furnish that person with a copy of the order and of any relevant map or plan.

(4) The duties of a water undertaker under this paragraph shall be enforceable under section 18 of this Act by the Secretary of State.

(5) In this paragraph "relevant locality", in relation to any compulsory works order, means—

> (a) any locality which is affected by any provision made by the order for the purpose of enabling any engineering or building operations to be carried out; and
>
> (b) where provision is made by the order for the purpose of enabling discharges of water to be made, each locality in which the place of any of the discharges is situated or in which there appears to the undertaker which applied for the order to be any inland waters or underground strata the flow, level or quality of water in which may be affected by any of the discharges.

### *Compulsory acquisition provisions*

6.—(1) Without prejudice to the provisions of Schedule 14 to this Act—

1965 c. 56.

> (a) Part I of the Compulsory Purchase Act 1965;

1981 c. 67.

> (b) section 4 and Part III of, and Schedule 3 to, the Acquisition of Land Act 1981; and
>
> (c) the enactments for the time being in force with respect to compensation for the compulsory purchase of land,

shall apply in relation to so much of a compulsory works order as confers powers of compulsory acquisition as they apply in relation to a compulsory purchase order made by virtue of section 155 of this Act and, accordingly, shall so apply, where the case so requires, with the modifications made by Schedule 9 to this Act.

(2) Subject to the provisions of sub-paragraph (6) below, if any person aggrieved by a compulsory works order containing powers of compulsory acquisition, or by a certificate given under the special land provisions in connection with such an order, desires—

> (a) to question the validity of the order, or of any provision of the order, on the grounds that any powers of compulsory acquisition conferred by the order are not authorised by this Act to be so conferred, or that any of the relevant requirements have not been complied with in relation to the order; or
>
> (b) to question the validity of the certificate on the grounds that any of the relevant requirements have not been complied with in relation to the certificate,

he may make an application for the purpose to the High Court at any time before the end of the period of six weeks beginning with the date on which notice of the making of the order is first published in accordance with paragraph 5 above or, as the case may be, notice of the giving of the certificate is first published in accordance with the special land provisions.

(3) On any application under sub-paragraph (2) above with respect to any order or certificate, the High Court—

> (a) may by interim order suspend the operation of the order, or any provision of the order, or of the certificate (either generally or in so far as it affects any property of the applicant to the High Court) until the final determination of the proceedings; and
>
> (b) if satisfied—

(i) that any powers of compulsory acquisition conferred by the order are not authorised by this Act to be so conferred; or

(ii) that the interests of that applicant have been substantially prejudiced by a failure to comply with any of the relevant requirements in relation to the order or the certificate,

may quash the order, or any provision of the order, or the certificate (either generally or in so far as it affects any property of that applicant).

(4) Except as provided by sub-paragraph (2) above, the validity of any such order or certificate as is mentioned in that sub-paragraph shall not, either before or after the order or certificate has been made or given, be questioned in any legal proceedings whatsoever.

(5) Subject to any order of the High Court under sub-paragraph (3) above, any such order or certificate as is mentioned in sub-paragraph (2) above shall become operative (except, in the case of an order, where it is subject by virtue of the special land provisions to special parliamentary procedure) on the date on which notice of the making or giving of the order or certificate is published as mentioned in the said sub-paragraph (2).

(6) Where an order such as is mentioned in sub-paragraph (2) above is subject to special parliamentary procedure, sub-paragraphs (2) to (4) of this paragraph—

(a) shall not apply to the order if it is confirmed by Act of Parliament under section 6 of the Statutory Orders (Special Procedure) Act 1945; and

1945 c. 18 (9 & 10 Geo. 6).

(b) in any other case, shall have effect as if the reference in sub-paragraph (2) of this paragraph to the date on which notice of the making of the order is first published in accordance with paragraph 5 above were a reference to the date on which the order becomes operative under the said Act of 1945.

(7) In this paragraph—

"the special land provisions" means the provisions, as applied by virtue of sub-paragraph (1) above, of Part III of the Acquisition of Land Act 1981 or, as the case may require, of Part II of Schedule 3 to that Act; and

1981 c. 67.

"the relevant requirements", in relation to an order or certificate, means the requirements of this Schedule and such requirements of the special land provisions or of any other enactment as are applicable to that order or certificate by virtue of this paragraph.

*Compensation in certain cases of compulsory acquisition*

7. Where—

(a) in connection with any engineering or building operations to which a compulsory works order relates, a licence under Chapter II of Part II of the Water Resources Act 1991 is granted, or is deemed to be granted, to the water undertaker in question; and

1991 c. 57.

(b) that licence is a licence to abstract water or to obstruct or impede the flow of any inland waters,

no compensation shall be payable by virtue of sub-paragraph (1) of paragraph 6 above in respect of any land or interest injuriously affected by the carrying out of those operations, in so far as that land or interest is injuriously affected by the abstraction of water, or the obstruction or impeding of the flow, in accordance with the provisions of the licence.

*Compensation in respect of powers other than acquisition powers*

8.—(1) If the value of any interest in any relevant land is depreciated by the coming into force of so much of any compulsory works order as—

(a) confers compulsory powers, other than powers of compulsory acquisition, for the purpose of enabling any engineering or building operations to be carried out; and

(b) grants authority for the carrying out of the operations,

the person entitled to that interest shall be entitled to compensation from the applicant for the order of an amount equal to the amount of the depreciation.

(2) Where the person entitled to an interest in any relevant land sustains loss or damage which—

(a) is attributable to so much of any compulsory works order as—

(i) confers compulsory powers, other than powers of compulsory acquisition, for the purpose of enabling any engineering or building operations to be carried out; and

(ii) grants authority for the carrying out of the operations;

(b) does not consist in depreciation of the value of that interest; and

(c) is loss or damage for which he would have been entitled to compensation by way of compensation for disturbance, if his interest in that land had been compulsorily acquired under section 155 of this Act in pursuance of a notice to treat served on the date on which the order comes into force,

he shall be entitled to compensation from the applicant for the order in respect of that loss or damage, in addition to compensation under sub-paragraph (1) above.

(3) Where any damage to, or injurious affection of, any land which is not relevant land is attributable to so much of any compulsory works order as—

(a) confers compulsory powers, other than powers of compulsory acquisition, for the purpose of enabling any engineering or building operations to be carried out; and

(b) grants authority for the carrying out of the operations,

the applicant for the order shall pay compensation in respect of that damage or injurious affection to every person entitled to an interest in that land.

(4) A person who sustains any loss or damage which is attributable to any discharge of water made by a water undertaker in pursuance of a compulsory works order shall be entitled to recover compensation from the undertaker in respect of the loss or damage.

(5) For the purposes of sub-paragraph (4) above any extra expenditure—

(a) which it becomes reasonably necessary for any water undertaker or public authority (other than the undertaker making the discharge) to incur for the purpose of properly carrying out any statutory functions; and

(b) which is attributable to any such discharge of water as is mentioned in that sub-paragraph,

shall be deemed to be a loss sustained by the undertaker or public authority and to be so attributable.

1961 c. 33.

(6) Any question of disputed compensation under this paragraph, shall be referred to and determined by the Lands Tribunal; and in relation to the determination of any such compensation the provisions of sections 2 and 4 of the Land Compensation Act 1961 shall apply, subject to any necessary modifications.

(7) For the purpose of assessing any compensation under this paragraph, so far as that compensation is in respect of loss or damage consisting in depreciation of the value of an interest in land, the rules set out in section 5 of the Land Compensation Act 1961 shall, so far as applicable and subject to any necessary modifications, have effect as they have effect for the purpose of assessing compensation for the compulsory acquisition of an interest in land.

SCH. 11

1961 c. 33.

(8) Where the interest in land in respect of which any compensation falls to be assessed in accordance with sub-paragraph (7) above is subject to a mortgage—

  (a) the compensation shall be assessed as if the interest were not subject to the mortgage;

  (b) a claim for compensation may be made by any mortgagee of the interest, but without prejudice to the making of a claim by the person entitled to the interest;

  (c) no such compensation shall be payable in respect of the interest of the mortgagee (as distinct from the interest which is subject to the mortgage); and

  (d) any such compensation which is payable in respect of the interest which is subject to the mortgage shall be paid to the mortgagee, or, if there is more than one mortgagee, to the first mortgagee, and shall in either case be applied by him as if it were proceeds of sale.

(9) In this paragraph "relevant land", in relation to a compulsory works order, means any land which is not land in relation to which powers of compulsory acquisition are conferred by the order but is—

  (a) land where any operations for which authority is granted by the order are to be carried out;

  (b) land in relation to which compulsory powers are conferred by the order; or

  (c) land held with any land falling within paragraph (a) or (b) above.

### *Protection of public undertakings*

9. The provisions of section 186 of this Act and of Part I of Schedule 13 to this Act shall apply, as they apply in relation to the carrying out of works in exercise of powers under this Act, in relation to the carrying out of works by virtue of an authority granted by so much of any compulsory works order as makes provision other than provision conferring powers of compulsory acquisition.

### *Interpretation*

10. In this Schedule—

  "bridleway" and "footpath" have the same meanings as in the Highways Act 1980;

1980 c. 66.

  "compulsory works order" means an order under section 167 of this Act;

  "powers of compulsory acquisition" means any such powers as are mentioned in subsection (4)(a) of section 167 of this Act;

and references to a tenant for a month or for any period of less than a month include references to a statutory tenant, within the meaning of the Landlord and Tenant Act 1985, and to a licensee under an assured agricultural occupancy, within the meaning of Part I of the Housing Act 1988.

1985 c. 70.

1988 c. 50.

# SCHEDULE 12

COMPENSATION ETC. IN RESPECT OF PIPE-LAYING AND OTHER WORKS POWERS

*Compensation in respect of street works powers*

1.—(1) This paragraph applies, in relation to a relevant undertaker, to the powers conferred on it in relation to streets by sections 158, 161 and 162 of this Act.

(2) It shall be the duty of every relevant undertaker—

(a) to do as little damage as possible in the exercise of the powers to which this paragraph applies; and

(b) to pay compensation for any loss caused or damage done in the exercise of those powers.

(3) Any dispute as to whether compensation should be paid under sub-paragraph (2) above, or as to the amount of any such compensation, shall be referred to the arbitration of a single arbitrator appointed by agreement between the parties to the dispute or, in default of agreement, by the Secretary of State.

1991 c. 22.

1950 c. 39.

(4) Until the coming into force of Part III of the New Roads and Street Works Act 1991, a payment of compensation under this paragraph shall be treated for the purposes of section 32 of the Public Utilities Street Works Act 1950 (provisions against duplication of compensation) as made under an enactment passed before that Act of 1950; but nothing in this sub-paragraph shall be taken to prejudice the power of the Secretary of State under that Act of 1991 to make an order bringing Part III of that Act into force on different days for different purposes (including the purposes of this paragraph).

*Compensation in respect of pipe-laying works in private land*

2.—(1) If the value of any interest in any relevant land is depreciated by virtue of the exercise, by any relevant undertaker, of any power to carry out pipe-laying works on private land, the person entitled to that interest shall be entitled to compensation from the undertaker of an amount equal to the amount of the depreciation.

(2) Where the person entitled to an interest in any relevant land sustains loss or damage which—

(a) is attributable to the exercise by any relevant undertaker of any power to carry out pipe-laying works on private land;

(b) does not consist in depreciation of the value of that interest; and

(c) is loss or damage for which he would have been entitled to compensation by way of compensation for disturbance, if his interest in that land had been compulsorily acquired under section 155 of this Act,

he shall be entitled to compensation from the undertaker in respect of that loss or damage, in addition to compensation under sub-paragraph (1) above.

(3) Where any damage to, or injurious affection of, any land which is not relevant land is attributable to the exercise by any relevant undertaker, of any power to carry out pipe-laying works on private land, the undertaker shall pay compensation in respect of that damage or injurious affection to every person entitled to an interest in that land.

(4) The Secretary of State may by regulations make provision requiring a relevant undertaker, where it is proposing or has begun, in a prescribed case, to exercise any power to carry out pipe-laying works on private land, to make advance payments on account of compensation that will become payable in respect of the exercise of that power.

(5) In this paragraph "relevant land", in relation to any exercise of a power to carry out pipe-laying works on private land, means the land where the power is exercised or land held with that land.

(6) In this paragraph the references to a power to carry out pipe-laying works on private land are references to any of the powers conferred by virtue of sections 159, 161(2) and 163 of this Act.

*Assessment of compensation under paragraph 2*

3.—(1) Any question of disputed compensation under paragraph 2 above shall be referred to and determined by the Lands Tribunal; and in relation to the determination of any such compensation the provisions of sections 2 and 4 of the Land Compensation Act 1961 shall apply, subject to any necessary modifications.

1961 c. 33.

(2) For the purpose of assessing any compensation under paragraph 2 above, so far as that compensation is in respect of loss or damage consisting in depreciation of the value of an interest in land, the rules set out in section 5 of the Land Compensation Act 1961 shall, so far as applicable and subject to any necessary modifications, have effect as they have effect for the purpose of assessing compensation for the compulsory acquisition of an interest in land.

(3) Where the interest in land in respect of which any compensation falls to be assessed in accordance with sub-paragraph (2) above is subject to a mortgage—

    (a) the compensation shall be assessed as if the interest were not subject to the mortgage;

    (b) a claim for compensation may be made by any mortgagee of the interest, but without prejudice to the making of a claim by the person entitled to the interest;

    (c) no such compensation shall be payable in respect of the interest of the mortgagee (as distinct from the interest which is subject to the mortgage); and

    (d) any such compensation which is payable in respect of the interest which is subject to the mortgage shall be paid to the mortgagee or, if there is more than one mortgagee, to the first mortgagee, and shall in either case be applied by him as if it were proceeds of sale.

(4) Where, apart from this sub-paragraph, any person entitled to an interest in any land would be entitled under paragraph 2 above to an amount of compensation in respect of any works, there shall be deducted from that amount an amount equal to the amount by which the carrying out of the works has enhanced the value of any other land which—

    (a) is contiguous or adjacent to that land; and

    (b) is land to an interest in which that person is entitled in the same capacity.

*Compensation in respect of sewerage works etc.*

4.—(1) Subject to the following provisions of this paragraph, a sewerage undertaker shall make full compensation to any person who has sustained damage by reason of the exercise by the undertaker, in relation to a matter as to which that person has not himself been in default, of any of its powers under the relevant sewerage provisions.

(2) Subject to sub-paragraph (3) below, any dispute arising under this paragraph as to the fact of damage, or as to the amount of compensation, shall be referred to the arbitration of a single arbitrator appointed by agreement between the parties to the dispute or, in default of agreement, by the Secretary of State.

(3) If the compensation claimed under this paragraph in any case does not exceed £50, all questions as to the fact of damage, liability to pay compensation and the amount of compensation may, on the application of either party, be determined by, and any compensation awarded may be recovered before, a magistrates' court.

(4) Sections 300 and 301 of the Public Health Act 1936 (which relate to the determination of questions by courts of summary jurisdiction and to appeals against such determinations) shall apply for the purposes of and in relation to a determination on an application under sub-paragraph (3) above as they apply for the purposes of and in relation to a determination by a magistrates' court under that Act.

(5) No person shall be entitled by virtue of this paragraph to claim compensation on the ground that a sewerage undertaker has, in the exercise of its powers under the relevant sewerage provisions, declared any sewer or sewage disposal works, whether belonging to that person or not, to be vested in the undertaker.

### *Compensation in respect of metering works*

5.—(1) Without prejudice to section 148 of this Act or to paragraph 11 of Schedule 6 to this Act or paragraph 1 above, where a person authorised by any relevant undertaker carries out any works by virtue of section 162 of this Act on any premises, the undertaker shall make good, or pay compensation for, any damage caused by that person or by any person accompanying him by or in connection with the carrying out of the works.

(2) Any dispute between a relevant undertaker and any other person (including another such undertaker)—

    (a) as to whether the undertaker should pay any compensation under this paragraph; or

    (b) as to the amount of any such compensation,

shall be referred to the arbitration of a single arbitrator appointed by agreement between the undertaker and that person or, in default of agreement, by the Director.

### *Compensation in respect of discharges for works purposes*

6.—(1) It shall be the duty of every water undertaker—

    (a) to cause as little loss and damage as possible in the exercise of the powers conferred on it by section 165 of this Act; and

    (b) to pay compensation for any loss caused or damage done in the exercise of those powers.

(2) For the purposes of subsection (1) above any extra expenditure—

    (a) which it becomes reasonably necessary for any other water undertaker or any sewerage undertaker or public authority to incur for the purpose of properly carrying out any statutory functions; and

    (b) which is attributable to any discharge of water under section 165 of this Act,

shall be deemed to be a loss sustained by the undertaker or public authority and to have been caused in exercise of the powers conferred by that section.

(3) Any dispute as to whether compensation should be paid under sub-paragraph (1) above, or as to the amount of any such compensation, shall be referred to the arbitration of a single arbitrator appointed by agreement between the parties to the dispute or, in default of agreement, by the President of the Institution of Civil Engineers.

SCHEDULE 13 Section 183.

PROTECTIVE PROVISIONS IN RESPECT OF CERTAIN UNDERTAKINGS

PART I

PROVISIONS APPLYING GENERALLY ·

*General provisions protecting undertakings*

1.—(1) Nothing in this Act conferring power on a relevant undertaker to carry out any works shall confer power to do anything, except with the consent of the persons carrying on an undertaking protected by this paragraph, which, whether directly or indirectly, so interferes or will so interfere—

(a) with works or property vested in or under the control of the persons carrying on that undertaking, in their capacity as such; or

(b) with the use of any such works or property,

as to affect injuriously those works or that property or the carrying on of that undertaking.

(2) Without prejudice to the construction of sub-paragraph (1) above for the purposes of its application in relation to the other provisions of this Act, that sub-paragraph shall have effect in its application in relation to the relevant sewerage provisions as if any use of, injury to or interference with any sluices, floodgates, sewers, groynes, sea defences or other works which are vested in or under the control of the NRA or an internal drainage board were such an interference with works or property vested in or under the control of the NRA or that board as to affect injuriously the works or property or the carrying on of the undertaking of the NRA or of that board.

(3) A consent for the purposes of sub-paragraph (1) above may be given subject to reasonable conditions but shall not be unreasonably withheld.

(4) Subject to the following provisions of this Schedule, any dispute—

(a) as to whether anything done or proposed to be done interferes or will interfere as mentioned in sub-paragraph (1) above;

(b) as to whether any consent for the purposes of this paragraph is being unreasonably withheld; or

(c) as to whether any condition subject to which any such consent has been given was reasonable,

shall be referred to the arbitration of a single arbitrator to be appointed by agreement between the parties to the dispute or, in default of agreement, by the President of the Institution of Civil Engineers.

(5) The following are the undertakings protected by this paragraph, that is to say-

(a) the undertakings of the NRA, the Civil Aviation Authority, the British Coal Corporation and the Post Office;

(b) the undertaking of any relevant undertaker;

(c) any undertaking consisting in the running of a telecommunications code system, within the meaning of Schedule 4 to the Telecommunications Act 1984; 1984 c. 12.

(d) any airport to which Part V of the Airports Act 1986 applies; 1986 c. 31.

(e) the undertaking of any public gas supplier within the meaning of Part I of the Gas Act 1986; 1986 c. 44.

(f) the undertaking of any person authorised by a licence under Part I of the Electricity Act 1989 to generate, transmit or supply electricity; 1989 c. 29.

(g) the undertaking of any navigation, harbour or conservancy authority or of any internal drainage board;

(h) the undertaking of any railway undertakers;

(i) any public utility undertaking carried on by a local authority under any Act or under any order having the force of an Act.

(6) For the purposes of this paragraph any reference in this paragraph, in relation to any such airport as is mentioned in sub-paragraph (5)(d) above, to the persons carrying on the undertaking is a reference to the airport operator.

### *Protection for statutory powers and jurisdiction*

2. Nothing in any provision of this Act conferring power on a relevant undertaker to carry out any works shall confer power to do anything which prejudices the exercise of any statutory power, authority or jurisdiction from time to time vested in or exercisable by any persons carrying on an undertaking protected by paragraph 1 above.

### *Special protection for certain undertakings in respect of street works*

3.—(1) Subject to the following provisions of this paragraph and without prejudice to the other provisions of this Schedule, the powers under the street works provisions to break up or open a street shall not be exercisable where the street, not being a highway maintainable at public expense (within the meaning of the Highways Act 1980)—

1980 c. 66.

(a) is under the control or management of, or is maintainable by, railway undertakers or a navigation authority; or

(b) forms part of a level crossing belonging to any such undertakers or to such an authority or to any other person,

except with the consent of the undertakers or authority or, as the case may be, of the person to whom the level crossing belongs.

(2) Sub-paragraph (1) above shall not apply to any exercise of the powers conferred by the street works provisions for the carrying out of emergency works, within the meaning of Part III of the New Roads and Street Works Act 1991.

1991 c. 22.

(3) A consent given for the purposes of sub-paragraph (1) above may be made subject to such reasonable conditions as may be specified by the person giving it but shall not be unreasonably withheld.

(4) Any dispute—

(a) as to whether a consent for the purposes of sub-paragraph (1) above should be given or withheld; or

(b) as to whether the conditions to which any such consent is made subject are reasonable,

shall be referred to the arbitration of a single arbitrator appointed by agreement between the parties to the dispute or, in default of agreement, by the President of the Institution of Civil Engineers.

(5) If any relevant undertaker contravenes, without reasonable excuse, the requirements of sub-paragraph (1) above, it shall be guilty of an offence and liable, on summary conviction, to a fine not exceeding level 3 on the standard scale.

1870 c. 78.

(6) The restrictions contained in paragraphs (1) to (5) of section 32 of the Tramways Act 1870 (protection of tramways) shall apply in relation to any exercise of a power conferred by the street works provisions—

(a) as they apply in relation to the powers mentioned in that section; and

(b) as if references in that section to a tramway included references to a trolley vehicle system.

(7) In this paragraph "the street works provisions" means so much of sections 158, 161 and 162 of this Act as relates to powers exercisable in relation to streets.

(8) Until the coming into force of section 52 of the New Roads and Street Works Act 1991, sub-paragraph (2) above shall have effect as if the reference to Part III of that Act were a reference to the Public Utilities Street Works Act 1950; but nothing in this sub-paragraph shall be taken to prejudice the power of the Secretary of State under that Act of 1991 to make an order bringing that section 52 into force on different days for different purposes (including the purposes of this paragraph).

### *Protection for telecommunication systems*

4. Paragraph 23 of Schedule 2 to the Telecommunications Act 1984 (which provides a procedure for certain cases where works involve the alteration of telecommunication apparatus) shall apply to every relevant undertaker for the purposes of any works carried out by that undertaker in exercise of any of the powers conferred by any enactment (including, in the case of a statutory water company, section 1 of the Statutory Water Companies Act 1991).

1984 c. 12.

1991 c. 58.

## PART II

### FURTHER PROTECTIVE PROVISIONS IN RESPECT OF SEWERAGE POWERS

#### *Protection for dock undertakers*

5.—(1) Subject to the provisions of this paragraph, nothing in the relevant sewerage provisions shall authorise a sewerage undertaker, without the consent of the dock undertakers concerned—

 (a) to interfere with any river, canal, dock, harbour, basin, lock or reservoir so as injuriously to affect navigation thereon or the use thereof or the access thereto, or to interfere with any towing path, so as to interrupt the traffic thereon;

 (b) to interfere with any bridges crossing any river, canal, dock, harbour or basin;

 (c) to carry out any works in, across or under any dock, harbour, basin, wharf, quay or lock, or any land which belongs to dock undertakers and is held or used by them for the purposes of their undertaking;

 (d) to carry out any works which will interfere with the improvement of, or the access to, any river, canal, dock, harbour, basin, lock, reservoir, or towing path, or with any works appurtenant thereto or any land necessary for the enjoyment or improvement thereof.

(2) For the purposes of this paragraph dock undertakers shall be deemed to be concerned with any river, canal, dock, harbour, basin, lock, reservoir, towing path, wharf, quay or land if—

 (a) it belongs to them and forms part of their undertaking; or

 (b) they have statutory rights of navigating on or using it or of demanding tolls or dues in respect of navigation thereon or the use thereof.

(3) A consent under this paragraph shall not be unreasonably withheld.

(4) Any dispute as to whether or not consent under this paragraph is unreasonably withheld shall be referred, if either party so require, to the arbitration of a single arbitrator appointed by agreement between the parties or, in default of agreement, by the President of the Institution of Civil Engineers.

(5) Upon an arbitration under this paragraph, the arbitrator shall determine—

 (a) whether any works which the sewerage undertaker proposes to carry out are such works as under this paragraph the undertaker is not entitled to carry out without the consent of any dock undertakers;

 (b) if they are such works, whether the injury, if any, to the undertakers will be of such a nature as to admit of being fully compensated by money; and

(c) if the works are of such a nature, the conditions subject to which the sewerage undertaker may carry out the works, including the amount of the compensation (if any) to be paid by the sewerage undertaker to the dock undertakers.

(6) The sewerage undertaker in question shall not proceed to carry out any proposed works if, on an arbitration under this paragraph, the arbitrator determines—

(a) that the proposed works are such works as the sewerage undertaker is not entitled to carry out without the consent of the dock undertakers; and

(b) that the works would cause injury to the dock undertakers of such a nature as not to admit of being fully compensated by money,

but, in any other case, the sewerage undertaker may carry out the works subject to compliance with such conditions, including the payment of such compensation, as the arbitrator may have determined.

(7) Nothing in this paragraph shall be construed as limiting the powers of a sewerage undertaker under this Act in respect of the opening and the breaking up of streets and bridges for the purpose of constructing, laying and maintaining sewers, drains and pipes.

### *Protection for airports, railways etc.*

6.—(1) Subject to the provisions of this paragraph, nothing in the relevant sewerage provisions shall authorise a sewerage undertaker, without the consent of the Civil Aviation Authority or, as the case may be, of the airport operator or railway undertakers concerned, to carry out any works along, across or under—

(a) any property of the Civil Aviation Authority;

1986 c. 31.
(b) an airport to which Part V of the Airports Act 1986 applies; or

(c) any railway of any railway undertakers.

(2) Sub-paragraphs (3) to (7) of paragraph 5 above shall apply for the purposes of this paragraph as they apply for the purposes of sub-paragraph (1) of that paragraph but as if references to the dock undertakers were references, as the case may require, to the Civil Aviation Authority, to the relevant airport operator or to the railway undertakers.

### *Saving for Part I and other powers*

7. The provisions of this Part of this Schedule are without prejudice to the provisions of Part I of this Schedule or to any power conferrred on a sewerage undertaker otherwise than by the relevant sewerage provisions.

Section 188.

## SCHEDULE 14

### MINERAL RIGHTS

### *Acquisition of mineral rights*

1.—(1) This paragraph applies in each of the following cases, that is to say—

(a) where a relevant undertaker acquires any land (whether compulsorily in exercise of any power conferred by or under this Act or otherwise); and

(b) where a relevant undertaker carries out any works in relation to any land for the purposes of, or in connection with, the carrying out of any of its functions.

(2) Subject to sub-paragraph (3) below, a relevant undertaker shall not, by virtue only of its acquisition of the land or the carrying out of the works, become entitled to any mines or minerals lying under the land; and, accordingly, any such mines or minerals shall be deemed to be excepted from any instrument by virtue of which the land vests in the relevant undertaker unless express provision to the contrary is contained—

(a) where the land vests in the relevant undertaker by virtue of a conveyance, in the conveyance; or

(b) where the land is acquired by the relevant undertaker in pursuance of any power of compulsory acquisition conferred by or under this Act, in the order authorising the acquisition.

(3) A relevant undertaker shall be entitled to such parts of any mines or minerals that lie under the land as it may be necessary for it to dig, carry away or use in carrying out any works for the purposes of constructing, making, erecting or laying any part of its undertaking.

### Notice required for the working of underlying mines

2.—(1) If the owner of any mines or minerals underlying any part of a relevant undertaker's undertaking proposes to work them, he shall, not less than thirty days before the commencement of working, serve notice of his intention to do so on the relevant undertaker.

(2) On receipt of a notice under sub-paragraph (1) above the relevant undertaker may cause the mines or minerals to be inspected by a person designated by it for the purpose.

(3) Subject to sub-paragraph (5) and paragraph 3 below, if, where notice has been served under this paragraph, the relevant undertaker—

(a) considers that the working of the underlying mines or minerals is likely to damage any part of its undertaking;

(b) is willing to compensate the owner of the mines or minerals for the restriction imposed by virtue of this sub-paragraph; and

(c) serves notice to that effect on the owner of the mines or minerals before the end of the period of thirty days mentioned in sub-paragraph (1) above,

the owner shall not work the mines or minerals except to such extent as may be determined by the relevant undertaker, and the relevant undertaker shall so compensate the owner.

(4) Any dispute as to the amount of any compensation payable by virtue of sub-paragraph (3) above shall be referred to and determined by the Lands Tribunal.

(5) If before the end of the period of thirty days mentioned in sub-paragraph (1) above, no notice has been served under sub-paragraph (3)(c) above by the relevant undertaker, the entitlement of the owner of the mines and minerals to work them shall be an entitlement to work them by proper methods and in the usual manner of working such mines or minerals in the district in question.

(6) If any damage to the undertaking of a relevant undertaker is caused by the working otherwise than as authorised by this paragraph of any mines or minerals underlying any part of its undertaking—

(a) the owner of the mines or minerals shall, at his own expense, forthwith repair the damage; and

(b) the relevant undertaker may, without waiting for the owner to perform his duty, repair the damage and may recover the expenses reasonably incurred by it in doing so from the owner.

*Mining communications*

3.—(1) If the working of any mines or minerals is prevented by reason of any of the preceding provisions of this Schedule, the owner of the mines or minerals may cut and make such communication works through the mines or minerals, or the strata in which they are situated, as are required for the ventilation, drainage and working of mines or minerals which are not underlying any part of the undertaking of the relevant undertaker in question.

(2) Communication works cut or made under this paragraph—

(a) shall not, in a case where—

(i) the part of the undertaking in question was constructed, made, erected or laid in pursuance of an order made under any enactment or is situated on land acquired by the relevant undertaker in pursuance of any powers of compulsory acquisition; and

(ii) the order authorising the works or acquisition designates dimensions or sections for the communication works,

exceed those dimensions or fail to conform to those sections; and

(b) in any other case, shall not be more than 2.44 metres high or more than 2.44 metres wide.

(3) Communication works cut or made under this paragraph shall not be cut or made on the land where the part of the undertaking is situated so as to cause damage to that part of the undertaking.

(4) Where works carried out under this paragraph by the owner of any mines or minerals cause loss or damage to the owner or occupier of land lying over the mines or minerals, the relevant undertaker shall pay full compensation to him for the loss or damage.

(5) Sub-paragraph (4) above shall not apply where the person sustaining the loss or damage is the owner of the mines.

(6) In this paragraph "communication works" means airways, headways, gateways or water levels.

*Compensation relating to severance*

4.—(1) Where mines or minerals underlying any part of a relevant undertaker's undertaking are situated so as, on two or more sides of that land, to extend beyond the land on which that part of the undertaking is situated, the relevant undertaker shall from time to time pay to the owner of the mines or minerals (in addition to any compensation under paragraph 2 above) any expenses and losses incurred by him in consequence of—

(a) the severance by the undertaking of the land lying over the mines;

(b) the interruption of continuous working of the mines in consequence of paragraph 2(3) above;

(c) the mines being so worked in accordance with restrictions imposed by virtue of this Act or any order made under this Act,

and shall pay for any minerals not purchased by the relevant undertaker which cannot be got or won by reason of the part of the undertaking in question being situated where it is or by reason of the requirement to avoid damage to any part of the relevant undertaker's undertaking.

(2) Any dispute as to whether any sum should be paid under this paragraph or as to the amount payable shall be referred to the arbitration of a single arbitrator appointed by agreement between the relevant undertaker and the owner of the mines or minerals or, in default of agreement, by the Secretary of State.

*Powers of entry*

5.—(1) Any person designated in writing for the purpose by a relevant undertaker may, for any purpose specified in sub-paragraph (2) below—

   (a) enter on any land in which the mines or minerals are, or are thought to be, being worked, and which is in or near to the land where any part of that undertaker's undertaking is situated; and

   (b) enter the mines and any works connected with the mines.

(2) The purposes mentioned in sub-paragraph (1) above are—

   (a) carrying out any inspection under paragraph 2(2) above;

   (b) ascertaining whether any mines or minerals have been worked so as to damage the undertaking of the relevant undertaker in question; and

   (c) carrying out any works and taking any other steps which the relevant undertaker in question is authorised to carry out or take under paragraph 2(6) above.

(3) A person authorised to enter any premises under this paragraph may—

   (a) make use of any equipment belonging to the owner of the mines or minerals in question; and

   (b) use all necessary means for discovering the distance from any part of the undertaking of the relevant undertaker to the parts of the mines or the minerals which are, or are about to be, worked.

(4) Part II of Schedule 6 to this Act shall apply to the rights and other powers conferred by this paragraph.

*No exemption for injury to mines and minerals*

6. Nothing in any provision of this Act or of any order made under this Act shall be construed as exempting a relevant undertaker from any liability to which it would, apart from that provision, have been subject in respect of any damage to any mines or minerals underlying any part of its undertaking or in respect of any loss sustained in relation to any such mines or minerals by a person having an interest therein.

*Interpretation*

7.—(1) In this Schedule—

   "conveyance" has the same meaning as in the Law of Property Act 1925;     1925 c. 20.

   "designated distance", in relation to any part of a relevant undertaker's undertaking, means, subject to sub-paragraph (6) below, thirty-seven metres;

   "mines" means mines of coal, ironstone, slate or other minerals;

   "owner", in relation to mines and minerals, includes a lessee or occupier; and

   "underlying", in relation to any part of the undertaking of a relevant undertaker, means lying under, or within the designated distance from, that part of that undertaking.

(2) For the purposes of this Schedule the undertaking of a relevant undertaker shall be taken to consist of so much of any of the following as is for the time being vested in or held by that undertaker for the purposes of, or in connection with, the carrying out of any of its functions, that is to say—

   (a) any buildings, reservoirs, wells, boreholes or other structures; and

   (b) any pipes or other underground works particulars of which fall or would fall to be incorporated in any records kept under section 198 or 199 of this Act.

SCH. 14

(3) References in this Schedule to the working of any mines or minerals include references to the draining of mines and to the winning or getting of minerals.

(4) For the purposes of this Schedule land shall be treated as acquired by a relevant undertaker in pursuance of powers of compulsory acquisition if it—

1973 c. 37.

    (a) was so acquired by a water authority established under section 2 of the Water Act 1973 or any predecessor of such a water authority or by a predecessor of a statutory water company; and

    (b) is now vested in that undertaker in accordance with a scheme under Schedule 2 to the Water Act 1989 or Schedule 2 to this Act or otherwise.

1989 c. 15.

(5) In relation—

    (a) to any land treated by virtue of sub-paragraph (4) above as acquired in pursuance of powers of compulsory acquisition; or

    (b) to any land acquired by a statutory water company before 1st September 1989 in pursuance of any such powers,

references in this Schedule to the order authorising the acquisition include references to any local statutory provision which immediately before 1st September 1989 had effect in relation to that land for the purposes of any provisions corresponding to the provisions of this Schedule.

(6) For the purposes of this Schedule where—

    (a) any part of a relevant undertaker's undertaking was constructed, made, erected or laid in pursuance of an order made under any enactment or is situated on land acquired by the relevant undertaker in pursuance of any powers of compulsory acquisition; and

    (b) the order authorising the works or acquisition designates any distance for the purposes of any enactment relating to mines or minerals underlying that part of the undertaking,

then for the purposes of this Schedule that distance shall be the designated distance in relation to that part of the undertaking, instead of the distance specified in sub-paragraph (1) above.

Section 206.

## SCHEDULE 15

### DISCLOSURE OF INFORMATION

#### PART I

##### PERSONS IN RESPECT OF WHOSE FUNCTIONS DISCLOSURE MAY BE MADE

Any Minister of the Crown.

The Director General of Fair Trading.

The Monopolies Commission.

The Director General of Telecommunications.

The Civil Aviation Authority.

The Director General of Gas Supply.

The Director General of Electricity Supply.

A local weights and measures authority in England and Wales.

#### PART II

##### ENACTMENTS ETC. IN RESPECT OF WHICH DISCLOSURE MAY BE MADE

1968 c. 29.

The Trade Descriptions Act 1968.

1973 c. 41.

The Fair Trading Act 1973.

The Consumer Credit Act 1974.

The Restrictive Trade Practices Act 1976.

The Resale Prices Act 1976.

The Estate Agents Act 1979.

The Competition Act 1980.

The Telecommunications Act 1984.

The Airports Act 1986.

The Gas Act 1986.

The Consumer Protection Act 1987.

The Electricity Act 1989.

SCH. 15
1974 c. 39.
1976 c. 34.
1976 c. 53.
1979 c. 38.
1980 c. 21.
1984 c. 12.
1986 c. 31.
1986 c. 44.
1987 c. 43.
1989 c. 29.

Any subordinate legislation made for the purpose of securing compliance with the Directive of the Council of the European Communities dated 10th September 1984 (No. 84/450/EEC) on the approximation of the laws, regulations and administrative provisions of the member States concerning misleading advertising.

## Table of Derivations

*Notes:*

1. The following abbreviations are used in this Table:—

| | |
|---|---|
| 1936 | = The Public Health Act 1936 (c. 49) |
| 1937 | = The Public Health (Drainage of Trade Premises) Act 1937 (c. 40) |
| 1945 | = The Water Act 1945 (c. 42) |
| 1948 | = The Water Act 1948 (c. 22) |
| 1961(F) | = The Factories Act 1961 (c. 34) |
| 1961 | = The Public Health Act 1961 (c. 64) |
| 1963(L) | = The London Government Act 1963 (c. 33) |
| 1973 | = The Water Act 1973 (c. 37) |
| 1974 | = The Control of Pollution Act 1974 (c. 40) |
| 1977 | = The Criminal Law Act 1977 (c. 45) |
| 1980 | = The Highways Act 1980 (c. 66) |
| 1981 | = The Water Act 1981 (c. 12) |
| 1981(SC) | = The Supreme Court Act 1981 (c.54) |
| 1982(CA) | = The Civil Aviation Act 1982 (c. 16) |
| 1982(CJA) | = The Criminal Justice Act 1982 (c. 43) |
| 1985(LG) | = The Local Government Act 1985 (c. 51) |
| 1985 | = The Water (Fluoridation) Act 1985 (c. 63) |
| 1986(AA) | = The Airports Act 1986 (c. 31) |
| 1986(GA) | = The Gas Act 1986 (c. 44) |
| 1989 | = The Water Act 1989 (c. 15) |
| 1989(EA) | = The Electricity Act 1989 (c. 29) |
| 1990(FS) | = The Food Safety Act 1990 (c. 16) |
| 1990(EP) | = The Environmental Protection Act 1990 (c. 43) |
| 1991(NR) | = The New Roads and Street Works Act 1991 (c. 22) |
| R: (followed by a number) | = The recommendation so numbered as set out in the Appendix to the Report of the Law Commission (Cm. 1483). |

2. The functions originally vested in the Minister of Health under 1936 and 1937 have become vested in the Secretary of State as a result of the following transfer of functions orders ("TFOs"): SI 1951/142; SI 1951/1900; SI 1965/319; 1970/1681. Other TFOs, where applicable in relation to a provision re-enacted in this Bill, are specified at the appropriate place in column 2 of this Table.

3. General provisions contained in section 32 of the Magistrates' Courts Act 1980 (c. 43) and section 46 of the Criminal Justice Act 1982 (c. 48) provide, respectively, for the maximum fine on summary conviction of an either way offence to be the statutory maximum and for a reference to the amount of the maximum fine to which a person is liable in respect of a summary offence to become a reference to a level on the standard scale. Where the effect of one of these enactments is consolidated it is not referred to separately in column 2 of this Table.

| Provision of Act | Derivation |
|---|---|
| 1 | 1989 s. 5. |
| 2 | 1989 s. 7(1) - (4). |
| 3 | 1989 ss. 8(1) - (3), (5) - (7) & 20(8)(a)(i) & (c). |
| 4 | 1989 ss. 9 & 20(8)(a)(i) & (c); 1990(EP) Sch 9 para 17(2). |
| 5 | 1989 s. 10; 1990(EP) Sch 9 para 17(3). |

| Provision of Act | Derivation |
|---|---|
| 6 | 1989 s. 11(1) - (3), (5) & (8). |
| 7 | 1989 ss. 11(4)(part), (6) & (7) & 12 (2). |
| 8 | 1989 s. 13(1), (2)(part), (3), (5) & (7). |
| 9 | |
| (1) | 1989 s. 13(2)(part). |
| (2) | 1989 s. 13(4). |
| (3) & (4) | 1989 s. 12(3) & (4). |
| (5) | 1989 s. 12(4) & (6). |
| 10 | 1989 s. 13(6). |
| 11 | 1989 s. 14(1), (3) & (8) - (10). |
| 12 | 1989 s. 14(2), (6) & (7). |
| 13 | 1989 s. 15. |
| 14 | 1989 s. 16. |
| 15 | 1989 s. 17. |
| 16 | 1989 s. 18. |
| 17 | 1989 s. 19. |
| 18 | 1989 s. 20(1) - (4) & (7) - (10). |
| 19 | 1989 s. 20(5), (6) & (8). |
| 20 | 1989 s. 21. |
| 21 | 1989 s. 22(1) - (3). |
| 22 | 1989 s. 22(4) - (8). |
| 23 | 1989 s. 23(2), (3), (8) & (9). |
| 24 | 1989 s. 23(1), (4) - (7) & (9). |
| 25 | 1989 s. 24(2). |
| 26 | 1989 ss. 24(1) & 23(9). |
| 27 | 1989 s. 26. |
| 28 | 1989 s. 6. |
| 29 | 1989 s. 27(1), (3) & (4). |
| 30 | 1989 s. 27 (2). |
| 31 | 1989 s. 28. |
| 32 | 1989 s. 29(1), (3) & (4). |
| 33 | 1989 s. 29(3), (5), (6) & (10). |
| 34 | 1989 s. 30(1) - (5). |
| 35 | 1989 ss. 29(2), (8) & (9) & 30(6). |
| 36 | 1989 s. 12(1), (5) & (6). |
| 37 | 1989 ss. 37 & 38(6). |
| 38 | 1989 s. 38(1) - (3). |
| 39 | 1989 s. 38(4). |
| 40 | 1989 s. 39. |
| 41 | 1989 s. 40(1) & (2) & (6) - (8). |
| 42 | 1989 s. 41(1), (2) & (8) - (10). |
| 43 | 1989 s. 41(3) - (7) & (9). |
| 44 | 1989 s. 40(3) - (5) & (8). |

| Provision of Act | Derivation |
| --- | --- |
| 45 | 1989 ss. 42(1),(2) & (5), 44(1), (4) & (5) & 176. |
| 46 | 1989 ss. 42(3) - (5) & 44(1) & (4) - (6). |
| 47 | 1989 s. 43(1) & (2). |
| 48 | 1989 s. 43(3). |
| 49 | 1989 s. 43(4) - (6). |
| 50 | 1989 s. 43(7). |
| 51 | 1989 ss. 42(6), 44(2), (3) & (7) & 176. |
| 52 | 1989 s. 45(1) - (5). |
| 53 | 1989 s. 45(6). |
| 54 | 1989 s. 45(7) & (8). |
| 55 | 1989 ss. 46(1) - (3), (7) - (9) & 49(1)(part). |
| 56 | 1989 s. 46(4) - (6). |
| 57 | 1989 s. 47(1), (2), (4) - (9) & (11). |
| 58 | 1989 s. 47(3) & (6) - (11). |
| 59 | 1989 s. 48. |
| 60 | 1989 s. 49(1) - (3). |
| 61 | 1989 s. 49(1) & (4) - (6). |
| 62 | 1989 s. 49(1) & (7). |
| 63 | 1989 s. 49(8) & (9). |
| 64 | 1989 s. 50. |
| 65 | 1989 s. 51(1) - (4) & (7) - (9). |
| 66 | 1989 s. 51(5), (6) & (10). |
| 67 | 1989 s. 65. |
| 68 | 1989 s. 52; 1990(FS) s. 55(2). |
| 69 | 1989 s. 53; 1990(FS) s. 55(2). |
| 70 | 1989 s. 54. |
| 71 | 1945 s. 14(9), (10) & (12); 1948 s. 5(4); 1977 Sch 6; 1989 Sch 25 para 7(1). |
| 72 | 1945 s. 21(1), (3) & (4); 1989 Sch 25 para 7(4)(a) & (d); R: 21. |
| 73 | 1989 s. 61. |
| 74 | 1989 s. 62(1) - (4), (6) & (7) & Sch 26 para 19. |
| 75 | 1989 s. 63. |
| 76 | 1945 s. 16(1) - (4); 1977 Sch 6; IA s. 17; 1989 Sch 25 para 7(3)(a) - (c). |
| 77 | 1989 s. 56(1) & (4) - (6). |
| 78 | 1989 s. 56(2) & (3); 1990(FS) s. 55(3). |
| 79 | 1989 ss. 55 & 56(2)(part). |
| 80 | 1989 ss. 57 & 164(3); 1990(FS) s. 55(4). |
| 81 | 1989 s. 58(1) - (4). |
| 82 | 1989 s. 58(5) - (10). |
| 83 | 1989 s. 164. |
| 84 | 1945 ss. 21(2) & (2A), 53 & 59; 1963(L) Sch 11 Pt I para 27; 1989 ss. 59(2) & 62(4) & Sch 25 para 7(4)(b) & (c). |

| Provision of Act | Derivation |
|---|---|
| 85 | 1989 s. 59(1), (4) & (5). |
| 86 | 1989 s. 60(1) - (4) & (6). |
| 87 | 1985 ss. 1 & 5; 1989 Sch 25 para 73. |
| 88 | 1985 ss. 2 & 5; 1989 Sch 25 para 73. |
| 89 | 1985 ss. 4 & 5; 1989 Sch 25 para 73. |
| 90 | 1989 s. 172. |
| 91 | Introduces Sch 7. |
| 92 | 1989 s. 171. |
| 93 | 1989 ss. 66 & 164(3) & Sch 19 para 11; 1990(FS) s. 55(5) & (6). |
| 94 | 1989 ss. 67 & 68(6). |
| 95 | 1989 s 68(1) - (3). |
| 96 | 1989 s. 68(4). |
| 97 | 1989 s. 73 & Sch 25 para 3. |
| 98 | 1989 s. 71(1) - (3), (7) & (8). |
| 99 | 1989 s. 72(1), (2) & (8) - (10). |
| 100 | 1989 s. 72(3) - (7) & (9). |
| 101 | 1989 s. 71(4) - (6) & (9). |
| 102 | 1936 s. 17(1), (2) & (4) - (6); 1973 s. 14; 1989 Sch 8 para 1. |
| 103 | 1936 s. 17(7) - (9); 1973 s. 14; 1989 Sch 8 para 1; R: 1. |
| 104 | 1936 s. 18(1) - (4); 1973 s. 14; 1989 s. 176 and Sch 8 paras 1 & 2(1). |
| 105 | 1936 ss. 17(3) & 18(4) - (6); 1973 s. 14; 1989 s. 176 and Sch 8 paras 1 & 2(1). |
| 106 | 1936 ss. 34(1) & (3) , 303 - 302 & 343(1)(part); 1961(F) s. 184 & Sch 6 para 1; 1973 s. 14 & Sch 8 para 37; 1989 Sch 8 paras 1 & 2(6)(a). |
| 107 | 1936 ss. 36 & 291 - 294; 1973 s. 14; 1974 Sch 2 para 9; 1982(CJA) s. 38; 1989 Sch 8 paras 1 & 2(7). |
| 108 | 1936 s. 34(2) & (4); 1973 s. 14; 1989 Sch 8 paras 1 & 2(6)(b). |
| 109 | 1936 ss. 34(5) & 291 - 294; 1973 s. 14; 1974 Sch 2 para 8; 1982(CJA) s. 38; 1989 Sch 8 paras 1. |
| 110 | 1989 s.70(3) - (5). |
| 111 | 1936 ss. 27, 297 & 343(1)(part); 1974 Sch 2 para 7. |
| 112 | 1936 s. 19; 1989 Sch 8 para 2(2). |
| 113 | 1936 ss. 42, 90(1)(part) & 300 - 302; 1973 s. 14; 1974 s. 43(6); 1989 Sch 8 paras 1 & 5(1)(a). |
| 114 | 1936 ss. 48 & 343(1)(part); 1973 Sch 8 para 39; 1989 Sch 8 para 1. |
| 115 | 1936 s. 21; 1973 s. 14; 1980(H) Sch 24 para 4(b); 1985(LG) Sch 4 para 47; 1989 Sch 8 paras 1 & 2(3). |
| 116 | 1936 s. 22; 1973 s. 14; 1989 Sch 8 paras 1 & 2(4). |
| 117 | 1936 ss. 30, 31, 90(5), 283 & 343(1); 1963(L) Sch 11 Pt I paras 1 & 24(b); 1973 s. 14; 1989 ss. 71(2) & (9), 72(7)(part) & Sch 8 para 1. |

| Provision of Act | Derivation |
|---|---|
| 118 | 1937 ss. 1 & 2(5) & (5A); 1961 s. 69(1); 1973 s. 14; 1989 Sch 8 paras 1 & 3(1)(c); R: 2. |
| 119 | 1937 s. 2(1); 1973 s. 14; 1989 Sch 8 paras 1 & 3(1)(a). |
| 120 | 1989 Sch 9 paras. 1(1),(2), (4) & (5), 5 & 9. |
| 121 | 1937 ss. 2(3), (5) & (5A) & 14(1); 1961 ss. 1(3) & 59; 1973 s. 14; 1989 Sch 8 paras 1 & 3(1)(b) & (c). |
| 122 | 1937 s. 3; 1961 ss. 61 & 66(2); 1973 s. 14; 1989 Sch 8 paras 1 & 3(2) & (3). |
| 123 | 1989 Sch 9 para 1(3) - (6). |
| 124 | 1961 s. 60(1) - (4), (6) & (8); 1973 s. 14; 1989 Sch 8 para 1. |
| 125 | 1974 s. 45(1) - (3); 1989 Sch 8 para 5(3). |
| 126 | 1961 s. 60(5) - (7) & 66(2); 1973 s. 14; 1974 s. 45(4); 1989 Sch 8 paras 1 & 4(2) & (4) & 5(3) & (4). |
| 127 | 1989 Sch 9 para 2. |
| 128 | 1961 s 62; 1973 s. 14; 1989 Sch 8 paras 1 & 4(2). |
| 129 | 1936 s. 90(5); 1937 ss. 7(1) & (2) & 14(2); 1973 s. 14; 1989 Sch 8 para 1; R: 2. |
| 130 | 1989 Sch 9 para 1(1), (4) & (5) & 5. |
| 131 | 1989 Sch 9 para 2. |
| 132 | 1989 Sch 9 paras 3, 4(3) & 7. |
| 133 | 1989 Sch 9 para 4 & 5. |
| 134 | 1989 Sch 9 para 6. |
| 135 | 1989 Sch 8 paras 3(4) & 4(3). |
| 136 | 1961 s. 67(1). |
| 137 | 1961 s. 66(1); 1981(SC) Sch 5. |
| 138 | 1989 s. 74; 1990(EP) Sch 15 para 28. |
| 139 | 1961 s. 64; TFOs: SI 1965/319; SI 1970/1681. |
| 140 | Introduces Sch 8. |
| 141 | 1936 s. 283; 1937 ss. 13 & 14(1); 1961 ss. 1(3) & 63(1); 1973 s. 14; 1989 Sch 8 paras 1 & 4(5) . |
| 142 | 1989 s. 75. |
| 143 | 1989 s. 76. |
| 144 | 1989 s. 77 & Sch 26 para 16(10). |
| 145 | 1989 s. 80. |
| 146 | 1989 s. 79. |
| 147 | 1989 s. 81. |
| 148 | 1989 Sch 10 para 2(1) - (3) & (5) & 5. |
| 149 | 1989 s. 78(2) & (3). |
| 150 | 1989 s. 82. |
| 151 | 1944 (c. 26) s. 1(1), (4) & (5); 1955 (c. 13) s. 1; 1971 (c. 49) s. 1; 1989 Sch 25 paras 6 & 21; TFOs: SI 1951/142; SI 1951/1900; SI 1965/319; SI 1970/1681. |
| 152 | 1989 s. 170(7). |
| 153 | 1989 s. 25. |
| 154 | 1989 s. 184. |

| Provision of Act | Derivation |
|---|---|
| 155 | 1989 s. 151. |
| 156 | 1989 s. 152; 1990(EP) Sch 8 para 8 & Sch 9 para 17(4). |
| 157 | 1989 ss. 158 & 186. |
| 158 | 1989 Sch 19 paras 1(1) & 2(1) - (3), (7) & (8). |
| 159 | 1989 Sch 19 paras 1(1) & 4. |
| 160 | 1936 ss. 275 & 291 - 294; 1945 Sch 4; 1973 s. 14; 1989 Sch 8 para 1. |
| 161 | 1989 s. 154 & Sch 19 paras 1(2), 2(1)(c) & (d) & 4(1)(c) & (d). |
| 162 | 1989 Sch 10 paras 1(1) - (3), (5) & (7) & 5 & Sch 19 para 1(5). |
| 163 | 1989 Sch 19 para 5. |
| 164 | 1945 ss. 15, 53 & 59(1); 1963(L) Sch 11 Pt I para 27; 1972 (c. 61) s. 18(6); 1973 Sch 8 para 49; 1989 Sch 25 para 7(2). |
| 165 | 1989 Sch 19 paras 1(1) & 8(1), (5) & (6). |
| 166 | 1989 s. 176 & Sch 19 para 9(1) & (3) - (8) & Sch 26 para 43(1). |
| 167 | 1989 ss. 155 and 157(1). |
| 168 | 1989 Sch 19, para 10(1) - (3). |
| 169 | 1989 s. 156(1) - (5). |
| 170 | 1945 ss. 16(5) & 21(2); 1948 s. 6; 1989 ss. 62(4) & 64(1) - (3) & (5) & Sch 25 para 7(3)(d) & (4); 1990(FS) s. 55(2). |
| 171 | 1936 s. 287; 1937 s. 10; 1973 s. 14; 1974 Sch 3 para 10; 1989 Sch 8 paras 1, 2(9) & 3(7). |
| 172 | 1961 s. 67(2); 1989 Sch 10 para 1(1) & (4). |
| 173 | 1989 s. 180. |
| 174 | 1945 s. 35(4); 1977 s. 31(6); 1989 s. 167 & Sch 25 para 7(5)(b). |
| 175 | 1989 Sch 10 para 3(1) & (2). |
| 176 | 1989 Sch 10 paras 3(3) & (4) & 5. |
| 177 | 1989 Sch 10 paras 3(5) & (6) & 5. |
| 178 | 1936 ss. 288 & 289; 1982(CJA) ss. 35 & 38. |
| 179 | 1945 s. 35(2); 1989 s. 153, Sch 19 para 1(1) & Sch 25 para 7(5)(a). |
| 180 | Introduces Sch 12. |
| 181 | 1989 s. 162(1) - (5), (10) & (11). |
| 182 | 1989 s. 162(6) - (10). |
| 183 | Introduces Sch 13. |
| 184 | 1936 s. 330 & 332; 1973 s. 14; 1982(CA) Sch 2 para 1(2); 1986(AA) Sch 2 para 2; 1989 Sch 8 para 1. |
| 185 | 1989 s. 161. |
| 186 | 1936 ss. 331, 332, 334 & 339; 1973 s. 14; 1989 s. 160(4) - (7) & (9) & Sch 8 para 1. |
| 187 | 1936 s. 340; 1989 Sch 19 para 7; TFO: SI 1970/1537. |
| 188 | 1989 s. 159. |
| 189 | 1936 s. 276; 1973 s. 14; 1989 Sch 8 para 1. |

| Provision of Act | Derivation |
|---|---|
| 190 | 1989 s. 163; 1990 (c. 11) Sch 2 para 81(2). |
| 191 | 1989 s. 157(2) - (4). |
| 192 | 1936 s. 328; 1989 Sch 19 paras 1(3), (4) & (6) & 11. |
| 193 | 1989 s. 35. |
| 194 | 1989 s. 36. |
| 195 | 1989 s. 31. |
| 196 | 1937 s. 7A; 1989 Sch 8 para 3(5). |
| 197 | 1989 Sch 19 para 9(2) & (8). |
| 198 | 1989 s. 165. |
| 199 | 1989 s. 166(1), (2), (3)(b) & (5) - (9). |
| 200 | 1989 s. 166(3)(a), (4) & (8) & (9). |
| 201 | 1989 s. 34. |
| 202 | 1989 s. 32. |
| 203 | 1989 s. 33. |
| 204 | 1937 s. 9; 1973 s. 14; 1974 Sch 2 para 14; 1982(CJA) s. 38; 1989 Sch 8 para 1. |
| 205 | 1989 Sch 10 paras 4 & 5. |
| 206 | 1961 s. 68; 1989 s. 174 & Sch 9 para 8; R: 11. |
| 207 | 1945 s. 45; 1989 s. 175 & Sch 25 para 7(8); R: 12. |
| 208 | 1989 s. 170(1) - (6) & (9). |
| 209 | 1981 s. 6; 1986(GA) Sch 7 para 2(6); 1989 Sch 25 para 63; 1989(EA) Sch 16 para 1(5); 1990 (c. 11) para 46; 1991(NR) Sch 8 para 106. |
| 210 | 1989 s. 177; R: 13. |
| 211 | 1936 s. 298; 1973 s. 14; 1989 Sch 8 para 1. |
| 212 | 1989 s. 182. |
| 213 | 1936 s. 319; 1946 (c. 36) ss. 4(3) and 5(2); 1974 s. 104; 1989 s. 185. |
| 214 | 1936 ss. 283; 1937 s. 14(2); 1961 s. 1(3); 1973 s. 14; 1989 s. 189 (definition of "prescribed") & Sch 8 paras 1, 3(7) & 4(6). |
| 215 | 1936 s. 318; 1989 s. 181 & Sch 8 paras 1 & 2(10). |
| 216 | 1989 s. 187; R: 14. |
| 217 | 1989 s. 188. |
| 218 | 1989 s. 189(2) & (3); R: 21. |
| 219 | 1936 ss. 90(4) & 343(1)(part); 1961 s. 67(3); 1989 ss. 43(8), 77(5), 78(4), 160(3), 166(9), 167(7) & 189 & Sch 8 para 2(12), Sch 10 para 6 & Sch 19 paras 1, 3(6), 8(8) & 11; 1991(NR) Sch 8 para 116(3); R: 15 & 17 - 20. |
| 220 | 1989 s. 191(6). |
| 221 | 1936 s. 341; 1989 s. 192 & Sch 8 para 1; 1990 (c. 11) Sch 2 para 81(3). |
| 222 | 1985 s. 5(2); 1989 s. 193 & Sch 25 para 73. |
| Sch 1 | 1989 Sch. 3 paras 1 - 5. |
| Sch 2 | 1989 Sch 5. |
| Sch 3 | 1989 Sch 6. |

| Provision of Act | Derivation |
|---|---|
| Sch 4 | 1989 Sch 4 paras 1 - 5. |
| Sch 5 | 1989 Sch 7. |
| Sch 6 | |
| Pt I | 1936 ss. 287 & 288; 1945 s. 48; 1961(F) s. 184 & Sch 6 para 1; 1973 s. 14; 1989 Sch 8 para 1. |
| Pt II | 1989 ss. 59(3), 60(5), 62(5), 64(4) & (5), 156(6), 178 & 179, Sch 10 para 1(6), Sch 19 para 10(4) & (5) & Sch 21 para 5(4); 1991(NR) Sh 8 para 116(4). |
| Sch 7 | 1985 ss. 3 & 4. |
| Sch 8 | 1937 ss. 4(4) & 7(4) & (5); 1961 s. 63(8); 1973 s. 14; 1974 Sch 3 para 9; 1989 Sch 8 paras 1, 3(2) & (4), 4(2) & 5(2). |
| Sch 9 | 1989 Sch 18. |
| Sch 10 | 1989 Sch 24. |
| Sch 11 | 1989 Sch 20. |
| Sch 12 | 1936 ss. 278 & 303; 1973 s. 14; 1989 Sch 8 para 1, Sch 10, paras 1(2), 2(4) & 5 & Sch 19 paras 2(4) - (6), 6 & 8(2) - (4). |
| Sch 13 | 1936 ss. 333 & 334; 1973 s. 14; 1982(CA) Sch 2 para 1(2); 1986(AA) Sch 2 para 2; 1989 s. 160(1) - (3) & (6) - (8) & Sch 8 para 1, Sch 10 para 1(2) & Sch 19 para 2(9) & 3; 1989(EA) Sch 16 para 37; 1991(NR) Sch 8 para 116(4). |
| Sch 14 | 1989 Sch 21. |
| Sch 15 | 1989 s. 174(2)(d) & (3). |

Printed in the United Kingdom for Her Majesty's Stationery Office
Dd. 0509017   3/92   C15   4073   Ord. 191358

PRINTED IN ENGLAND BY PAUL FREEMAN
Controller and Chief Executive of Her Majesty's Stationery Office and
Queen's Printer of Acts of Parliament.
1st impression August 1991
2nd impression March 1992